Rich/Poor Man's Guide to Pittsburgh

with

"I Love Pittsburgh!
Pull-Out
Sight-Seeing Guide"

SEVENTH EDITION

by Dorothy A. Miller

A Complete & Unique Guide to the City
For Pittsburghers & Visitors

New Pittsburgh Publications
Publishers of "Pittsburgh Walking Map & Guide"
and "Pittsburgh Pleasures Events Calendar"
Box 81875, Pittsburgh, PA 15217

Welcome to the 7th Edition of the *Rich/Poor Man's Guide*, designed to help you discover all of the wonderful things that make Pittsburgh so special.

What's happening in Pittsburgh?

Incredible changes are taking place. In the wake of Renaissance II, all three riverfronts are exploding with new life . . . from the fabulous Sandcastle Water Park on the Mon to the fascinating new Carnegie Science Center on the North Shore . . . from new riverwalks and parks to the long-awaited Strip— Down by the Riverside development. Add to this, resurging new night life in the South Side, Strip and Mt Washington and Pittsburgh's recreational/riverfront renaissance is here!

These changes are all reflected in the Guide, including a completely new section on Boaters/Marinas/Waterfront restaurants. Visitors tell us the best thing about the city is its variety of ethnic cuisines, now highlighted in the Famous Pittsburgh Foods section. Biggest surprise of all is the growth of exotic Asian restaurants since our last edition. You'll find more than 50 in the new Oriental/Asian section.

Scenically set at the Point of three rivers and rated the most livable city in the U.S. by Rand McNally, Pittsburgh is a fascinating blend of ethnic heritages, big corporations, sophisticated cultural attractions, championship sports and —the city's hallmark—friendly people . . . a big city with a small town feel!

For 12 years, the *Rich/Poor Man's Guide* has shared with more than 100,000 readers a genuine love for the city and its hidden secrets. And visitors from all over the world, amazed at Pittsburgh's beauty, have written us how much the *Guide,* our *Walking Map* and *Pittsburgh Events Calendar* have helped them discover real Pittsburgh.

They come from all walks of life . . . natives keeping up with city changes, business executives, young professionals, new high-tech workers, students, people temporarily stationed here, former 'burghers, conventioneers, visitors, tourists—they all fell in love with the city.

Let the *Guide* help *you* fall in love with Pittsburgh and discover what makes it such a great place to live, work and visit!

TABLE OF CONTENTS

**I LOVE PITTSBURGH!
Pull-Out
SIGHTSEEING GUIDE**

A Special Section
to help you
Enjoy the city to the fullest!

**Visitor's Special
5 Easy Ways To Fall
In Love with the City**
plus

RENAISSANCE II BLDG
WATCHER'S GUIDE

REAL PLEASURES OF PITTSBURGH

HOW TO USE THIS GUIDE

It starts with you! This 7th Edition of the *Rich/Poor Man's Guide* is divided into 17 sections with numbered tabs on each page for quick, easy use. To get the most from the Guide begin with:

Reviews 1 & Rich Man's Dining 3

These restaurants and experiences of the city are all special Pittsburgh places with extraordinary cuisine, wonderful atmosphere or unusual ethnic food. **To help you discover the city's best these sections are indexed by geographic area, type of cuisine, connoisseur dining, nights of romance, fabulous buys, and shopping/experiences of the city.**

Sections 2,4,5,6-17

These sections are easily found in the Table of Contents.

General Index

A comprehensive, alphabetical index including all entries can be found in the back of the Guide.

Companion Pieces

The *Guide* and the *I Love Pittsburgh! Pull-Out Sightseeing Guide* are best used in conjunction with the *Pittsburgh Walking Map & Guide,* an invaluable aid in getting around the city, and the *Pittsburgh Pleasures Events Calendar* with listings of 850 things to do in Greater Pittsburgh and 13 spectacular color photos of the city.

For suggestions in planning a special day/night in Pittsburgh or a celebration within your budget call us at (412) 681-8528.

KEY

AE	Amer Exp	Inexp	Under $10
D	Discover	Mod	$10-$20
DC	Diner's Club	Exp	$20 & over
MC	Master Charge	(dinner per person)
V	Visa		

♿ Accommodates wheelchairs entrances, tables, restrooms

REVIEWS, RICH MAN'S DINING BY CATEGORY

GEOGRAPHIC

This is an independent publication, not connected with or financed by any business establishment. Prices, checked up to the eve of publication, are subject to change, as are policies and management. All opinions expressed are the author's.

CONNOISSEUR DINING

NIGHT OF ROMANCE

FABULOUS BUYS

SHOPPING/EXPERIENCES OF THE CITY

Pittsburgh is a "diner's town" with one of the highest number of restaurants per capita in the country. Here are some of the city's most unique, exciting eateries....all special Pittsburgh places with charm, great cuisine, ethnic touches. The reviews tell you when to go, what to order, what to wear with inside information on the best values in town.

Allegheny Brewery & Pub

Wunderbar! Fun At Oldtime Beer Hall

Allegheny Brewery & Pub

Troy Hill Road, North Side. Across 16th St Bridge. Tues-Sat 11am-midnite. AE,MC,V. **237-9402.** [♿]

We loved this touch of old Heidelburg in Pittsburgh, a German beer hall in a wonderful setting—the atmospheric old Eberhardt & Ober Brewery on Troy Hill, an old German section of the city. You pass through the gate into a stone courtyard—shades of Frankenstein—the brewery's brooding walls high above. Inside a German pub has been recreated complete with wooden beams, high windows, smooth tables & benches made by owner Tom Pastorius...the only drawback—the benches are backless! But while you're eating you can watch Penn Pilsner's old time beer-making in gleaming copper vessels behind a glass wall. (This is the first 'tied house'—brewery attached to a restaurant—in Pennsylvania since Prohibition...brewing pure German beer without additives.) Already bursting at the seams, in summer the Pub spills out into a breezy courtyard garden with taps & long tables. Zany German & jazz bands add to the fun. We loved it!

When To Go: Definitely for live bands Wed-Sat 7:30-11:30. Watch for Five Guys Named Moe and German bands. Young/old love 'em!

What To Order: Wonderful wursts, sauerbraten, smoked pork chops, roast pork, soups, chicken and an interesting salad plate... served with your own loaf of dark sourdough rye & butter ...and authentic versions of sauerkraut, spaetzle (tiny German dumplings), apple sauce, sweet & sour red cabbage and of course—German potato salad.
We suggest you prepare your palate with **freshly brewed beer**—wonderful tasting Penn Pilsner ($1.75) with a **salty, soft pretzel** hot from the oven & horseradish mustard. The Fruit/Cheese Plate ($4.50) is also a good beginning. Our entree choice is the **Wurst Plate** ($6.50) **with two big wonderful German sausages**—a firm pale pork and a big brown link bursting with flavour. They're served with potato salad & sauerkraut but we like them with the **mealy, buttered spaetzle and tangy red cabbage.** Also good are the **Sauerbraten** (marinated beef roast) $9.50, **Smoked Pork Chop** $7.75 and **Potato Pancakes** $2.75. And who can resist old-fashioned bread pudding, apple strudel, Linzer torte or Black Forest cheesecake ($2-$2.75.)

Prices: are right! Lunch under $5, Dinner under $10. 2/$25 with beer/dessert.

What To Wear: It's a mixed crowd, young & old, preppy, peppy, grandpappy—all having a wonderful time. Come as you are...welcome!

Recommended: German Cuisine, Fabulous Buys, Outdoor Dining, Late Supper, Pgh After Dark.

The Exotic Tastes of Thai

Bangkok House

Bangkok House, *Dormont: 3233 W Liberty Ave. Sun-Fri 5-10, Sat 5-11:30.* **341-8888. Bangkok Taste,** Downtown: 428 Forbes. Mon-Fri 11:30-9, Sat 2-8. **338-9111.** AE,MC,V.

This is exciting, four-star dining with Thai gourmet dishes in a very special atmosphere...in Dormont, a beautiful second floor room with a splashing central fountain, muted lighting, colorful Far East decor and a soothing Oriental soundtrack. This restaurant was so successful that a second was opened downtown, an elegant, downstairs room (where De Foro's used to be), a popular lunchtime spot for a super noon buffet or dinner. You couldn't find a better introduction to the taste of Thai than these two restaurants.

When To Go: Dinner at leisure in Dormont. Downtown Lunch Buffet.

What To Order: What are the tastes of Thai? Borrowing from nearby India and China, it has derived its own inimitable cuisine... sweet, hot to mild laced with coconut, peanuts, fruits, hot chilis, ginger root, lime, mint...most subtle. If Thai food is new to you we suggest you sample its uniqueness at the Downtown Bangkok Taste Buffet Mon-Fri from 11-2. Here for $6.95 you can try delicious soups, hot appetizers, meat, fish & vegetable dishes and desserts that change daily. Dinner at either site has the same incredible variety of pork, beef, seafood, rice, vegetarian, **curries and the traditional Phad-Thai noodles** all $6.95...try the noodles fried with shrimp, chicken, ground peanut & bean sprouts. Also good introductions are the Dinner Specials for 2 at the Dormont House where you can sample a wide range of mild to hot tastes i.e. the **Bangkok House Treat** which includes spring rolls, wonton soup, Thai beef salad, hot chicken green curry, shrimp broccoli and steamed rice...$19.95 for 2! Good buy. Another choice is the **Siamese Lady Treat**— spring rolls, hot chicken coconut soup, shrimp & chicken salad, BBQ pork ribs, shrimp snow peas, babycorn (delicious), mushroom and steamed rice...again 2 for $22.95. The most expensive of the dinners for 2, the **Royal Treat,** is still a bargain at $26 for 2.

If you like it hot try the **Volcano Chicken** "on fire" with chili ($9.95) or the **Siamese Fish,** a hot halibut in a zesty sauce ($12.95). Good eating awaits you.

What To Wear: These are mostly dress-up restaurants.

Prices: Dormont: Dinner $6-$11. Downtown: Lunch Buffet $6.95, Dinner $6-$10.

Recommended: Thai Cuisine, Connoisseur Dining, Fabulous Buys, Late Supper (Dormont).

Pittsburgh
Victoriana

Brady St Bridge Cafe

2228 E Carson St at foot of bridge, South Side. Mon-Thur 11:30-10, Fri til 11:30. Sat 5-11:30. Parking lot to left. AE, DC, MC. **488-1818.**

This Victorian restoration is one of the most unique rooms in the city. A seven-year dream of architect John Martine, designer of the Old Birmingham sign on South Side, it's a labor of love and a monument to Pittsburgh's past. More than $300,000 went into remodeling with memorabilia collected from all over the city. There's a greenhouse addition with beautifully-etched glass windows from an old schoolhouse and a glass roof buttressed with lintels and columns from old wooden Victorian porches. And nostalgic to many—a swinging galley door from the dance hall in old West View Park. All are blended into a charming, greenery-filled room with pale wooden tables, green padded chairs—a pleasant environment reminiscent of that 'best restaurant' of which every neighborhood used to boast.

Don't miss the ceiling in the bar, a colorful reproduction of an Egyptian theme that really glows. Many more surprises await you. Fans of old Victoriana will love it.

When To Go: Try the patio for lunch, dinner, late supper.

What To Order: The casual atmosphere encourages you to take it easy and enjoy your surroundings. There's an engaging new menu—fish, chicken, pasta and veal.

To get a really good look at the decor we suggest daylight hours or early supper. Lunches features burgers, delicious soups and an interesting Steak Salad. Dinners include everything from Grilled Pineapple Chicken at $10.75 to Angus Sirloin at $18.50 with two good dishes—**Fettuccine San Marco with Seafood** and **Norwegian Salmon with Champagne Cream Sauce**—around $13.

For a late afternoon or night snack try the delicious **Gourmet Pizzaelles,** 10-inch, thin crusted pizzas—with fresh basil, garlic and provolone or the zesty **Creole with provolone, artichokes and Cajun andouille sausage** for $4.75.

Soups are also delicious here as is another unique house specialty, Clam Bread $3. In summer you can dine outdoors in a pleasant enclosed patio.

Prices: Lunch $4-$7, Dinner $10-$18.50.

What To Wear: Informal will definitely do.

Recommended: American Cuisine, Outdoor Dining, Late Supper.

**Romantic Greenery,
Late Night Eatery**

Brandy's
*Penn Avenue & 24th Street, Strip District. Mon-Thur
11:15-2am, Fri-Sat til 2:30am, Sun 3-11. Parking after 5 in lot
next door—enter from street behind. AE,DC,MC,V.* **566-1000.**

The restaurant that started Pittsburgh's wave of charming
new eateries has settled in as a favorite for businessmen
and late night snackers. (A Brandy Van brings hotel guests
to and from downtown.) The city's first after-hours restaurant with class, Brandy's is all charm from its remodeled
three-story brick facade to the unique interior with its flickering fireplaces, skylight roof, hanging plants and old time
bar...one of the best ambiences in town.

When To Go: Business lunch, Late snacks, breakfast Fri-Sat til 2am.

What To Order: Just five minutes from town, Brandy's lends itself to a relaxing lunch. Besides fish, beef, chicken entrees, there's a
good Spinach & Bacon Salad for $4.75, and hearty hot
sandwiches—a popular Crabmeat Devonshire, Hefty Ham,
Roast Beef—all served with fries and slaw. For lunch we
recommend $5-$6 daily specials, Italian, Greek and Cajun
dishes such as **Stuffed Eggplant, Blackened Red Fish,
Stuffed Peppers, Shellfish.**

Dinners range from $10-$16 for surf & turf but you can get
snacks for much less. Still a good lunch/late nite buy are
the juicy half pound **Brandyburgers** around $4-$5—especially the cheese bacon specials. And you can dessert on
heady 151 proof **Brandy-laced Rum-Raisin Ice Cream** concoctions in a huge 17-oz snifter $3.75. You won't need a
drink with these.

This is still a perfect place for breakfast at unpredictable
hours or to end a romantic night out...with breakfasts from
$3.25 to $5.25 for the **Hungry Man's Breakfast**—bacon/
ham/sausage, French toast, home fries, two eggs and
coffee.

Try out the unique **Human Jukebox** (25¢ song, 5/$1)—call-
ins to a record connoisseur with a collection of 80,000 all
time greats from 1922 to the present. Friday nights you can
join in the friendly barroom sing-a-long.

Prices: Lunch $3.25-$7; Dinner $10-$14, Breakfast $3.25-$5.25.

What To Wear: Casual best, informal or 'suit' the occasion.

Recommended: American Cuisine, Night of Romance, Party Rooms, Late
Supper.

Bravo! Trattoria

**Theatre Bistro
Draws Raves**

Bravo! Trattoria

134 Sixth Ave, Downtown. Lunch Mon-Fri 11-5, Dinner Mon-Sat 5-11. Sun 4-8 for Heinz Hall, Benedum Ctr performances. AE,DC,MC,V. **642-7600.**

First there was Bravo! Franco, a successful bandbox of a restaurant whose superb food and style was an instant success. Across the street from Heinz Hall on Penn, it's glossy interior was always crowded with business lunchers and people on their way to and from the theatre. Often it was SRO and owner Luigi Caruso had to turn people away at the door. So he decided to open the Trattoria around the corner on 6th (on the site of former Lizzie Farrell's). And now we have another success story. We prefer the more casual ambience of this second restaurant which still has the NY spiffiness of the first—crisp black napkins marching on white clothed tables, black runged chairs creating a pleasing symmetry...but there's a less hurried feel here and a leisurely upstairs room. The bistro-like first floor also has a friendly bar at the entranceway. Both Bravos get applause for their deft career waiters/waitresses.

When To Go: Anytime, great for before/after theatre.

What To Order: There are many of the same superb dishes that made Bravo! Franco famous and some new ones...marvelous foccaccia bread, delicious wedding soup, wonderful pastas and antipastas, great veals—scallopine, hearty osso buco—grilled chicken and fish, delicious **Crab Cakes with mustard sauce.** (Bravo! Franco's menu is a little more elaborate—up to $19 for dinner). But our favorite way to eat at the Trattoria is to savour small course by small course...the delicious **Wedding Soup** ($1.75-$2.50). Then one of the fine salads...the beautifully constructed **House Salad,** great with generous dollops of blue cheese dressing...then possibly a small order of the day's pasta ($3.95)...and you'll still meet the minimum dinner charge. After 8pm you also have a choice of some great sandwiches at $7 including a divine **Turkey Breast, Bacon and Swiss Cheese on foccaccia.** This kind of eating leaves you room to appreciate "la dolci vita" in this case the dessert menu (dolci) with Italian sweets it would be a sin to bypass...**Cassatta alla Siciliano,** chocolate cake layered with ricotta topped with whipped cream & almonds, **Tiramisu,** chocolate zabaglione and rum flavored with mascarpone or a "deliciously thin" **Gelato**—Italian ice cream. One of the world's pleasures is savoring a fine Italian dessert with an espresso or cappuccino laced with Galliano. Lunch here has smaller versions of the same wonderful food.

Prices: Lunch $5.75-$8.25, Dinner $12-$16, Late Supper $5 & up.

What To Wear: Downtown/theatre attire.

Recommended: Italian Cuisine, Connoisseur Dining, Late Supper.

**Inspired
Riviera Cuisine**

Cafe Allegro

51 S 12th Street, South Side. Lunch Mon-Fri 11:30-3. Dinner Tues-Thur 4:30-10:30, Fri & Sat til 12. Sun 4:30-9:30. Reser. MC,V. **481-7788.**

With cuisine that is truly 'allegro'—lively and inventive—this restaurant has brightened the entire Pittsburgh dining scene. A family affair of gusto and love, Allegro is an intimate two-story restaurant tucked away in South Side's old Market Square. The surroundings are pleasant and romantic, the tables white-clothed and flower bedecked, and the food, inspired by French/Italian Riviera cuisine, at times transcends. There's a light touch and terrific new tastes in the dishes here—prepared 'fresca expresso,' fresh and fast with lots of wonderful herbs and spices.

When To Go: A lovely long dinner, weekday or weekend.

What To Order: A complimentary hors d'oeuvre, which might be anything from pate to roasted peppers, gets your meal off to a happy start...along with the bright, pleasant service. Tempting main entrees—unique versions of salmon, roast leg of lamb, tuna, chicken, veal ($9-$19) change weekly. But we've never been able to get beyond the superb a la carte dishes.

Ranging from a modest $3-$9, special soups, vegetables, salads, appetizers, pastas have some unforgettable tastes and make a delightful eclectic meal, a favorite of the 'lite' cafe go-er. There are rare dishes from which to choose...Roasted Pepper Soup, Eggplant Crepe and an incomparable **Roasted Sweet Pepper Salad with Asiago, our nomination as the city's best**—with calamata olives & prosciutto on bibb with olive oil ($3.25). Another wonderful offering which can be shared is the **Vegetable Platter**— unique versions rendolent with herbs and spices. Look for the sauteed **Swiss Chard** exquisitely seasoned with tomatoes, wine and fennel, toasted with cheese and bread crumbs...a dish fit for a king! Another plus—the pastas are available in full ($5.95) and half orders ($3.50) fitting beautifully into your a la carte meal. And don't miss the **Pasta del Sole** with tomatoes, cream, shallots and Romano cheese. The gourmet desserts are also in a class by themselves.

These entrees give you some idea of the uncommon cuisine in this little kitchen—our hats are off to Chef 'Red' Rayner for his light, sure hand and the Rayner-Cardamone family for proving once again that connoisseur dining can be had in Pittsburgh at reasonable prices. Don't miss it!

Prices: Lunch $6-$8, Dinner $14-$19.

What To Wear: Something nice. This will be an occasion you won't forget.

Recommended: French/Italian Cuisine, Connoisseur Dining, Fabulous Buys, Night of Romance.

REVIEWS

Cafe Azure

From the Terrace On Craig Street

Cafe Azure

317 S Craig Street, Oakland. Lunch Mon-Sat 11:30-3. Dinner Mon-Thur 6-10, Fri & Sat til 10:30. Reser sugg. AE,DC,MC,V. **681-3533.**

This sleek cafe with its high terrace overlooking South Craig's busy university/museum scene is what dining is all about. There's a wonderful European feel under the low tan awning...a lazy, summer ambience in which you can forget time and place and while away an hour...an afternoon... an evening with a glass of wine at sunset. As darkness falls and candlelight casts shadows on the blue-clothed tables, this is one of the city's most romantic settings. And the cuisine and fluid service play their roles to perfection. The restaurant's interior is also beguiling, classic lines blended in restful shades of tan and beige, soft light filtering through louvered blinds. Piano music from the small, colorful bar adds to the romantic mood Wed-Sat from 7.

When To Go: Lunch. Try 1:30-2 after peak hours or a relaxing light dinner at 8 or 9. The terrace is open Mar-Oct in good weather.

What To Order: The menu offers American-style French cuisine—Coquille St Jacques (scallops), Salmon en papillote (cooked in parchment paper) and gourmet versions of shrimp, chicken, fish, and steak in the $17-$20 range. But there's also a delicious **Grilled Duck Breast with Cherry Red Wine Sauce, Cinnamon & Clove** ($15) and a **Black Peppercorn Fettuccine** with chicken and sun-dried tomatoes in a delicate garlic cream sauce for $12. If budget allows, add hors d'oeuvres or French Onion Soup $4-$6.
Lunch or afternoon tea on the terrace is also delightful on a sunny day...and moderate for extraordinary entrees, soups, salads, pastas and a new menu item—pizza...here brushed with a gourmet touch and labeled "foccacia." Try the delicious **Provencale**—roasted sweet & hot peppers, sun-dried tomatoes & Asiago cheese, served with the tender house salad, $6.75. Bene! Or you can get a perfect **Croque Monsieur,** a traditional baked French bistro sandwich of ham, turkey and Jarlsberg with a Dijon mustard sauce. And wine is a necessity with your meal...try a blush zinfandel $3.75 glass. There are also beautiful salads such as Romaine & Hearts of Palm $4.25, and the **Blackened Chicken Caesar,** $7 plus superb French bread, cut diagonally and served with little crocks of sweet cream butter, a subtle touch. The Cafe also has some of the best coffee in the city. Cappuccino with some rare glacees (ice creams) and delicate sorbets makes a fine finale.

Prices: Lunch $6-$12, Dinner $12-$20.

What To Wear: Informal to elegantly casual by day or night.

Recommended: French Cuisine, Connoisseur Dining, Night of Romance, Outdoor Dining, Late Supper, Rich Man's Guide.

**Delightful Dining
On European Patio**

Cafe 401

401 Shady Avenue, Shadyside. Mon-Sat 11:30-2am. Sun Brunch 11-2. No reser. Valet Parking. AE,MC,V. **361-1900.**

The joy of dining outdoors has reached its peak in Pittsburgh with this smart new cafe at the site of the former Red Bull Inn. Its blue & white umbrellas bobbing above the greenery are an inviting sight from the avenue. At last this is real patio dining! There are at least 18 big round tables and room for 80 in this friendly yet discreet outdoor court with a real European feel. A concept of several local restaurateurs, it has become an instant success and a natural gathering place for Shadyside sophisticates—a delightful new "street scene." At night the patio becomes a romantic fairyland as hundreds of tiny lights illuminate the big tree in the center of the court. The large inside restaurant seats 200 with a big square wooden bar area and a very stylish diningroom carrying out the patio theme...handsome blue & white striped upholstery and marble table tops amid shades of wine and pale blue...a very restful room.

When To Go: Sunny Lunch/Brunch, Dinner, great for Late Snack.

What To Order: The cuisine has an Italian flavour with appetizers, salads, seafood and meat entrees all in a very reasonable range. The restaurant's forte, however, is its breads and pastas. Supper begins with a very fresh, sesame-covered Italian bread and the menu features several **Foccaccias** ($5-$8)— just right, mealy yet light and tender ...a must. The Garlic/Rosemary/Romano/ Parmesan is delicious but be forewarned...very garlicky...the **Roasted Peppers/Goat Cheese/Fresh Herb** version is tasty and fragrant. The Grilled Chicken Foccaccio, teamed with a salad (try the **Caesar with Grilled Chicken**) could easily become a meal. There are shrimp, sole and steak entrees but two of the most popular are Chicken Saltimbocca—Chicken Breast rolled with prosciutto, asiago and sage—and our favorite, a **Chicken Monterey** stuffed with cornbread, jalapenos and Monterey Jack ...both in the $11-$12 range. Best of all though are the pastas—great meals for $8-$12—especially the delicious **Penne with Grilled Chicken and Smoked Tomato** in a pink cream sauce with lots of Parmesan...our favorite...for $8.95! Desserts...wonderful at night with an espresso under the umbrellas...are very special at $2.95, particularly the Kahlua Cheesecake and a delectable **Strawberry/Mandarin Orange Tart!**

Prices: Reasonable. Lunch $4.50-$9, Dinner $9-$18.

What To Wear: Informal with lots of dress-up.

Recommended: Ital/Amer Cuisine, Night of Romance—Patio, Outdoor Dining, Sunday Brunch, Late Supper.

**Creative Cuisine
At Gourmet Cafe**

Cafe Sam

5242 Baum Boulevard, Oakland. Lunch Mon-Fri 11:30-4, Dinner Sun-Tues 5-10, Wed & Thur til 11, Fri & Sat til 12. Reser sugg. AE,MC,V. **621-2000.**

Get your reservations and join Pittsburgh's smart diners at this charmer in an awninged brick house which exudes an oldtime '30s flair. There's a small, cozy bar in the snug foyer, a good stop before dinner. And the romantic living/dining room has just the right touch—flowers, candles on the tables, smiling service. In short a very relaxing atmosphere which, along with the wonderful prices for extraordinary cuisine, is drawing Pittsburgh's beautiful people and seasoned diners. In summer a blue-awninged rooftop patio atop a new addition adds to the charm.

When To Go: Any night for a relaxing experience.

What To Order: Affordable creative cuisine is the surprise here. Strip steak, veal, duck, trout, grilled salmon, bouillabaisse are all from $11-$15 and lighter entrees and pastas from $4-$7.50. Adventuresome diners and lovers of light cuisine will find this place a mecca for combining inventive a la carte items. How about **Angel's Hair and Chipped Duck Breast** ($4.95) with a wonderful **Caesar Salad** with shrimp ($3.95), or a classic **French Onion Soup** baked with three cheeses ($3.25) combined with a delicious **Black Bean Venison Chili** or the **Smoked Salmon Scrambled Eggs** with potato pancakes—both under $7. These dishes are a labour of love by Chef/Owner Andrew Zins. For late snackers there's an hors d'oeuvres platter changing daily, grilled gourmet veal burgers, **Chicken Fajitas** and of course delectable desserts i.e. Chambord Cheesecake, Bittersweet Chocolate Mousse, Ice Cream Crepe with Raspberry Sauce from $2.75-$3.50

This is the kind of restaurant that gourmets—budget or otherwise—would design for themselves. . . imaginative cuisine that fits both the pocketbook and the trend to lighter dining without sacrificing taste. You can comfortably come back not just for a special occasion but often for dinner. No wonder so many East Enders have already made it their own.

Prices: Lunch $5-$8, Dinner $8-$15.

What To Wear: Some come informal, many dress up.

Recommended: Continental Cuisine, Connoisseur Dining, Fabulous Buys, Outdoor Dining, Late Supper.

Stylish New Italian Star

Caffe Giovanni

Hartwell Building, corner Walnut/Aiken, Shadyside. Lunch Mon-Sat 11:30-3, Dinner Mon-Tues 4:30-10, Wed-Sat til 11. Sun 4:30-9. Reser sugg. AE,DC,MC,V. **621-8881.**

A new dining star has emerged in Shadyside serving mouth-watering North & South Italian cuisine in style. A worthy successor to Clearwater, the new Caffe fills the beautiful architectural space of the Hartwell Building's third level, intriguingly designed for for a sweeping yet intimate feel. Angled views of the building's bold, clean lines, glimpsed from the curved stairway or glass elevator, are worth the trip alone! This is beautiful space and Giovanni's, the restaurant debut of John Vennare, former chef at the popular Pasta Piatto, couldn't have a better environment. By day the room is sunnily lit from the long windows along Aiken. And by night candles throw soft shadows on the formal white-clothed tables setting an exciting dining mood.

When To Go: Romantic dinner, sunny lunch.

What To Order: A big blue dinner menu, red ribboned, makes interesting gastronomic reading, quite a selection of painstakingly pre-pared specialty dishes: 10 appetizers, 2 soups, 4 salads, 16 pastas!, 7 veals, 5 chickens, 7 seafood, 4 beef, and one lamb dish. You'll be confused but it's sweet confusion. Many of the dishes are recipes from Vennare's family including the house's **"own sweet sausage,"** a good beginning as an appetizer grilled with red & green peppers & served with goat cheese $5.50. But then so are the **Sweet Roasted Peppers** with fontina and olives $5.95. The sausage makes another entrance with **Spaghettini** along with red & green peppers in a good, spicy sauce. But best pasta of all is a divine **Granchio, Spinaci e Pignoli— Angel Hair Pasta with crabmeat, spinach and pine nuts** in a delicate, beautifully blended cream sauce, an inspired dish worth every bite of $16.95. Veal is the test of Italian and Giovanni's is first rate—Romano, in port wine, with roasted peppers...or for a hearty change...with gnocchi in a veal sauce. The chicken dishes, all around $12, are also unusual, particularly the **Breast of Chicken in a creamy Galliano with peaches, grapes and pistachio nuts.** These are real adventures in eating. Affordable lunches...Mama's Gnocchi $6.25, Antipasto with squid, shrimp, artichoke, caponata, olives, sausage, prosciutto & fontina...all for $7.50 guarantee noonday attendance. And for lunch or dinner is the great **Gorgonzola Salad** with crunchy walnuts (a Vennare signature) $4.50. Treat yourself!

Prices: Lunch $4.50-$7.95, Dinner $8.25-$20.

What To Wear: Dress up to the food, decor.

Recommended: Italian Cuisine, Connoisseur Dining, Late Supper.

Cardillo's Club Cafe

**Great Jazz, Food
At Supper Club**

Cardillo's Club Cafe

56 S 12th Street, South Side. Tues-Sat 6pm-2am. Weekend reser sugg. AE,MC,V. **381-3777.**

This stylish, sophisticated club has a NY ambience with a unique Pittsburgh flair—the pianos of Bobby Cardillo, long-time local favorite, and son Harry, the only father-son jazz piano duo in the country. It was Bobby's dream and it's pure pleasure when the two hold forth at twin Steinways on a raised dais in this stylish yet intimate room. The club is a sleek renovation of South Side's renowned old Club Cafe (made famous in the movie "Dominick and Eugene"). There's space for listening and mixing at the long bar, at stools around high tables and at a small serpentine bar facing the music. And there's a pleasant white-clothed dining area. This is a great place for relaxing and impressing your out-of-town guests with Pittsburgh night life at its best!

The Cardillos perform singly or together Tues-Thur 8:30-12 with mellow sets for diners Fri & Sat from 7:30-9. Then young Harry & his combo take over for some of the most exciting jazz sounds in the city . . . this piano is terrific! Weekends there are also guest artists. Local and visiting musical talent gravitates here late at night. It gets crowded, so be sure to make reservations well ahead.

When To Go: Dinner/Late snack. Catch the Cardillo duo weekends 7:30-9. Stay on for listening.

What To Order: The best way to enjoy the music is while supping on some very good dishes, the menu is small but choice—charbroiled NY strip, shrimp, lemon chicken, a fish of the day, a very good **Chicken Veronique** in puff pastry with cream sauce & grapes, or **Chicken/Shrimp Dijon,** both $13.95. Dinners come with an excellent house salad, vegetable and rice, potato or pasta. We suggest a side dish of the **homemade pasta, tender and delicious.** Full pasta orders include canneloni, fettucini and a special **Pasta Marrianna** (named for Bobby's late wife). For late nighters there's wedding soup, an array of appetizers and excellent salads as they should be made. Try the red leaf lettuce, artichoke hearts, black olives and peppers with the house's generous blue dressing, only $4.95.

Price: Where else can you get dinner & great jazz for $15-$20 person? (Weekend $2 cover waived for diners.) Dinners $11-$14. Late appetizers, salad, soup $4-$7. Drinks: Mod.

What To Wear: Informal to dress-up—go in style.

Recommended: American Cuisine, Night of Romance, Late Supper, Pgh After Dark.

Pittsburgh's Room at The Top

Christopher's

1411 Grandview Avenue, Mt Washington. Mon-Thur 5-11, Fri & Sat til midnite. Valet parking. Reser. AE,D,DC,MC,V. **381-4500.**

Get out your imaginary top hat, white tie and tails and get set for a marvelous evening on top of the town at this spectacular restaurant 1000 feet above the city. The star-studded ride to Mt Washington via the incline or a drive up McArdle Roadway will put you in a festive mood and as you approach the top of Grandview Ave at twilight, the ceiling lights of this glass-walled restaurant add excitement to the night. The thrill continues with your ride in the outside glass elevator up ten flights to the rooftop. Neither the view nor the restaurant will disappoint you.

Steel, glass, aluminum, coal—Pittsburgh trademarks—have been used in this dramatically lit, multi-level room with the glamour of a 30's Hollywood musical set. The glass walls, tallest in the country, afford elegantly framed views of Pittsburgh at its best—by night—and despite the ultra-sophisticated setting, a smooth unobtrusive staff will make you feel at home. This is the place to show visitors New Pittsburgh. Explore city views from various levels, checking out the 20-ton, 60-ft wall of coal in the dining room, the Sports Hall of Fame in the back lounge and the mini-museum of Pittsburgh artifacts at the door.

When To Go: Any night for an elegant outing, by dusk or dark.

What To Order: The menu's also 'top flight' and expensive, but with the help of the maitre d'—ask for George—we've worked out an affordable fling. Entrees can go as high as $35 but there are many choices in the $19-$22 range—**Chicken Solaro**—oven braised in parmagiana/reggiano crumbs with Galliano liqueur ($20), a delicious **Pork with Prunes and Port Wine** ($19) and Grilled Swordfish & Scallops with roasted peppers ($21) all served with a vegetable and a starch.

Or, if you feel adventuresome, you can enjoy a unique dinner of house specialties. Begin with the delicious **Onion Soup** $4.50. Then share a marvelous **Greek Salad** $4.50, or the unusual Duck Salad $5.95...and for an entree, the tasty **Lobster Shrimp & Crab Cake in sun-dried tomato sauce** ($9.95) or the Pasta of the Day $15-$18. With wine at $4 a glass, dinner for two is around $50. Add a wonderful dessert—**Cherries Jubilee,** $9 for 2, or splurge on a bottle of Cook's Champagne $19 to celebrate your night at the top.

Prices: Dinner $18-$35.

What To Wear: Be a superstar...shiny or subdued...match the setting.

Recommended: Continental Cuisine, Connoisseur Dining, Night of Romance, City Views, Rich Man's Guide.

Craig Street Shops

Craig Street Walk & Shop

Craig Street Shops
South Craig between Forbes & Fifth. Hours: Mon-Sat 10-5:30. Some shops open Thur til 8. Parking in lot behind Gallery Shops off Winthrop or at The Carnegie.

This street of shops, in the heart of Oakland's museum-university complex, packs a lot of charm into a small, walk-able area. Houses in the short blocks up from the Carnegie Museum have been remodeled into galleries, boutiques, import shops...with intriguing new restaurants and side-walk cafes adding a European air. The area is worth a holiday visit when trees lining the street sparkle with a fairyland of lights.

Our shopping tour begins at the Museum Art Shop in the Scaife Gallery with its beautiful gifts and objects d'art and fascinating children's gifts at the nearby Natural History Museum Shop. Art browsing continues up Craig with the **Wargo Gallery** and the new **Calaban Book Store** for rare books. The building across the street with the bright yellow two-story pencil (by Lubutz Architects) is Top Notch Art Supplies and farther up the street is the studio of famous Pittsburgh sculptor **Virgil Cantini.** In the next block there's unusual browsing at **Macondo**—clothing, jewelry, folk art from around the world. Then on to the Gallery Shops...fine, one-of-a-kind ceramics and jewelry by top US artisans in **Made By Hand,** lovely woolens and wares of the **Irish Design Center,** fascinating antiques at **Apropos Interiors,** and fine women's apparel at Berkeley Square. Next door in the Craig Square Shops are the intriguing papers of **Papyrus,** the unique gifts of **Watermelon Blues.**

Here you can stop for a relaxing break at **Kane's Courtyard**...pastries & sandwiches in the little outdoor courtyard or in the indoor solarium. Or try a delicious sticky bun, ice cream or coffee from **Bunznudders.**
Don't miss the small shops around the corner on Winthrop including the **Bryn Mawr-Vassar** used book store, a favorite haunt of book lovers. Across the street is the **Phantom of the Opera** for comic book collectors.

When To Go: Wonderful walk for a Saturday or off-day afternoon. A beautiful setting during Christmas light-up nights.

What To Wear: Your leisure best.

Where To Eat: **Ali Baba,** *404 S Craig. Lunch: Mon-Fri 11:30-2:30, Dinner 7 days 4-10. AE,MC,V.* **682-2829.**
Popular Mid-East fare in quiet surroundings. Great a la carte items—falafil, tabooli, hummus, baba ghanooj, spinach pie, Greek Salad, baklava, Arabic coffee $2-$4.50. Dinners—shish kebab, lamb shank, cous-cous & more, $5.75-$10. Bring your own wine. Best buy on street.

Craig Street Shops

Bunznudders, *305 S Craig. Sun-Thur 8am-10pn, Fri & Sat til midnite.* **683-9993.**
An extraordinary bakery/ice creamery with hot-from-the-oven cinnamon buns, yogurt, muffins, meat & veggie croissants, pink lemonade, outside tables in summer. A real treat $1-$3.50.

Cafe Azure, *317 S Craig. Lunch Mon-Thur 11:30-2:30, Fri-Sat til 3. Dinner Mon-Thur 5:30-9:30, Fri-Sat til 10:30. AE,DC,MC,V.* **681-3533.**
Wonderful place for afternoon lunch on the terrace in museum-university center. Beautifully served French provincial cuisine plus croissant sandwiches, quiche, desserts. Lunch $6-$10, Dinners $12-$20. Fine dining. (See Review)

Great Scot, *413 S Craig. Mon-Thur 11-11, Fri-Sat til 12. Sun 10-10. AE,DC,MC,V.* **683-1450.**
A high class "Cheers." Great place for comfort, cuisine, celebration; big brass bar, wooden tables & a menu with all the staples—great burgers, surprisingly fine cuisine. Lunch $3-7, Dinner $12-$15. (See Review, Brunch)

Kane's Courtyard, *Gallery Shops, 303 S Craig Street. Mon-Fri 7-6, Sat 10:30-6.* **683-9988.**
Pastries, great sandwiches, salads at little tables in the Gallery Courtyard or inside in the 'greenhouse,' $1-$4. Take-out.

Museum Cafe, *Scaife Gallery, The Carnegie. Lunch Tues-Fri 11:30-2:30, Dinner Fri only 5:30-8:30. Sun Brunch 12-2. AE,DC,MC,V.* **622-3144.**
A beautiful place to lunch & watch the waterfall by the glass window in the main cafe. Nice sandwiches, salads, soups in $6-$7 range. Fri Dinner $10-$17. Great Sun Brunch. (See Review)

Paradise on Craig, *420 S Craig. Mon-Sat Lunch 11:30-2:30, Dinner 5:30-9:30. AE,MC,V.* **681-9199.**
The area's newest with natural grain, vegetarian cuisine, lots of delicious surprises, outdoor tables in summer, bakery treats. Lunch $2.50-$6, Dinner $5-$14.

Star of India, *412 S Craig. Lunch Mon-Sat 11:30-2:30, Dinner Sun-Thur 5-10, Fri-Sat til 10:30. No liquor. AE,MC,V.* **681-5700.**
The pungent tang of curry wafts up the avenue from this Indian eatery. Soups, appetizers, delicious breads, curries, vegetarian delights, Tandoori, BBQ chicken $8-$15. (See Review)

YumWok, *400 S Craig. Mon-Sat 11:30-10.* **387-7777.**
Unique Chinese cafeteria in pleasant setting; the real thing, great food/prices $3-$6; daily $3.25 dinner specials.

Darbar

Inexpensive Indian Feast

Darbar
4519 Centre Avenue, Oakland. Lunch Mon-Sat 11:30-2:30, Dinner 5-10, Fri & Sat til 10:30. Sun 5-10. AE,MC,V. **687-0515.**

This neighborhood restaurant has given local gourmets another opportunity to discover the subtle and tangy spices of India in an informal, homey setting at economical prices. Pleasant and unpretentious, Darbar features dishes mainly from India's Northern Punjab region, but has all of the Indian staples. While the service may sometimes be uneven, dishes here can be outstanding! Spice levels range from one to ten so if you're new to the Indian cooking start with a three or four level.

When To Go: Noon Lunch Buffet Mon-Fri, Dinner any night.

What To Order: Begin with the **fragrant, delicately spiced Indian masala tea,** a perfect prelude to dinner, and with it. . .one of the highlights of Indian cuisine. . .delicious breads from the tandoor clay oven. . .wonderful unleavened nan and whole wheat bread—plain, puffed or stuffed with cauliflower and potatoes. Our favorites are the crisp, peppery lentil **Papadam,** and the moist, savory **Onion Nan**. . .delicious dipped into the small dishes of mild sweet fruit and hot green mint chutney that accompanies you through dinner.

Some of India's most popular cooking is from the **Tandoor** oven which locks in flavour for mildly spiced, juicy chicken, lamb and shrimp. The **Curries** are another familiar taste.

But most of all we love the exciting flavors of the vegetarian dishes. . .the perfume of the **Matar Paneer,** Indian home-made cheese gently cooked with tender peas in a subtle cream sauce, $7.25, and the popular **Navrattan Korma,** nine vegetables with nuts cooked in cream $8.95. Another wonderful taste is the spicy **Chicken Biryani,** long grain rice with saffron seasoning, $6.95.

The delicate desserts, bland at first sitting, soon become an acquired taste. . .the smooth sweetness of **Rasmalai,** cottage cheese & milk flavored with rose water or the **Gulab Jaman** milk pastry with a thick honey syrup or delightful **Kulfi Almond/Pistachio Ice Cream**. . .a cool end to your meal with the fragrant tea. A good way to sample many tastes here is at the noon buffet Mon-Fri featuring a dish from the tandoor, two vegetable dishes, rice, raita (cucumber yogurt), salad and dessert. . .a bargain at $6.95. Don't forget to take a spoonful of anise seeds at the door.

Prices: Lunch Buffet $6.95, Dinner $5.95-$8.95.

What To Wear: Informal.

Recommended: Indian Cuisine, Fabulous Buys.

Downtown Home Away From Home

DelFrate's

971 Liberty Ave, Downtown. Mon-Fri 11-10. Lounge til 2. AE,DC,MC,V. **391-2294.**

This Pittsburgh family restaurant, in the same old-world yellow brick building at Liberty and 10th for 60 years, suddenly finds itself in the midst of Renaissance II's Convention and Vista/Liberty Center activity. Right across the street from the Vista, it has become a 'home away from home' for businessmen and travelers seeking the comforting warmth of home cooking after a hard day 'on the road' or at the conference table. And that's what owner Dan DelFrate excels at...welcomes. He says his parents, immigrants from Lucca, Italy who started the restaurant, used to say, "People come to our house to eat the good food we make...more importantly they come because they are our friends. We feed them, serve them drinks and make them feel at home." To relax its guests the restaurant has a mellow atmosphere...candles...soft lighting and a robust menu of Italian favorites at good prices. Next door a take-out deli is run by brother Frank.

When To Go: Lunch or a relaxing dinner by candlelight.

What To Order: The dinner menu features veal, steak, seafood, chicken and pastas made from scratch from old family recipes. There's a wonderful **Spaghetti Marinara** with the house's zesty sauce...with or without meatballs...and for those who appreciate its plain, good, taste—**Spaghetti al Olgio, with olive oil, garlic...and anchovies** if you want them...both in the $8-$9 range. Other favorite dishes are **Chicken Marsala** with mushrooms in a delicate wine sauce (only $5.45) and in season a big **California Fruit Salad** with sherbet. Perhaps the best dish is a spirited **Francesco Scallopini,** veal with mushrooms, peppers, zucchini, pimentos in a robust wine sauce, $13.45, served with potato, rice pilaf or salad and a vegetable. A very good house wine ($2.25 a glass) helps you unwind and for dessert there's homemade **Double-Fudge Cake and Apple Pie** made by Dan's wife Marion. No wonder this has become a home away from home! For lunch ($3.95-$6) there's a delicious **Marinated Chicken Salad** and one of the best **Monte Cristo Sandwiches** we've found, a big, triple-decker, batter-dipped, deep-fried ham and turkey on white, topped with bacon, tomato & cheese sauce...for $4.95! (Antipasto meats & cheeses are fresh the NY-style Dilly Dally Deli next door. A favorite breakfast spot, open 6-5 Mon-Fri, it's known for its corned beef & pastrami on rye and comforting favorites i.e. Yankee pot roast and hot turkey sandwich with mashed potatoes and gravy.

Prices: Lunch $4.50-$6, Dinner $7.45-$14.95, less for sandwiches.

What To Wear: You're downtown but you can be comfortable here.

Recommended: Italian Cuisine.

D'Imperio's

**Unforgettable
4-Star Dining**

D'Imperio's
3412 William Penn Highway, Wilkins Twp. Dinner Tues-Sun 5-11. Lounge til 2. Reser sugg. AE,MC,V. **823-4800.**

When your palate craves the very best. . . that memorable meal that makes dining a joy. . . hie on out to D'Imperio's (Monroeville Exit 14 off Parkway East, one mile on the right) for some of **the very best cuisine in the Pittsburgh and Western Pa area.** This rare restaurant with its three beautiful dining rooms has more than great food. The best definition of a truly elegant restaurant is that it makes the diner feel comfortable. And that's the secret of D'Imperio's. Dining is raised to an art in this gracious old-world setting. . . beautiful table settings, shining silver and a peerless staff all orchestrated by owner Tony D'Imperio who personally sees to the comfort of his guests. You'll love the warmth here. After dinner you can linger for music and dancing in adjoining Joe's Jazz Lounge.

When To Go: Romantic dinner, night on the town.

What To Order: The menu is laden with unforgettable dishes. . . tastes that can spoil you. All of the North Italian classics are superbly done— succulent osso buco, veal scaloppine, lamb, steak, lobster, fish flown in daily, plus perfecto pastas. . . ravioli with fresh tomato basil, pasta ribbons in light cream tomato, spaghettini with pignoli, basil and Parmesan. And the wines—superb!

For lunch we love to twin a pasta with the house's **great Antipasto,** an exquisite example of the cuisine here—a medley of marinated mushrooms, pungent caponata (cold eggplant salad), tarragon shrimp, tart sweet peppers and salmon mousse. . . each distinct taste blending into a wondrous whole. It's divine with the house's **heavenly garlic cheese bread**. . . a glass of wine. . . and thou. (And maybe the addition of the fabulous **Cioppino**—Italian fish soup!) Lunch specials—entree, appetizer, dessert, soft beverage are a bargain $9.95.

Our dinner favorite is one of the least expensive entrees— **Cornish Hen with wild rice and raspberry sauce** ($14.95). There's also a tender **Veal Scaloppine** ($18.95), or daily specials i.e. salmon, swordfish, beef Wellington, tuna steak—with antipasto, soup, pastry. . . a bargain at $24.95. The dessert cart, needless to say, is irresistible. . . especially the **Tiramisu,** a light froth of espresso, cognac and mascarpone cream cheese. If you're serious about food don't miss dining at D'Imperio's!

Prices: Reasonable, considering the cuisine. Dinner $14-$25. More with wines but worth it.

What To Wear: The food deserves your best—business or pleasure.

Recommended: Continental Cuisine, Connoisseur Dining, Rich Man's Guide, Pgh After Dark.

Big Beautiful Eating/Meeting Place

Dingbat's City Tavern

Lower Plaza, Oxford Centre, Downtown. Mon-Thur 11-12, Fri & Sat til 1. Bar til 2 nightly. Parking in Oxford Centre garage. AE,D,DC,MC,V. **392-0350.** 🔥

This handsome, spacious restaurant, the hub of the Grant Street business crowd, is a big, friendly place. Designed for socializing, it's centered around a big brass and marble bar. Borrowing elements from the Frank Lloyd Wright prairie school of architecture, it has a brass, burnished look with mosaic tile floor, dark wood, deep green fabrics and beautiful stoneware table settings. There's also a sunken patio with umbrellaed tables where in fine weather you can enjoy the terraced greenery off Grant—one of the loveliest outdoor dining experiences in the city.

You can also order from a lobby take-out window and eat at tables with a wonderful view of the glass-roofed Oxford Atrium. This is a good place to be when you feel like being part of the crowd.

When To Go: Lunch, Dinner, Before/After theatre. Join the five o'clock cocktail rush.

What To Order: There's a tantalizing menu, the same day/night with lots of entrees and a la carte specialties til the wee hours of the morning. It includes some unique, big salads from $5 to $7, and some Mexican and Cajun i.e. the **Blackened Mexican Chicken Steak Salad.** Also featured are char-broiled seafood/steak, a tempting array of sandwiches including a very good classic Club with French fries & slaw plus tuna, chicken & shrimp croissants and the 'Waterworks'—grilled turkey breast, melted Swiss, bacon, lettuce and tomato on homemade grilled Italian bread ($5.95). Quiche, omelettes, all kinds of pizza, pastas and specialty drinks to suit your fancy round out the varied menu that has made Dingbat's a happy name in Pittsburgh. (The restaurant also participates in the Dining with Heart 500 Club.)

A good economical dinner choice is the **Angel Hair Pasta & Grilled Chicken** in tomato sauce with Italian sausage, mushrooms and pepper ($7.95) or the Char-Broiled Steak Sandwich with mushrooms, onion & provolone with big Texas fries and cole slaw ($7.25). Also good is the **Chicken Quesadilla,** a tortilla with grilled chicken, cheeses, guacamole & sour cream ($5.95) and a specialty of the house, the **Giant Onion Ring Loaf,** $2.25 a half.

Don't resist temptation, succumb to the delicious **Mud Pie**—coffee ice cream, almonds and chocolate topped with hot fudge $3, or **Strawberry Yogurt Pie** $2.50.

Prices: Lunch/Dinner $5.75-$11.

What To Wear: Downtown casual. You'll see and be seen.

Recommended: American Cuisine, Outdoor Dining, Late Supper.

Emilia Romagna Ristorante

**Italian Find
In Upper Room**

Emilia Romagna Ristorante
942 Penn Avenue, Downtown. Lunch Mon-Fri 11:30-2, Dinner Mon-Thur 5-10, Fri & Sat til 11. AE,DC,MC,V. **765-3598.**

This restaurant is a real sleeper, a big slow room with a quiet air—and when the busy lunch rush is over it's a good place to sit and savour the exquisite cuisine of the Northern Italian Emilia-Romagna region. There's a welcome unhurried pace—a calm, continental atmosphere that bespeaks the experience of owner/operators Don and Chef Roberta Karanovich. Food is painstakingly prepared fresh and hot from the oven and served with lots of love on starched white linen tablecloths. Some of the dishes really excel... the veal, the cold plates and the **delicious flat Tuscan bread done to a golden brown and fragrant with olive oil—one of the best breads in town.** Eating well is what this place is all about.

When To Go: Lunch, preferably late if you're serious about food, or dinner.

What To Order: Lunch includes several specialties prepared to perfection, tasty **Frittatas**—scrambled eggs with green peppers and tomatoes, **Funghi Ripieni**—mushroom caps stuffed with a mixture of cheeses, a delicious **Fettucine al Pomodoro** in a delicate tomato cream sauce and a unique **Fettucini con Friggione** with zucchini, hot sausage, green peppers and tomatoes, plus delicious veal dishes—all reasonably priced from $6.95 & up.

Our luncheon choice however is one of the prize-winning **Cold Plates**—works of art—the **Carpaccio,** thinly sliced marinated raw sirloin, or the **Antipasto Supremo,** both $8.50, served with fresh vegetables and the delicious bread...with coffee and tax $14-$15 for 2.

Dinners include fettucine, shrimp, trout, chicken and broiled strip steak with beautiful North Italian touches. And for the Italian cognoscenti, the chef loves to create made-to-order dishes. Our choice, however, hands down, is the veal—some of the best in town—**Stuffed Veal Breast, Osso Buco, or Veal Cutlet** with vegetable and house salad, $13.95, with good house wine add $2.50-$3. Worth the extra are delicious homemade desserts—lemon ice, rum-espresso pound cake or a delectable Florentine cake with whipped cream and cherries.

Prices: Lunch $5-$6.50, Dinner $12-$15.

What To Wear: Downtown casual.

Recommended: Italian Cuisine, Fabulous Buys.

**On The Trail of
The Great Steak**

Fatigati's

Miller's Run Road, Cuddy. Mon-Sat 11:30-11. AE,DC,MC,V.
221-4444.

Steak lovers take note. You haven't enjoyed a real steak until you've eaten at Fatigati's. The restaurant's about a half hour away from town and difficult to reach, but you'll be glad you made the trip. Take the Parkway West to I-79S, get off at Bridgeville exit, at first stop sign turn left onto Rt 50. When you pass 84 Lumber look for the Miller's Run Road sign about a quarter of a mile down the road...turn right on Miller's Run. Two miles up the road is Fatigati's, a big, old building with a parking lot to the left. This is old coal mining country and on the way you'll pass thru two small towns—Sygan, then Morgan (unmarked) to reach Cuddy (pop. 500). Not to hurry. Fatigati's has been in the same place for 65 years and they're not going anywhere. What you see is what you get—a big old house, plain tables, a rather scrubby view. But oh what food—the steaks are inches high, in fact so big that you can easily get two— maybe three—to a steak...you're in steak lover's heaven.

When To Go: Give yourself lots of time for the trip.

What To Order: Steak of course. Fatigati's fame has spread. The first thing people ask is where they get their prime, succulent, melt-in-your-mouth beef. (It comes from the Midwest via a Greensburg food service.) The menu carries a staggering number of Italian/American dishes—chops, seafood, pastas from $6-$27 including a very popular $5.95 chicken-in-the-basket.

But go for the **thick, thick flame-broiled steaks from 3-5 pounds** - a single steak enough for two or three sliced horizontally ($1 plate charge). Says Manager Ivo Fatigati, ''It depends on the appetite. I've seen some people eat a whole steak by themselves. Smaller eaters can go three to a steak.'' All the steaks are priced at $27 including T-bones, strip and a 3-4 pound prime rib. They're done to your own turn and served with big glass bowls of salad—greens, tomato, cucumber—and big French fries or spaghetti. 'Mom,' Yolanda Fatigati from Pisa, makes all of the pasta including ravioli and tender gnocchi, and brother Bill's at the bar.

We heartily recommend Fatigati's—steak lover or not—it's a real experience. Your dinner—with two on a steak—is just around $30, plus a 12-oz glass of wine $2.50 or a 13-oz draft beer $1.25.

Prices: Dinner $6-$27—a real bargain when you share a steak.

What To Wear: Something comfortable...you're in the country.

Recommended: American Cuisine, Fabulous Buys.

Froggy's

'Spiffy Place for Nifty People'

Froggy's

100 Market St at 1st Ave (across Blvd of Allies), Downtown. Mon-Thur 11:30-12, Fri & Sat til 1. Bar til 2. Sun—Steeler home games. Reser sugg. AE,DC,MC,V. **471-FROG (3764).**

A popular downtown meeting place, Froggy's, from its spiffy brown coronet awnings to the last detail of service, is a setting in which to lose yourself and your troubles in an aura of bygone days. Enter by the Market Street door with the green, glass frogs overhead into the F. Scott Fitzgerald barroom with its long oak bar, overhead fans and open brick grill. Then on to the adjoining dining room with its round oak tables, claw foot chairs, Casablanca fans and hanging plants. Beautiful reproductions of barroom mirrors interlaced with local sports photos cover the walls. Upstairs there's a **romantic third floor roof patio** for cooling drinks in summer under Cinzano-umbrellaed tables. This restaurant is a feast for the senses even before you taste a bite.

Originally the site of one of the city's oldest taverns, this renovated warehouse is the creation of Steve 'Froggy' Morris of Zelda's Greenhouse fame. His dream was to create "a palace of fun and food to pleasure nifty people from all over...with a decor so splendiferous it would knock your eye out." And Froggy's does just that.

When To Go: Lunch after 1. Better get reservations. Late supper after 8. Jazz pianist Tues-Thur & Sat.

What To Order: The short, sweet Steaks & Chops menu is available all day from $5.95 to $18.95 for filet mignon. And there's an excellent a la carte menu, luncheon specials and burgers from $4.25 to $12. For a budget meal we suggest the **Bullfrog Burger** $5, or the **Chef's Grumpy Duffy Salad**—with house dressing—a crisp, sharp, vinegary, antipasto-like salad with ham, cheese, peppers, olives, red cabbage, **and onions** if you ask for them—$5.50. Either item comes in around $12 for 2—$20 with drinks. A good alternate is the popular **Steak Salad** at $6.75.

A favorite haunt of the city's fourth estate, Froggy's drinkers mean business and these are the biggest drinks in town from the long bar—4-oz liquor for $4, a 12-oz wine for $3.75 and beer $2.25 & up.

Prices: Lunch/Dinner $5.95-$18.95.

What To Wear: Keep up the Fitzgerald illusion. Match the beautiful setting with sweaters, tweeds or after-theatre weeds.

Recommended: American Cuisine, Late Supper.

Sumptuous New Shops A Delight

Galleria
1500 Washington Road at Gilkeson, Mt. Lebanon. Shops Mon-Sat 10-9:30. Sun 10-5. Restaurants, cinemas later. **561-4000.**

This sumptuous shopping center lifts your spirits with its Mediterranean design centered around a beautiful 50-ft clock tower inside a five-story atrium. Patterned after a 19C Milan marketplace, the pale salmon walls, terra cotta touches, teal green tiles and shining marble floors are a beautiful background for some first-class, upscale shopping. It's a browser's feast for the eyes! The $35 million renovation, on former Kaufmann's site, houses 50 unique specialty shops, four restaurants and six cinemas. Architecturally the second level of the Atrium is the best vantage point for a close-up of the tower, the tall palm trees, brass lion head railings and a view of the gleaming first level below. This place with its subdued richness could teach Trump Tower a thing or two about upscale design. And the shops are a delight...many come just to see the beautiful high-fashion stores...these windows are gorgeous...**Harve Bernard, Polo/Ralph Lauren, Perry Ellis, Venetia, Mondi** and **Lillie Rubin** and the exquisite designs of **Laurel.** Many other shops are also quite affordable...Fantasies Lingerie, The Gap, Stylegate, Benetton, Talbot's, Sincerely Yours cards & Christmas Store. Be sure to see the magnificent and unique stones in **What on Earth** on the first level. The splendid atmosphere makes it a real pleasure to come just for a movie and a delicious, fresh-baked bun at **Cinnamon Jim's** on the balcony level...you'll find your way by the wonderful aroma. There's also great take-out at H & M Gourmet Foods at the 2nd level entrance.

Where To Eat:

The Good Earth *First level. Mon-Thur 9-10, Fri-Sat 8-11. Sun 8-9. AE,MC,V.* **343-7808.**
All fresh food, it's good and its's good for you. Fish, meat, vegetarian dishes, pasta, salads, hot/cold sandwiches, good country breakfast; finest of ingredients. $3-$9.

Hot Licks *Second Level. Mon-Thur 11:30-10, Fri-Sat til 12. Sun 12-10. AE,DC,MC,V.* **341-7427.**
A Pgh original for mesquite ribs, chicken & burgers; fajitas, salads, sandwiches, desserts. $3.75-$10. Kids 83¢ on Sun.

L & N Seafood Grill *First Level. Mon-Thur 11:15-10, Fri-Sat til 12. Sun 11-9. Brunch 11-2. AE,DC,MC,V.* **343-6855.**
Popular seafood house with bar, booths, nautical look and fabulous biscuits. Broiled/grilled shrimp, fish, seafood, beef, poultry, pasta, salads. Lunch $5-$9, Dinner $7.50-$22.

Mark Pi's China Gate *Second Level. Mon-Thur 11:30-10, Fri til 11. Sat 12-11. Sun 12-9. AE,MC,V.* **341-9582.**
A beautiful restaurant on the mezzanine with excellent Szechwan, Hunan, Mandarin specialties. Lunch $3.75-$7, Dinner $5-$12.50.

REVIEWS

Gandy Dancer

**Happiest Hour,
Biggest Bargain
In Town**

Gandy Dancer

Station Square, Carson at Smithfield St. Bridge. Mon-Thur 11:30-1am, Fri & Sat til 2. Sun 2:30-10. AE,D,DC,MC,V. **261-1717.**

Celebrities, office workers, Pittsburgers of all ages and backgrounds gravitate to this lively saloon off the elegant Grand Concourse restaurant. On the site of the former baggage room of the restored P&LE Station, it gets its name from itinerant railroad workers called 'gandy dancers' after a legendary Irish boss named Gandy. And some of the old railroad spirit lives again in this bustling bar with wonderful food, fun and camaraderie.

You can sit at the Oyster Bar for quick service, enjoy a booth in the back for less lively moments or join in the happy crowd at the piano from 4:30-1. Local favorite Reid Jaynes plays til 8:30, Larry Beile til 1.

When To Go:
Happy Hour Monday thru Friday 4:30-6:30. In addition to music there are free hors d'oeuvres.

What To Order:
Prices are always right for delicious seafood, pasta, sandwiches, soups and finger foods. Everything's good and everything's a bargain...famous **Charley's Chowder** just $2.25 a tub, $1.75 a crock—a meal in itself with the house's deliciously flavoured **pizza bread,** some of the best in the city.
There's rock shrimp, deep-fried for $7.75, peel 'n eat for $7.25, the house special—**Pasta with red or white clam sauce** served with salad and homemade bread for $7.75, and two new pastas—primavera with crisp vegetables $7, or with shrimp and scallops for $9.75.

Traditionally there are even bigger bargains through the week: **Mondays—Mussels for $3.25, Wednesdays—Peel 'n Eat Shrimp for $5.25, Thursdays—Oysters & Clams on the Half Shell $4.50-$5.50 and Fridays—Big Fish Sandwich for $3.50.** Even without the specials you can eat here easily for $15 for 2. Given the prices and the quality of food it's no wonder this place is always humming.

While you're at the Square, exit by the back door to explore the big Bessemer converter and the antique railroad cars in the nearby museum court. This is a very special Pittsburgh place.

Prices:
Same all day menu $2-$14.

What To Wear:
You'll see everything from jeans to button-down Brooks Brothers.

Recommended:
American Cuisine, Fabulous Buys, Happy Hour, Late Supper, Pgh After Dark.

**Elegant Early Bird
At Pgh Showcase**

Grand Concourse

*One Station Square, Carson Street at Smithfield Street
Bridge. Lunch Mon-Fri 11:30-2:30. Dinner Mon-Thur 4:30-10,
Fri & Sat til 11. Sun Brunch 10-2:30, Dinner 4:30-9.
Parking—East Lot off Carson. Reser. AE,D,DC,MC,V.*
261-1717.

This Pittsburgh showcase is one of the most beautiful
restaurants in the city. . .and the U.S. The splendidly
restored old P&LE railroad station with its soaring stained
glass ceiling, grand marble staircase and yesteryear elegance has been transformed into a wide, palm-treed dining
room with the feel of a Grand Hotel. This is a marvelous
setting for a special occasion or a celebration. And if you're
in a romantic mood, it's worth the wait for a seat in the
River Room to watch the lights of the city reflected in the
water at dusk. Nightly piano music helps sustain the romantic mood.
And in an era of rising costs, the Concourse still offers the
grandest early dinner of them all, a veritable phoenix among
early birds, Mon thru Fri from 4:30-6 and Sun 4:30-9.

When To Go: Take advantage of early prices. Seating by 5:45.

What To Order: Early dinner here includes a choice of 15 elegant entrees
from $9.95-$15. For fish lovers alone there's Boston Cod,
Rainbow Trout, New Bedford Fish Cakes, Nantucket Blue-
fish, Flounder, Poached Salmon, Shrimp Artichoke Pasta,
and Garlic Shrimp. There's also Veal Piccata, Pork Tenderloin, NY strip, Chicken Dijon, Linguini Primavera, London
Broil, Petite Filet Mignon. Who could ask for anything more?
Dinners come with a choice of appetizer, salad or soup,
vegetable or starch, plus dessert and beverage. First
timers—don't miss **Charley's Chowder, an unforgettable
fish soup par excellence.** Wine at an economical $2.50
brings your dinner to around $30 for 2. . .**making this fabu-
lous restaurant accessible to more and more Pittsburgh
families and visitors.**

Regular dinners are relatively moderate for a plethora of
fresh fish, meat, seafood and pasta made on the premises,
from $12-$20. There are also luscious desserts i.e. **Pep-
pered Strawberries with Cream Pernod & Grand Marnier**
$6.50 or the unique **Espresso and Pastry** with a petite torte
and pizelle for $4.25. Another delightful addition is the **Chil-
dren's Menu** for 12 and under—burgers, fish, chicken,
grilled cheese with chips, fries and beverage $2-$3.25, a
great boon for family diners.

Prices: Lunch $8-$12.50, Dinner $12-$20—Early Birds $10-$15.

What To Wear: Your very best to match the elegant atmosphere.

Recommended: American Cuisine, Connoisseur Dining, Night of Romance,
City Views, Fabulous Buys, Brunch, Party Rooms.

Great Scot

High Class
Neighborhood
Cheers

Great Scot

413 S Craig Street, Oakland. Mon-Thur 11-11, Fri & Sat til 12. Bar til 2. Sun Brunch 10-3:30, Dinner til 10. AE,DC,MC,V. **683-1450.**

A high class neighborhood 'Cheers,' this popular eating house is the liveliest on Craig Street. A big, handsome room with wooden tables & lots of brass, its friendly bar attracts the avenue's business & professional crowd, and a surprisingly refined kitchen has earned a reputation for inventive, delicious cuisine. The warm ambience is the well-thought-out work of Jack Camphire, an experienced Pittsburgh restaurateur—always on the scene.

When To Go: Lunch, Dinner, After Work, Late Supper—good anytime.

What To Order: Favorite items seldom change here. . .a good sign as the menu has lots of winners that would be missed. Always a good bet are the **burgers—close to if not *the* best in the city,** plain or with cheese, mushrooms, sprouts, wonderful toppings, a meal in themselves ($6-$7) served with regular or unique sweet potato chips—the house's signature—cole slaw and a great gourmet mustard.

Other standouts are the Grilled Chicken Breast, Turkey Devonshire and Beer Batter Fish sandwiches ($6), a **great San Francisco Stir Fry Salad**—lots of rice, shrimp & veggies. For late snackers there are great appetizers—Coconut Beer Shrimp, Chicken Fingers with cherry mustard sauce, Steak Tartare and Buffalo Chicken Wings. . .all in the $5-$6 range. Don't miss the **very special soups**. . .some hot. . .some cold. . .a unique sampling of all three for $2.95.

Lunches are also gourmet. A great choice is the chicken or fresh fish of the day, always unique—**Maryland Style Crab Cakes** or our favorite delicious **Belgian Waffle with Fresh Fruit and Sausage** ($5.75).

An innovative dinner menu offers varied versions of chicken, steak and fish served with a fresh touch on vegetables. And everything from the smallest to the largest entree is beautifully served. Desserts are also inviting. . .two of the city's best are a luscious **Mississippi Mud Pie**—ice cream, hot fudge, whipped cream, almonds—and a hearty **Bread Pudding laced with Whiskey Sauce,** both worth the $3.95 tab.

Prices: Great for the quality. Lunch/Late Supper $5-$8, Dinner $12-$15.

What To Wear: Casual or business—you'll feel right at home.

Recommended: American Cuisine, Brunch, Late Supper.

Big, Brassy & Beautiful

Houlihan's Old Place

Freight House, Shops at Station Square. Sun-Thur 11-11, Fri-Sat til 12:30am. Lounge til 2. Sunday Brunch 10:30-2:30. AE,D,DC,MC,V. **232-0302.**

Big, bold, brassy and beautiful describes Houlihan's, the hub of Station Square. This lush restaurant-bar with a glorified pub atmosphere has a plethora of paraphernalia from the past—mostly from England—a cheery bar with a big brass espresso machine, lots of wood and front tables with a foggy view through frosted antique glass...a London-like illusion. There are comfortable, colorful dining rooms and a small DJ dance floor that comes alive at 8. One of Gilbert/Robinson's charming chain—'convivial food and the largest collection of pub mirrors in the world'—this place can adapt itself to everything from a snack to a full fledged, affordable fling.

When To Go: Leisurely lunch around 2. Dinner, Late Supper.

What To Order: Just reading the menu here is an appetizing pastime. You can opt for a traditional dinner ($9-$13) but the excitement's in a la carte appetizers, snacks, new light low-cal dishes, hot new salads and delicious Cajun & Mexican items...all well below the $10 mark. Some of the best are the spicy **Buffalo Chicken Wings, the Cajun Shrimp Dinner, and Cashew Chicken Salad.** There's also Shrimp Linguine for $8.25.

We especially enjoyed the award-winning Fajitas (faheetas), tortillas you fill yourself with char-grilled beef or chicken served on a sizzling skillet with bell peppers, guacamole, cheese, sour cream & salsa $9.75, and the new **Appetizer Combo**—buffalo wings, zucchini sticks and potato skins $6.95. The **Baby Back Ribs** are also especially good here with fries and slaw at $11.95. Portions are generous, so if you mix & match your orders, you can eat well for under $20 for 2.

Specialty drinks and luscious desserts like **Hot Apple Strudel Pie** and **Cappuccino Cake** may lure you into a higher bracket but there's no better place for a food fling than Houlihan's!

Prices: Lunch $5.95-$7.95, Dinner $7.95-$9.95.

What To Wear: Go in style...your style. Anything goes.

Recommended: American Cuisine, Fabulous Buys, Brunch, Late Supper, Pgh After Dark.

Jacqie's/Jacqueline's

Elegant, Urbane City Dining

Jacqie's/Jacqueline's

Webster Hall, 4415 5th Ave, Oakland. **Jacqie's** *Lunch Mon-Sat 11:30-3. Dinner Mon-Thur 5:30-10, Fri & Sat til 11.* **683-4344.** **Jacqueline's** *Dinner Tues-Thur 6-10, Fri & Sat til 11. Sun 5-9.* **683-4525.** *AE,DC,MC,V.* 🦽

Warm wood paneling now covers the glass walls and elegant brass signs herald Jacqie's and Jacqueline's, worthy successors to the famed La Normande/Le Bistro duo in Webster Hall. Carrying on the tradition of fine dining is Manager Toni Pais who greets old friends at the door while NY Chef Steve Cortez reigns in the kitchen. Jacqie's, an elegant modern room, is now warmed by soft terra-cotta walls and muted lighting but the long bar remains the same along with the nightly piano music. Nothing has been spared in presentation whether you choose the more informal Jacqie's for modern Italian or the blue-draped, chandeliered Jacqueline's for classical French cuisine.

When To Go

Lunch/dinner at Jacqie's is a good beginning.

What To Order

For all of its formality Jacqie's has a very versatile menu. You can enjoy all of the amenities of first class service and yet eat economically from appetizers, soups, pastas—half orders $6-$7 or whole $12-$15—choice renditions of ravioli with veal & wild mushrooms, agnolotti with spinach and ricotta, fettuccine and capellini and our hands down favorite, the deliciously smooth taste of the **Tagliatelli with Cognac, Cream & Mushrooms.** Lunch also offers some fascinating pizzas i.e. **Pizza Antonito—sun-dried tomatoes and artichoke hearts** ($5.75), a great light lunch idea paired with the **Roasted Pepper/Mozzarella Salad** ($4.25) and shared by two. Calzones & tempting gourmet sandwiches, refined salmon, fish, chicken and veal entrees are $6-$13. Dinner has other revelations from **Chicken with Hot Sausage & Hot Peppers** ($15) to wonderful meat and fish renditions from the grill ($19-$26).

There's more haute classical cuisine at adjoining Jacqueline's, a stately French manor house setting with a blue and gold motif, sparkling crystal and silver service. Prices are not that much higher but this is formal, special occasion dining, each course painstakingly prepared and splendidly presented....epicurean entrees such as **Guinea Hen with Apples and Ginger, Filet Mignon with Foie Gras and Truffle Sauce** around $23, a superfine wine list and an attentive staff catering to every need. (See Rich Man's Guide)

Prices:

Jacqie's—Lunch $5.25-$13, Dinner $15-$26, less a la carte. Jacqueline's—Dinner $23-$27.

What To Wear:

Dress up for the occasion.

Recommended:

French/Italian Cuisine, Connoisseur Dining, Night of Romance, Late Supper, Rich Man's Guide.

Wining, Dining Italian Style

Juno Trattoria

One Oxford Centre, Downtown. Mon-Thur 11:30-10, Fri & Sat til 12. AE,DC,MC,V. **392-0225.**

Pittsburgh loves Italian—and one of the proofs is Juno's, a very popular trattoria in the beautiful glass-walled space of Oxford Centre's third level. The winning Juno formula—casual atmosphere, popular Italian dishes, hand-rolled pastas, homemade pastries & breads—is thriving downtown and in three other Juno's in Ross Park Mall, Robinson Town Centre and Fox Chapel's Waterworks. The marble tables and wood floors of the downtown site blend well with the ultra-modern Oxford setting for a bright, contemporary look. A winner of the National Pasta Association's 'best pasta in the city' award, Juno is the creation of Dominic Abbott and Joseph DeMartino, also the forces behind unique Abate's fish house in Fox Chapel and four popular Dingbat's restaurants—one of them on Oxford's first level. There's now complimentary limo service to the theatre district and to Penguins' Civic Arena games.

When To Go: Anytime—lunch, supper.

What To Order: A voluminous menu offers a wide selection of appetizers, pizza, pasta, sandwiches, plus entrees in the $12-$13 range featuring chicken, beef, seafood and a slew of veals—a specialty here. There's Veal Florentine, Veal Sauteed with Eggplant, Osso Buco (braised veal shanks) and the menu's most expensive item—Grilled Veal Chops with mushrooms ($18.95). Superb pastas are more economical and come in two sizes—"piccolo" ($4.25-$7) and "uno" dinner serving ($8-$12.50.) They lend themselves well to a la carte dining paired with one of the house's fine salads and dessert.

The casualness here also encourages building your own meal from wonderful hot & cold appetizers like Baked Stuffed Artichokes, Steamed Mussels, Hot Banana Peppers and a fragrant **Focaccia,** a pizza-dough turnover filled with cheese and sundried tomatos. Umm good. And for those who love their antipasto, this one's a treat—sausage-stuffed hot peppers, baked eggplant, deep-fried cheese/seafood filled mushrooms. Wonderful with the **delicious, aromatic garlic bread**...the provolone/Parmesan version's worth it at $2.50. Or match a salad with the **Cheese Manicotti** ($7.25) or share a delicious **Chicken and Broccoli Ravioli** ($8.50). Then end with delightful Italian dessert—homemade cannoli, rum cake and lemon Italian ices. You can take home many of the restaurant's menu items from the tempting take-out counter.

Prices: Lunch $4.95-$15, Dinner $7.95-$19.

What To Wear: Downtown casual.

Recommended: Italian Cuisine, Gourmet To Go.

Laforet

**Exquisite Fare
For Dedicated
Gourmet**

Laforet

*5701 Bryant Street, Highland Park. Dinner Tues-Thur 6-10,
Fri & Sat 5:30-11. Reser. AE,MC,V.* **665-9000.**

If ever a restaurant was designed to showcase the talents of
its creators—this one is—doubly so. Lettered on the menu
are the names of the Chef Michael Uricchio and wife Candace, Chef de Patisserie. . . the lights behind Laforet. The
young couple continue to delight diners with their originality,
creating fine food with a flair in this little two-story restaurant on the site of the former Chariot. The second floor dining room, warmed by deep shades of coral, is a lovely,
traditional Victorian setting for romantic dining. Many consider its inventive cuisine the best in the city.

When To Go: A lingering dinner—any night.

What To Order: Dishes are painstakingly prepared and beautifully
presented—part of the pleasure of dining here—in a charming, polished atmosphere. Prices are reasonable considering
the fare with appetizers $4-$6.50 for such epicurean items
as wild mushroom and chicken pate, lobster and scallop
mousse, and delicate salads with warm duck, asparagus
tips, roasted red peppers and toasted walnuts. An ever-
changing menu features several fish, chops, lamb, veal and
chicken for $18-$23. And for the enterprising there's a
nightly fixed price French provincial **Regional Dinner**. . .
6 courses for $35. . . a good gourmet buy.

We highly recommend one of the specialties of the house,
the tender, tender **Loin Lamb Chops marinated in whole
grain mustard, garlic and lemon,** then flame grilled—ours
were medium-rare and the best we ever had—for $23. Or
try inventive seafood dishes i.e. **Sea Scallops with
Avocado,** Striped Bass with Hazelnuts, a delicious **Norwegian Salmon with Smoked Salmon Mousse** $18-$25.
Meals are served with a small but potent medley of
vegetables—ours was a timbale of corn and spinach with
lyonnaise potatoes—and between courses a tangy grapefruit
sorbet.

The desserts are lovely to look at and delightful to
eat. . . like the **White Chocolate Fruit Tart** filled with creme
Anglaise and fresh fruit. . . a truly inspired sweet ($7.50).
These are the kind of touches you grow to expect here.
The lamb chops with blush zinfandel wine, $3.75 glass, will
bring dinner to around $55 for 2, over $60 with dessert but
for some extraordinary cuisine.

Prices: Dinner $18-$24.

What To Wear: Dress up.

Recommended: French Cuisine, Connoisseur Dining, Night of Romance,
Rich Man's Guide.

**There's A Small
. . . French Cafe**

Le Petit Cafe

*809 Bellefonte Street, Shadyside, Tues-Thur 11:30-9:30, Fri &
Sat til 10:30. Sun Brunch 11:30-3, 5:30-8:30. Weekend reser
sugg. AE,DC,MC,V.* **621-9000.** 🔗

This little Parisian cafe, with its elegant air, tiny bistro bar,
and outdoor tables in summer, has one of the best
ambiences in the city. Put this restaurant on your 'don't
miss' list. The food, the mood and the varied offerings make
it within everyone's price range—for lunch, wine or dinner
at seven. Off hours are the best to enjoy the restaurant's
charm. Try to arrive for an early 'aperitif' at one of the small
tables near the glass doorway with a view of Bellefonte St.
Here you can enjoy the restaurant's aura—the little bar, the
subtle hues of pale wine and mauve, the pastry table—a
chance to peruse the posted daily menu, and, if you read
French, to glance over a recent edition of 'Figaro.' This restaurant is small but potent in indefinable atmosphere. Good
restaurants strive not only to satisfy the palate but to deliver
diners from the exigencies of daily life. Petit Cafe's ambience
successfully induces an air of forgetfulness and pleasure.
One of the small Left Bank touches are the paper table-
clothes and crayons for dinnertime sketching. You can dine
at a small banquette with a good view of the room or by the
paned windows, beautiful at night by candlelight. And happily
the full menu is now also available at the outdoor tables.

When To Go: We suggest an off hour. Early for dinner—5:45—or late
lunch to enjoy the atmosphere.

What To Order: Lunch can be put together nicely from an a la carte menu
—a fried Monte Cristo sandwich, a hearty cheese-baked
onion soup, Caesar salad, wonderful omelettes and a beautiful salad nicoise, all in the $3.50-$7.50 range. Our sugges-
tion is a delicious house specialty, the **Angel Hair with
Mussels & Clams** ($6.50) or the **Crepe of the Day** ($7). . .
both served with crusty French bread and a crock of sweet
cream butter.
For dinner there are some delightful entrees—**Pork Loin
with Cream Garlic Sauce** $11.75, and two beautiful
chickens—**Chicken Breast with Red Currant & Apricot
Glaze** and **Roast Chicken filled with Brie with Raspberry
Sauce.** Chef Richard Willen is adding some California spa
fare i.e. grilled fish for under $16, and watch for the **Dinner
Specials,** a bargain $29.95 per couple for any salad, entree
and dessert of the day. There's a wonderful pastry tray
$3.75, or you can finish with a European cinnamon
espresso $1.25.

Prices: Lunch $5.75-$12, Dinner $7.50-$18.50.

What To Wear: Your romantic best.

Recommended: French Cuisine, Connoisseur Dining, Brunch, Outdoor Dining, Night of Romance.

REVIEWS

Le Pommier

**French Find On
The South Side**

Le Pommier

*2104 E Carson Street, South Side. Lunch Mon-Fri 11:30-2:30,
Dinner Mon-Thur 5:30-9, Fri & Sat til 10. Reser. AE,DC,MC,V.*
431-1901.

Le Pommier is reminiscent of the simple French country
inns found outside great cities where a chef retreats to
serve a number of fine dishes to gourmet patrons who know
and seek fine food in a quiet, unhurried atmosphere.
There's a delight in finding the same quiet charm and a
sure, deft hand in the kitchen of this elegant little in-city
restaurant where Owner/Chef extraordinaire Christine
Dauber's loving attention to ingredients makes each dish a
fresh experience. The decor behind the blue, lace-curtained
facade on Carson is deceivingly simple. . . unadorned brick
walls, candle-lit wooden tables, blue & white print
tablecloths—all conspire to create a cozy, comfortable setting. The small number of choices is pleasing to the connoisseur. . . you have confidence the day's menu was
planned around the freshness of the morning's market.

When To Go: Lovely for lunch or dinner.

What To Order: This is cuisine for the serious diner so give yourself time to
savour the tastes. The fare changes seasonally with inimita-
ble versions of fish, veal, poultry and steak. The soup, typi-
cally French, deliciously creamy or savory is $4 a large bowl
with inventive salads and appetizers $4.50-$6. A delicious
start is the **Braised Fennel Salad with carrots, onions and
Gruyere,** $5 wonderful with a Kir Royale—champagne and
Chambord to put you in a holiday mood ($5), or a glass of
fine house wine $3.75-$6. If your budget allows, try the outstanding **Pheasant Breast** or the **Braised Duck with Red
Wine and Morel Mushroom Sauce** or the **Grilled Steak
with Green Peppercorn Cream Armagnac** in the $23-$25
range. But the **Chicken Breast Stuffed with Bleu Cheese**
is equally delicious at $15.50 with flawless vegetables.

Le Pommier is also a delightful luncheon place with sunny
light from the curtained front windows. Elegant entrees
range from $4.50 for a pungent **Grilled Eggplant Sandwich
with roasted peppers and feta cheese** to $8.50 for
Salmon en Papilotte. Soups and salads are much less.
This is also a chocolate lover's haven with a daily **Chocolate Inspiration,** wonderful tarts, creme caramel, or Stilton
cheese to end your meal. P.S. Another good way to discover the cuisine here is at monthly regional dinners
($24.95 for four courses inc tax) or at cooking classes which
include lunch/wine for $27.50. (See Rich Man's Guide).

Prices: Lunch $4.50-$8.95, Dinner $15-$23.

What To Wear: Something casually fine.

Recommended: French Cuisine, Connoisseur Dining, Rich Man's Guide.

Mario's Southside Saloon

Hearty Italian Food, Fun

Mario's Southside Saloon

1514 East Carson Street, South Side. Mon-Sat 11-2am, Sun 1-10. AE,DC,MC,V. Reser. **381-5610.**

Not a restaurant for the faint-hearted, Mario's, from its pasta hung windows to its second floor gallery, is a home for the convivially intrepid. If you love being part of a crowd and don't mind the din and noise (especially on the balcony) this is the place to go for wonderful Italian fare at relatively low prices. Seekers of quiet can take the narrow back stairs to the small third floor rooms which accommodate the overflow. And the overflow seems constant at this popular neighborhood saloon-restaurant adopted by South Siders and Pittsburghers from all over.

When To Go: Lunch, Dinner, Late Supper—things are always humming here.

What To Order: Give yourself time to study a rambunctious menu jammed with unique daily specials and a variety of Italian dishes. The linguini, sauces, soups, dressings, pies are all made daily in Mario's kitchen. There's a full line-up of **pasta conveniently available by the whole or half order** ranging from $3.95 to $9.95 in a variety of sauces—marinara, garlic butter, pignola, red or white clam sauce, gorgonzola, Alfredo, carbonara, Florentine and top-of-the-line seafood and langostino.

One of the beauties of a half order—plenteous in itself—it leaves you room to sample some of the house specialties— fresh **Spinach Salad** $2.25, the **Antipasto** or great **Fried Calamari** at $4.95 or unique French fries with cheese or gravy $2.95. Sandwiches range from $2.95 for the fish Whale's Tale to $3.50 for the meatball-pepperoni-mushroom-cheese '**Too Full to Float Italian Boat**' and the **South Side Sicilian**—pepperoni, prosciutto and provolone with peppers and onions. And sooner or later you'll want to try a huge 36-oz **yard of beer** in a long, long glass flagon—around $6.25. It's good to find a fun restaurant that takes its food seriously. You'll like this super Italian saloon.

P.S. Nothing succeeds like success. Owner Robert Passolano, who also owns **Blue Lou's** next door, is opening another restaurant **Nick's Fat City** across the street.

Prices: Good a la carte buys, $3 up. Serious dinners $8-$12.

What To Wear: No need to bother too much. Unless you're expecting to meet company...come as you are and enjoy.

Recommended: Italian Cuisine, Fabulous Buys, Late Supper.

Max's Allegheny Tavern

Oldtime German Food, Atmosphere

Max's Allegheny Tavern
Corner of Middle and Suismon Sts, North Side. Mon-Thur 11-11, Fri-Sat til 11:30. Sun 11-8. No reser. AE,DC,MC,V. **231-1899.**

Turn back the clock, put on your appetite for hearty German dishes and get in the mood for rollicking fun. This old time North Side saloon has real Tiffany lamps, a unique player piano with a mini-orchestra under glass, superb food—and nostalgia for the time when North Side was the city of Old Allegheny. In operation since 1899 the tavern is a wonderful place to show visitors the real old Pittsburgh.

When To Go: Timing's important at Max's. This Pittsburgh German 'gaste-haus' is always crowded. We recommend **supper week-days** at 6 or 6:30. Give your name at the door. This should give you an ideal wait of 20 minutes at the bar and time to savour the atmosphere. Order draft **lite or dark from a great selection of beers,** $1.50 for a Mason jar full, or splurge on Beck's at $2.50. Scoop up some round pretzel bits. Take in the original mahogany mirrored bar, the wooden tables, the old mosaic tile floor and the bright Tiffany lamps above the wooden booths. That wonderful music is coming from the player piano past the bar. Wander back, beer in hand, to examine what surely must be one of Pittsburgh's wonders—percussion, tambourine and accordion squeezing in and out behind the piano's glass front. Play a few selections of honky-tonk or old favorites at 25¢ a throw. If you like crowds, wait for a table in the main room but three other rooms carry over the barroom feeling.

What To Order: Enjoy the menu, a replica of an 1898 *Allegheny Evening Record,* with sauerbraten and wursts all under $9. Our favorite and the biggest bargain on the menu is the **Brat-wurst Dinner,** a delicate veal and pork sausage for $5.25 including two side dishes—we suggest delicious **Sweet & Sour Cabbage** and the perfectly seasoned **German Potato Salad**—or the delectable **Potato Dumplings.** Homemade dark & light rye is served with generous crocks of apple butter. This food is good!

To top off dinner there's Bavarian Cheesecake with straw-berries ($2.75) or homemade **Apple Strudel** with ice cream ($2.50). Dinner with beer, strudel, beverage & tax...and two piano plays...comes in around $20 for 2—a real bargain for hearty cuisine.
In early evening walk off your hearty meal with a stroll around the Old Allegheny neighborhood with its tall houses and narrow passageways.

Prices: Lunch/Dinner $4.50-$10.

What To Wear: Comfortable clothes of your choice.

Recommended: German Cuisine, Fabulous Buys, Late Supper.

Serenity At The Scaife

Museum Cafe

Scaife Gallery, Carnegie Museum of Art, Forbes & Craig, Oakland. Lunch Tues-Fri 11:30-2:30. Dinner Fri only 5:30-8:30. Sun Brunch 12-2. Parking behind museum. AE,DC,MC,V. **622-3225.** Museum **622-3131.**

There are few places in Pittsburgh more satisfying than the serene glass and gray granite Scaife Gallery...perfectly blended into the older buildings of the famous Carnegie museums. The best approach is down the wide stone steps off Forbes, past the fountain to the main glass doors. New York may have its Metropolitan, Cleveland its fabled galleries, but Pittsburgh has the perfect planes of the Scaife by architect Edward Larabee...one of the most beautiful public spaces in the city. Matching the perfect setting is the lobby Cafe, a picturesque study in pink and green, its marble tables overlooking the outdoor fountain...a wonderful place to linger over lunch.

When To Go: The museum's open Tues-Sat 10-5, Sun 1-6 and new **Friday night hours til 9 pm.**

What To Order: The Cafe offers a beauteous lunch in the glass-walled dining area along Forbes. There's a good mix between light and hearty foods, fish, fowl and vegetable entrees, sandwiches & salads i.e. Warm Chicken Salad, Turkey Devonshire and healthful sandwiches with cream cheese & sprouts...all in the $6-$7 range. Friday night's menu has limited but choice mixed grills, fish, veal and pasta. For hungry kids there's a more basic cafeteria downstairs.

Begin your tour by ascending the wide, cantilevered staircase along the sheer glass wall overlooking the Sculpture Court. At the top to your left begins the Pittsburgh collection—the expansive white galleries a perfect background for **Monet's Waterlilies, Rouault's Old King, Milton Avery's** beautiful new **Dunes & Sea I,** and **Giacometti's tall, metal, solitary Walking Man.** And don't miss Segal's **Tightrope Walker,** precariously balanced on the high wire over the entrance by the Sculpture Court. In the Museum of Natural History next door are more marvels...the famous **Dinosaur Hall, Artic Exhibit, the new Walton Egyptian Hall** and the spectacular **Hillman Hall of Minerals & Gems**...one of the most beautiful exhibits in the world. In good weather you can enjoy the outdoor sculpture and the cooling waterfall. And don't miss items for adults and children in the bright & beautiful Museum Shops.

Cost: Museum Admission $5 adults, $4 Sr Cit, $3 students. Members free. Friday half price admission 3-9 pm. Cafe Lunch $5.95-$7.25, Dinner $10-$17.

What To Wear: Casual...or your Sunday best.

Recommended: American Cuisine, Experiences of the City.

**New Eateries
Boom With
North Side**

North Side

Across the Allegheny from Downtown.

North Side is one of the city's busiest spots nowadays with more and more eateries springing up to serve the area. The most intriguing of Pittsburgh's neighborhoods, "Old Allegheny"—once a city in itself—has become a second cultural center with the new Carnegie Science Center and its World War II submarine next to Three Rivers Stadium drawing more and more visitors. In cobblestoned Landmark Square are the acclaimed Pittsburgh Public Theater and the Children's Museum, with the Aviary just a block away. North Side's streets and hills with their tall brooding buildings and the gentrified houses of the Mexican War Streets/Allegheny West make for intriguing walking. . .as does Roberto Clemente Park along North Shore with its intriguing Sculpture Court and some wonderful camera views of the city across the river. (See Sightseeing Guide)

Where To Eat:

James St Tavern *422 Foreland & James. Mon-Thur 11-10, Fri-Sat til 12. AE,DC,MC,V.* **323-2222.** One of area's most ambitious, a few blocks west of Allegheny Center, with versatile menu and nighttime jazz tailor-made for visitors/ natives. Warm, brick/wood decor, excellent food make it ideal for before/after-theatre and events. Good fish, seafood, chargrilled chicken, steak, great lamb, Cajun soup and an 8-oz Prime Rib $11, 12-oz $14. Weekend jazz with your food. Lunch $3-$7, Dinner $8-$16.

Allegheny Brewery & Pub *Troy Hill Rd. Tues-Sat 11-12. AE,MC,V.* **237-9402.** Great food/fun in old German beer hall. Inexp-Mod. (See Review)

Billy's Bistro *1720 Lowrie. Sun-Thur 11:30-10, Fri-Sat til 11. AE,DC,MC,V.* **231-9277.** More than bistro food, sandwiches plus lobster, BBQ ribs, NY strip. $2-$11. DJ Thur. Inexp.

Clark Bar & Grill *503 Martindale St, Old Clark Candy Bldg near Stadium. Mon-Sat 11-2am. Also open Sun events. AE,D,MC,V.* **231-5720.** Good looking; hearty food, grills, chicken/ribs, pasta. Inexp-Mod.

Maggie Mae's *110 Federal St. Mon-Sat 11-11, Sun 3-9:30. AE,MC,V.* **231-8181.** Bouncy room, big bar with remnants of Pgh past. Eclectic menu, salads with fries & cheese. Inexp-Mod.

Max's Allegheny Tavern *Middle/Suismon. Mon-Thur 11-11, Fri & Sat til 12. Sun til 8. AE,DC,MC,V.* **231-1899.** Great German food, atmosphere. Inexp-Mod. (See Review)

Park House *403 E Ohio. Mon-Fri 11:30-2, Sat & Sun 5:30-2. AE,DC,MC,V.* **231-0551.** Old time barroom, imported beers, coffee. Good economical food—shrimp, soups, salads. Inexp.

One Oxford Centre

Sleek Skyscraper Visitor's Must

One Oxford Centre

301 Grant Street, Downtown. Shops open Mon-Thur 10-7, Tues-Wed, Fri 10-6, Sat 10-5:30. Restaurants later. Garage on Cherry Way connects to second level. **391-5300.**

This 46-story tower, a major Renaissance II addition, has changed the character of Grant Street with its sleek, silver lines. The stunning skyscraper, a great place for visitors and shoppers, is a true 'showcase of pedestrian pleasures.' The glass and aluminum octagon is centered around a graceful, five-story Atrium with a green-treed, white-tabled indoor plaza—a good place to rest and people-watch. Piano music in the main lobby Mon-Sat from 11-2 adds to the relaxing atmosphere. Smooth, steel escalators glide through the Atrium offering many-faceted views of the plaza and the glistening upper levels.

And the Gallery's high fashion shops and services make browsing and buying a delight. **At holiday time the Centre is a glittering sight both indoors and out.**

Some shops and sights not to be missed are **Mollie Moses'** statue-like, glass-enclosed mannequins encircling the Atrium's third level. . .the two-story, glass walls of **Polo/Ralph Lauren**. . .the colorful windows of **Benetton**. . .the showcases of **Ann Taylor, K Barchetti, Emphatics, Talbots** and **Gucci**. . .all wonderful browsing. There's also precious-gem jewelry at Hardy & Hayes, unusual gifts at Counterpoint, fashions at Jaz and melt-in-your-mouth chocolate chips at Mrs. Fields Cookies.

Where To Eat: Interspersed with first-class browsing are three popular, affordable restaurants, each a winner in its own right.

Dingbat's City Tavern *Lower Level. Lunch Mon-Sat 11:30-2, Dinner Mon-Sat 5-12. AE,D,DC,MC,V.* **392-0350.**
A handsome restaurant/gathering place with a long bar, good food and an outdoor cafe on the Grant St side. Take-out window off lobby. (See Review)

Juno Trattoria *Third Level. Mon-Thur 11:30-10, Fri-Sat til 11. AE,D,DC,MC,V.* **392-0225.**
Popular Italian restaurant with homemade pasta, pizza in beautiful, sleek setting on third floor. (See Review)

Warburton's
Delicious pastries, scones, meat/veggie savouries from this very British bakery and cafe. Inexp.

What To Wear: Be prepared for a very sophisticated setting.

Recommended: Shopping, Experiences of the City.

Orchard Cafe

Seafood Lover's Dream Buffet

Orchard Cafe

Pittsburgh Vista Hotel, Liberty Center, 1000 Penn Avenue, Downtown. Mon-Fri 6:30am-10:30pm, Sat & Sun 7am-10:30pm. Sun Brunch 11:30-2:30. AE,D,DC,MC,V. **281-8162.**

This lovely room on the second level of the Vista Hotel is well named...the Monet-like watercolors and flowered chintz in hues of peach, pink and salmon create a country garden setting. Luminous light through the diaphanous curtains at the floor-to-ceiling windows casts a rosy glow over all and etched glass partitions add to the airiness and give privacy in the spacious, comfortable room.

Part of the pleasure of dining here is exploring the luxury Vista Hotel beginning with the four-story atrium lobby with its transparent glass roof, Grecian marble floors and soft carpets...an aura of subdued elegance. Don't miss the wonderful chandeliers in the second floor ballroom.

When To Go: Anytime—breakfast, lunch or dinner but we recommend the Friday Sea Fest, Saturday Italian Feast or the superb Sunday Brunch.

What To Order: The menu features interesting appetizers, soups, sandwiches and salads for a reasonable $2.75-$9 and main courses ranging from $7.50 for Mushroom Lasagna to $18.95 for Medallions of Beef. **But the lavish Daily Buffets are the star of the show.** The Lunch Buffet features marvelous hot dishes plus smoked seafood, seafood and green salads, vegetables and a luscious array of desserts for $10.95. You can do the Soup 'n Salad Bar alone for $7.50. At night the salad bar's included with dinner.

Best way to discover the hotel's fabulous fish, however, is at the **Friday Night Sea Fest,** a seafood lover's dream and best buy of the house. At these feasts, modeled after the famous buffet in the Cape Cod Room of Vista's Chicago Drake Hotel, you can revel in delicacies such as **she-crab soup, smoked salmon, trout, sturgeon, shrimp, crab claws, fish pates, salmon mousse,** seafood salads **plus** an entree selection of **Rainbow Trout, Filet of Pike en Papillote, Broiled New England Scrod or Broiled/Poached Salmon** for $20.50 (for an additional $9 you can have Maine Lobster). Finish with some very special desserts at $2.50. Saturdays are another special night here—an Italian Buffet—osso buco, pork picatta, flank steak, leg of lamb, red snapper, your personal pasta plus wine and accordion music...another festive outing for $17.95.

Prices: Lunch/Dinner $7-$18.95.

What To Wear: It's informal but you'll be comfortable in your finest.

Recommended: American Cuisine, Connoisseur Dining, Fabulous Buys—Friday Night Sea Fest, Brunch.

Pittsburgh's Crystal Palace

PPG Place

Off Market Square, Downtown. Shops, Food Court Mon-Fri 10-6, Sat 10-5. Wintergarden open Mon-Fri 6am-7pm, Sat & Sun 9-7. Garage entrances on 3rd & 4th Aves. **434-3131.**

Already an architectural landmark, shimmering PPG Tower has become the visual center of downtown's Renaissance II...its glass spires creating a 'crystal palace' in the heart of the city. On a five-acre site adjacent to historic Market Square, the soaring 40-foot tower and the five smaller buildings exemplify the city's new human goal of creating not just office buildings but pleasurable urban spaces.
The vast, calm Plaza, reminiscent of the grand squares of Europe, is a wonderful place to watch the play of light and shadow on the glass walls enclosing it on all four sides. And the airy Wintergarden, the light from its high webbed-glass roof pouring down on a profusion of greenery, has become a popular Pittsburgh people place. Building Two, with an entrance off Market and Fourth, has shops with out-of-the-ordinary gifts—**Sincerely Yours, Children's Carousel** and fine leather goods from Specialty Luggage.

Where To Eat: You can stop for an economical lunch or shopping break at the International Food Court which seats 600 in Building Two's lower level. Here from the inviting cafe tables amid potted greenery you have a sweeping view of the two-level atrium. The Court has 12 eateries, some of the city's favorites...Greek food from the Grecian Isles, soups, salads, sandwiches from Strawberry Saloon, super pizza from Somma, Mexican fare from the Hat Dance, meats/sweets from the famous Warburton's bakery and Burgers Burgers & Chili from an eatery of the same name. In summer, **a pushcart serves lemonade to lunchers at outdoor tables off the Plaza.** Three sit-down restaurants are:

Euro Cafe
Two PPG Place. Mon-Sat 11-5, Bar open til l0pm. AE,DC,MC,V. **471-2907.**
A continental cafe with European specialties—soups, salads, sandwiches, entrees & dishes from a different European country every day, $3.50-$7.50.

River City Inn
Five PPG, Mon-Sat 10-10. AE,DC,MC,V. **391-1707.**
Sandwiches, lite fare $2.50-$4.75.

Ruth's Chris Steak House
Six PPG Place. Lunch Mon-Fri 11:30-3, Dinner Mon-Sat 5-11. Sun 5-9. Reser sugg. AE,DC,MC,V. **391-4800.**
'Home of serious steaks,' one of the nationally acclaimed chain. Lunch $6-$13, Dinner $14-$20. (See Review)

What To Wear: It's a business, shopping or sightseeing crowd.

Recommended: American Cuisine, Shopping/Experiences of City.

Paradise on Craig

**Vegetarian
Heaven**

Paradise on Craig

*420 South Craig Street, Oakland. Mon-Sat Lunch 11:30-2:30,
Dinner 5:30-9:30. AE,MC,V.* **681-9199.**

Good news for the city's health food/vegetarian fans, this
restaurant serves up natural, wholesome dishes—lots of
cheese, grains, veggies, fish and chicken in intriguing and
often surprisingly delicious ways. Everything from full-
fledged "regular" dinners to unique macrobiotic fare is
served in a spotless, sunny room with windows on Craig
Street...white walls enlivened with colorful art exhibits
...and a refined folk/classical sound track. A quartet of
young owners cook up the creative offerings. The entranceway serves as a small cafe for light snacks and homemade
goods from the Simple Treat Bakery case with tables moving to the sidewalk in good weather. Even reading materials
are provided...it's a nice place to while away time with a
cappuccino.

When To Go: An economical lunch/supper.

What To Order: We suggest you begin with the unique taste of the herbal
iced teas...wonderful red or lemon zinger, cinnamon
rose...as you peruse the menu and learn all about
balanced grains, beans, vegetables, masa, miso, nori and
tofu—all part of the natural scene here. Be adventuresome!
There are lots of great new tastes...salads with crunchy
seeds, alfalfa sprouts and a subtle tahini dressing, crisp nori
rolls (rice in sea vegetable wrappers) and great chewy
brown rice reminiscent of the wonderful fare at the old Cor-
nucopia restaurant. And don't miss the **whole wheat
rolls...delicious goodness** with a perfect crust. Our lunch
favorites are the **Paradise Greens**—fresh spinach and
vegetables topped with sunflower seeds, sprouts and
cheese ($4.50), the **homemade wholewheat "pitzas"**
($2.25 plus toppings), a great **Grilled Garden Sandwich—
shallots, mushrooms, green peppers, spinach with
melted provolone** or soy cheese, delicious on crisp toasted
whole wheat or Swedish rye...just $3.50.

Suppers are also reasonable with fish, chicken in flavourful
ways. But, good news for vegetarians, the roasted Vegetable Platters are inspired! How about eggplant, hot & sweet
peppers and new potatoes, or a medley of squash, pump-
kin, carrots and carmelized onions in a creamy walnut
sauce ($8.75.) Delicious!

Prices: Reasonable. Lunch $2.50-$6. Dinner $5-$14.

What To Wear: Informal—you'll see professionals, students, "students of
cuisine."

Recommended: American Cuisine, Outdoor Dining, Gourmet To Go.

Still the City's Italian Favorite

Pasta Piatto

736 Bellefonte Street, Shadyside. Mon-Sat Lunch 11:30-3, Dinner Mon, Tues, Thur 4:30-l0, Wed, Fri, Sat til 11. Sun 4:30-9. No reser. MC,V. **621-5547.**

People still declare, "Nothing beats the Pasta Piatto," #1 in the city for fine, N Italian dishes. This is the restaurant that took Pittsburgh by storm 10 years ago serving up fine cuisine in a white-tablecloth atmosphere at prices less than many a larger establishment. The Piatto took the starch out of dining in Pittsburgh and other restaurants have followed suit. It's still crowded—though now more comfortably—and there are still long lines and a "no reservations" policy. But the Piatto, reminiscent of the fine little Italian restaurants with their fresh flowers, attention to detail & service, is still serving up fine food at reasonable prices. Owner Linda Jeannette personally oversees the service and the making of the "best pasta between NY and Chicago" and the delicious breads and desserts.

When To Go: Lunch or Dinner. The "no reservations" policy results in long lines at peak hours but the short wait is worth it.

What To Order: There's a delicious variety of fine dishes—seafood, veal, salads and pastas of all kind including tortellini from a shiny machine from Italy. Lunches are from $3.50-$9 and dinners $9-$20 for a generous seafood dish **Granchi & Gamberi**, shrimp & lump crabmeat in wine and butter. We have many favorites—one more delicious than the other—the **heaping Antipasto** $8.25 (more than enough for dinner), the creamy **Fettuccini alla Carbonara** with butter, cheese and bacon, the **delicate Canneloni with Meat Sauce and Bechamel** and the **Linguini with Clam Sauce** topped with clams in the shell—a wonderful dish, all in the $10-$11 range... served with a perfect green salad and crusty house bread...for only about $13 a person, $16 with big goblets of house wine.

The **Gorgonzola Salad**—crisp, crisp romaine lettuce with walnuts and gorgonzola dressing—is a salad lover's dream for $4.75. Also worth the extra are the heavenly desserts— **Zabaglione** $3.25 and the **Pasta Delight**—whipped cream, vanilla cream, fresh fruit and toasted pecans $3.75. If you haven't discovered this fine restaurant you have a wonderful treat in store.

Prices: Lunch $3.50-$9, Dinner $9-$20.

What To Wear: Be comfortable and informal—the better to concentrate on the food.

Recommended: Italian Cuisine, Connoisseur Dining, Fabulous Buys, Late Supper.

The Primadonna

Provincial Eatery Makes Waves	**The Primadonna**

801 Broadway, West Park—McKees Rocks. Mon-Sat 4-11. AE,CB,DC,MC,V. **331-1001.**

Say hello to a provincial primadonna...a bountiful Italian restaurant that is sending gastronomic waves in the Greater Pittsburgh area. As many rebound from effete gourmet cuisine to hearty home cooking this neighborhood restaurant takes front and center. It's definitely Italian and folks from all over are heartened to see many McKees Rocks natives as regulars—who should best know good Italian!—cheek by jowl so to speak with the visitors. As usual with local successes, this is a family affair, in this case the Costanzo family, in evidence with Joe as official greeter, Pino as chef, cooking some of Mama's recipes in the kitchen, and their ancestors...keeping an eye on things from their oval frames on the walls. The restaurant with its portraits and flowered wallpaper resembles an old-fashioned diningroom in an Italian home. And the warm family feeling extends to the service with its honest concern that you have a most pleasurable meal. This and the good prices have led to long waits for a Primadonna table.

When to Go: No reservations so try to make it early or later than 6-7 but you'll probably have to wait anyway...in anteroom or bar.

What To Order: This is good, plain cooking...but the best of its kind. There are too many good things to be an accident. It's a big menu, from pastas beginning at $7.95 to NY Strip at $16.95...but most of the dishes are in the $8-$11 range. There are scores of pastas, some of the more interesting the **Spaghetti El Duce** with scallops, pepperoni & artichoke hearts and the **Veal Sicilian Pasta** with hot peppers, mushrooms & onions. There are some wonderful staples like tender **Homemade Gnocchi** with meatballs just like Mom used to make in a very good sauce ($8.50), and delicious homemade soup...the **Chicken Barley's** aroma brings back childhood memories of the family kitchen. Crusty Italian garlic bread is served with every meal and we heartily recommend the **Antipasto,** a generous arrangement of very fresh Italian meats and cheese over a bed of crisp greens with a **wonderful, zingy-sweet Italian dressing** ($6)...the small was enough for 2 with a meal. Portions are generous and dinners come with a salad, pasta/baked potato and vegetable. You can afford dessert $2-$3, and wine by the half carafe $6.50-$8. This is the kind of place you'll want to come back to to try out the house versions of linguine, ravioli, veal, seafood, spaghetti.

Prices: Dinner $7.95-$17, most in the $8-$11 range.

What To Wear: You can be comfortable.

Recommended: Italian Cuisine, Fabulous Buys, Late Supper.

Zesty Fare At Balcony Cafe

River Cafe

Second level, Freight House, Shops at Station Square. Sun-Thur 11:30-10, Fri-Sat til 11:30. AE,DC,MC. **765-2795.**

1

Word-of-mouth has spread news about this sleeper at Station Square. Patrons have been pleasantly surprised at the cuisine, the good prices, the generous portions and the San Francisco decor. This is a very pretty room, stretched out in an el along the balcony overlooking the Shops, bright and airy with ceiling fans and beautiful stained glass panels on loan from the Pgh History & Landmarks Foundation. The light fare of Amazing Grace, formerly on this site, has been replaced with a full-fledged menu of inventive dishes that have made the Cafe the surprise of the year. The traditional settings and service are enlivened with an informal air and the cordial concern of owner Richard Bozzo.

When To Go: Romantic lunch, dinner.

What To Order: This is a good place to take a group of enthusiastic eaters. "You've got to taste this" is a typical comment as patrons swap samples of the house's piquant dishes—many of them based on Cajun cookery. At various times we've traded tastes back and forth of the **New Orleans Sizzler Platter**—blackened shrimp, catfish and chicken...a real bargain at $10.95, the zingy **Catfish Salza** ($9.95), **Salmon with Saffron Pasta** ($12), the **Smoked Trout Appetizer** ($5), and the **Pasta Diablo** linguine with andouille sausage, mushrooms & peppers...a great dish...but almost too much and too "hot" for one person unless you have a Cajun palate. There's also Shrimp Diane, Linguini with Shell Fish & Artichokes & a Spinach Fettuccine Alfredo. A good selection of salads and sandwiches from $5-$7 round out the evening menu.

Extra touches make dining special here, a complimentary hors d'oeuvre—such as smoked turkey or pate—sourdough from the Breadworks, tender salad greens...try the raspberry vinaigrette...delicious smoked fish, poultry and fresh seafood fresh plus a dazzling dessert cart. So many goodies! This is also a popular lunch spot with smaller portions of the evening fare plus a wonderful Red Snapper Burger, Veal/Mushroom/Nutmeg Quiche, a Cajun Chicken Sandwich and an interesting Whole Wheat Pizza with andouille sausage, chicken, mushrooms, provolone and tomatoes...all in the $5-$6 range. You can also split lunches for a $1.25 plate charge.

Prices: Lunch $5.25-$8, Dinner $5.75-$13.

What To Wear: Informal to dress-up at night.

Recommended: Amer/Cajun Cuisine, Fabulous Buys, Late Supper.

Ruth's Chris Steak House

The Ritual of the Great Steak Dinner

Ruth's Chris Steak House

PPG Place, Downtown. Lunch Mon-Fri 11:30-3. Dinner Mon-Sat 5-11. Sun 4-8. Free evening parking PPG garage, enter Third or Fourth Ave. Reser sugg. AE,DC,MC,V. **391-4800.**

The famous Ruth's Chris has come to town and real steak lovers are doing obeisance to its noble heritage. This stylish, comfortable restaurant is one of 28 named for Ruth Fertel who purchased the Chris Steak House in New Orleans in 1965 and began franchising in '77. (Pittsburgh's was brought here by Jack Offenbach of The Samurai and Tequila Junction fame.) The setting, lots of warm cherry wood, glass and subtle lighting, is a fitting background for the ritual of the perfectly cooked steak and the painstaking dedication required to achieve it. First you take only only 'top of the top' U.S. prime (about 2% of all beef). Age in dry refrigeration (never freeze!) for 60 days to lock in flavour. Carefully hand cut just enough for each day's dining. Cook to order in a specially built, high temperature broiler that sears in juices at 1800 degrees. Place the steak, sizzling in butter, on a ceramic plate heated to 450 degrees...and serve with a flourish. Disciples say this meat just can't be beat!

When To Go: A weekend or Sunday dinner seems only fitting.

What To Order: These tasty, butter-soft morsels range from $16 for a **petite 8-oz filet** to $20 for a **12 to 14-oz filet or 16-oz ribeye. The porterhouse is $42 for 2** or $84 for four for a massive cut. So far, so good—but the steak you see is what you get for your money. Potatoes, vegetables, salads—and in some cases even sauces! are all extra. For instance an Italian salad $3-$4, a baked potato $3.25, and the house's delicious creamed spinach $3.50, can add $10 to your check. Actually the steaks are so big and good, a salad or potato alone should suffice. And since one good thing leads to another, how about rounding off your perfect dinner with **Blueberry Cheesecake, Apple or Pecan Pie a la mode or Bread Pudding with 80-proof Whiskey Sauce** ($3-$4).

If you're a steak lover you'll eventually come here to do homage anyhow.

(For non-beef eaters there's chicken, lamb and veal chops from $15-$23 and fresh fish and Maine lobster flown in daily—both at market price.) You can sneak a peek at this restaurant at lunch—a better bargain—with **NY Steak Sandwich** or a **Petite Filet** with fries & veggies $12.95, prime steak burger $5.95, and a great **Steak Salad** for $8.95.

Prices: Lunch: $6-$13, Dinner $15-$42.

What To Wear: Strictly downtown attire.

Recommended: American Cuisine, Connoisseur Dining, Rich Man's Guide, Late Supper.

Sarah's Restaurant

Ethnic Experience	**Sarah's Restaurant**

1

*52 S 10th St, South Side. Tues-Sat 5:30-9pm, Sun 4-8. Street parking, lots nearby. Reservations only. Groups preferred. No credit cards. **431-9307.***

Sarah's is an unofficial Pittsburgh landmark for its authentic Yugoslavian cuisine prepared fresh daily and lovingly by Sarah Evosevich herself. From noon on, bread is rising. . .strudel baking in preparation for the night's 'company'—dinner guests who will be served with a personal touch in this small charming South Side house.

Sarah's has a flat $20 fee for a family style dinner—and its fame, uniqueness and just plain good food for the money make it a natural Rich/Poor Man's feast. This is the place visiting firemen are taken to show off Pittsburgh's unique ethnic culinary heritage and to let real home cooking and homey atmosphere melt away road weariness. We suggest you take a group of hearty eaters to help you enjoy your meal and linger over the delicious dishes and table talk.

When To Go: Any night except Monday. Reservations are a must as each dinner is personally prepared.

What To Order: Sarah's home cooked meals are open ended. You can eat as much as you like of a series of dishes served in big bowls family style. Start off with a cocktail ($3) or a bottle of house wine ($20) from a cozy corner bar in the 'living room.' Food at Sarah's comes in generous portions and more or less in the following order. First the **Bread—some of the city's best—homemade, with a beautiful butter-browned crust** (just as delicious next morning if purloined for breakfast!) Then a cool, lightly marinated cole slaw followed by homemade soup—ours was Chorba, an old fashioned Serbian vegetable/barley. Then come the appetizers—as filling as a main course—**Spinach Pita,** delicate layers of filo dough with egg & cheese, and **Burek,** a tasty chicken and cheese casserole. Sometimes a tasty moussaka follows. Your plate runneth over!

And the main dishes are still to come—the unique taste of Podvarak—**turkey with sauerkraut stuffing,** Yanjatina—**delicate roast lamb with mushrooms, paprika potatoes** with a mysterious hint of garlic and fresh vegetables steamed to perfection. Dessert—unbelievably you still have room—is an **apple strudel** followed by a 'house liquor' of hot whiskey with honey & spices. Altogether a very satisfying meal that leaves you with a well-filled glow.

Prices: A bargain $20 complete dinner.

What To Wear: Comfortable clothes, suit coats for men.

Recommended: Yugoslavian Cuisine.

Shadyside Walk & Shop

Shadyside Shopping Spree

Walnut Street between Ivy and Aiken. Port Authority 77C bus stops at corner of Walnut & Ivy. 71B,C,D stop two blocks away on Fifth Avenue.

Shadyside, the city's finest specialty shopping center, has taken on new upscale sleekness. But the creative character of the street remains, an intriguing mix of elegance and off-beat charm...with just a little of Rodeo Drive thrown in. When East Enders talk about the 'Avenue' they usually mean Walnut Street—the place to see and be seen in the latest casual attire. There are some beautiful stores here...small one-of-a-kind speciality shops side by side with the sophisticated chains...and it all makes for delightful browsing and window shopping. The small area also abounds in famous eateries and night spots.

When To Go: Day off or Saturday afternoon for meeting, greeting people. Stores open Wed til 9.

Reserve a whole day, for there's beauty aplenty in this three-block area with its charming use of space including upstairs rooms and awninged byways. Nationally famous stores have brought new polish to the avenue—the beautiful windows of **Ann Taylor, e.b. Pepper,** alluring **Victoria's Secret** and **Laura Ashley** join **William Penn Hat & Gown Shop,** Talbot's Divine Knits, Basic Image, Kountz & Rider, men's Stylegate and the many fine small specialty shops creating a fashion mecca in a very small area. More down-to-earth shopping at **Express, The Gap, Benetton's** and the campy lure of **Banana Republic** add to the Avenue's cachet. Even the children are not forgetten with kids' fashions at Tots & Tweeds, Cradle & All and a bright new Gap Kids.

And along with the three tiers of wares in **Pier One** are unusual, unique shops—old fashioned **Shadyside Variety Store,** a tradition for odds & ends & kiddie delights, Rolliers, a super hardware store, **Annex Cookery** with its avant garde kitchen wares, Toadflax for antiques and hard-to-get gourmet goods and **Kards Unlimited** for probably the city's largest collection of unique gifts/cards. Urban Renewal (on the site of the muchmissed Ways & Means) has unusual housewares, furniture and some good half-price bargains in the lower level.

At the Aiken end of the street is Shadyside Village with the delightful **Pinocchio Bookstore.** And there's more shopping under the sunny, skylight roof of the **Theatre Mall.** Save time for browsing in the exclusive food shops in the small new malls with some of the best gourmet take-out in the city...dinner for one to 100! (See Gourmet to Go) A few blocks away Ellsworth Avenue is blooming with some of the old Shadyside village atmosphere—antique shops, art galleries and a new book store.

Where To Eat:

Artery *5847 Ellsworth. Tues-Sat 5-11, Sun til 10. AE,DC,MC,V.* **361-9473.**
Art gallery/restaurant with eclectic entertainment, brick patio in summer. Appetizers to entrees. $6-$12.

Callahan's Pub & Parlor *5505 Walnut, 2nd level. Mon-Sat 11am-2am, Sun 1-12. AE,MC,V.* **687-9212.**
Beautiful, upscale pool hall bar. Billiards $5 hr up; munchies/pizza/burgers/peel & eat shrimp. 75¢-$5.

Cappy's *5431 Walnut, Mon-Sat 11:30am-2am, Sun 12-2am. AE,DC,MC,V.* **621-1188.**
Mod, dim little restaurant/bar with creative sandwiches, great barbecue-grilled chicken. $3.50-$6.

Doc's Place *5442 Walnut. Mon-Fri 4-2am, Sat 11:30-2.* **Doc's Grille,** *Mon-Fri 5-2am, Sat 4-2am. AE,DC,MC,V.* **681-3713.**
Casual lounging, snacks in lively saloon at Doc's Place. Inexp. Delightful rooftop patio/upstairs diningroom. Grills, sandwiches, appetizers, entrees. Mod.

Elbow Room *5744 Ellsworth. Mon-Thur 11-12, Fri-Sat til til 1. Sun 11-11. AE,MC,V.* **441-5222.**
Good mix of food, folks keeps three rooms, bar, backyard patio crowded. Sandwiches, salads, dinners. $2-$12.

Hot Licks *Theatre Mall. Mon-Thur 11:30-10, Fri-Sat til 12. Sun 4:30-9. AE,DC,MC,V.* **683-2583.**
Headquarters for great mesquite ribs, grilled swordfish, chicken, burgers; salads, sandwiches, desserts. $3-$15.

Le Petit Cafe *Walnut/Bellefonte. Tues-Thur 11:30-9:30, Fri-Sat til 10:30. Sun 11:30-8:30. AE,DC,MC,V.* **621-9000.**
Beautiful little French cafe. Mod-Exp. (See Review)

Max & Erma's *5533 Walnut. Mon-Thur 11:30-11, Fri-Sat til 12. Sun til 10. AE,D,DC,MC,V.* **681-5775.**
Huge 2nd-fl with warm, brassy nooks; eclectic menu— burgers to light entrees, make-your-own sundaes. $2-$10.

Pamela's *5527 Walnut. Mon-Sat 8-4, Sun 9-2. No credit cards.* **683-1003.**
Breakfast specials, best hot cakes in town with sausage, bacon; sandwiches. $1.75-$3.50.

Pasta Piatto *736 Bellefonte. Lunch Mon-Sat 11:30-3. Dinner Mon, Tues & Thur 4:30-10, Wed-Sat til 11. Sun 4:30-9. MC,V.* **621-5547.**
Great N Italian cuisine at great prices. Lunch/Dinner $3.50-$20. (See Review)

Shadyside Balcony, *Theatre Mall. Mon-Thur 11:30am-12:30am, Fri-Sat til 1. Sun Brunch 11-3. AE,DC,MC,V.* **687-0110.**
Enjoy view of Avenue from glass-walled restaurant, innovative menu ($4.50-$10). Wonderful nightly jazz. (See Review)

Szechuan Gourmet, *709 Bellefonte, Mon-Thur 11:30-10, Fri-Sat til 11, Sun 4:30-10. AE,DC,MC,V.* **683-1763.**
Excellent Chinese cuisine, off-avenue setting. $7.95 up.

Shadyside Balcony

**Jazz Beat Goes
On at Balcony**

Shadyside Balcony

*Theatre Mall, 5520 Walnut Street, Shadyside. Mon-Tues
11:30-11, Wed & Thur til 12, Fri-Sat til 1. Sun Brunch 11-3.
Parking on, off Walnut Street. AE,DC,MC,V.* **687-0110.**

A Shadyside success story, the Balcony has expanded from
a small, glass-walled room to the entire second level of the
Theatre Mall with varied vistas and entertainment. It sets
the beat for Walnut Street, picking up the old Shadyside
jazz tradition six nights a week. Its big open space, broken
by the mall's main staircase, allows many uses—a quieter
dinner in the glass front restaurant with a bird's eye view of
the avenue...a livelier setting in the back cafe area where
you can enjoy music with your meal...or a visit to the long,
winding bar with plenty of room for stand-up conversation
and crowds spilling down the staircase. The Balcony's
music and ambience attracts a wide age range, a plus for
sophisticated partyers.

When To Go:
Don't miss the music weekdays from 8-12, weekends from
9-1am, Sunday Brunch 11-3.

What To Order:
The excellence of the food & service continues, thanks to
the hands-on management of young owners Muzz Meyers
and Bob Feldman. This is one of the city's most unusual a
la carte menus with an emphasis on deliciously simple,
healthful dishes. Our favorites include the **Vegetarian
Chef's Salad**—greens, cheeses, healthy sprouts & seeds—
and six delectable **Gourmet Pizza** including the **"Seventh
Inning Stretch" with marinated tomatoes, spinach, garlic, mozzarella & feta on crispy, slightly sweetened
dough—a zesty combination!** Both are in the $5-$6 range
which tells you something about prices here. There's a
delightful choice of beautifully crafted soups, salads &
unusual sandwiches including the **Flame-Grilled Salmon
BLT** on mixed greens with a lemon-dill sauce and the
Mushroom Plus—sauteed mushrooms, broccoli, walnuts,
raisins, apples & melted Muenster on Indian Harvest bread.
Paul's Hot Chili and innovative salad/soup/quiche combinations are as popular as ever.
Dinners have gotten even better with aromatic grilled versions of tuna, pork, shrimp, tenderloin or your own **"Combination Grill"** $12-$16. A longtime favorite, **Cashew
Chicken,** is still on the menu at $12.

Chocolate lovers get their just desserts here with one of the
city's best—**Balcony Hot Fudge** in your own little pitcher to
pour over French vanilla ice cream...heaven for $2.95.

Prices:
Lunch $5.45-$7, Dinner $6-$15.50

What To Wear:
Fashionable casual—Shadyside style.

Recommended:
American Cuisine, Fabulous Buys, Tea, Pgh After Dark,
Late Supper.

**French Cuisine—
Affordable Prices**

Simply French

1

346 Atwood Street, Oakland. Mon-Sat 4:30-9:30. AE,D,MC,V.
687-8424.

Bikki's Simply French restaurant is a perfect example of the
new 'informed informality'—good food in simple surroundings. Bikki (Bikkram Kochhar), a transplant from India's far-
off Himalayan highlands, is a bold and imaginative restaurateur (the former Taj in Squirrel Hill, The Wok Inn and Mai
Thai of Oakland). But this French table is the star of his
show and has held its reputation for excellence and its
popularity for several years. You have to savour the cuisine
and fantastic prices to understand the fervent fans and long
waiting lines. The atmosphere, though pleasant, isn't the
chief concern. Thanks to Chef Michael Hooker, who keeps
coming up with new and better creations, you can enjoy a
marvelous French fling at unheard-of prices. The 'bring your
own liquor' rule helps to reduce the dining tab.

When To Go: It's dinner only. Try around 5 or 8 to avoid the lines.

What To Order: Everything's good here, but we have our favorites.

Dinners range from $6.95—for a very good Mussels Dijon,
Spinach Gnocchi or Fettucine—to $15.95 for the most
expensive entree, Peppercorn Steak. And there are many
offerings in the $7-$9 range. Even with separate charges for
soup, appetizers, salads ($1.75-$5) you can let yourself go
and keep your tab at $15 a person. The mussels are a rave
here including both the **Mussels with White Wine & Shallots & Mussels Dijon** appetizers, both around $3. Also won-
derful tastes are the Apple, Onion or Cheddar Soup and a
delicious Roast Loin of Pork with mustard & brandied pears
or raisins $9.95. But our favorite of all favorites is the per-
fectly seasoned, done-to-a-crisp **Roast Duckling with Plum
Peppercorn Sauce**—possibly the best duck in town—for
$13.95! Another wonderful dish is the **Fettucine
Alfredo**—$6.95 as an entree, $3.50 as a side dish.

There's also a daily **Simply French Country Dinner** at
$9.95 with soup, salad, entree and dessert. . .a good bar-
gain. The house also boasts a new Simply Italian menu.

You'll be more than tempted by the extraordinary
desserts—**Chocolate Terrine with Pistachio Praline**, sorbets, or our own favorite, a cool **Orange Mousse** with
chocolate sauce. Bon appetit! You won't regret this visit.

Prices: Dinner $6.95-$16.95.

What To Wear: Comfort is the watchword. . .but you'll see all styles.

Recommended: French Cuisine, Connoisseur Dining, Fabulous Buys.

South Side Saturday Night!

South Side

East Carson Street from Birmingham Bridge to 10th St, 5 minutes from Downtown, Station Square & Oakland.

The historic "Birmingham" neighborhood continues to boom as more and more restaurants, art galleries and small shops open in the 20-block stretch within minutes of major city areas. South Siders are determined to keep their ethnic character amid the new sophistication, creating an interesting mix of urban charm and neighborhood nostalgia. The architecture alone is worth a visit. . . from the row houses in the 'flats' toward the river to Carson's tall, Victorian buildings with their ornamental ironwork, some of the best examples in the U.S. This is prime territory for browsers and collectors with some 32 art galleries and antique & craft shops mixed with storefronts harking back to the '30s/'40s.

But if you really want to see South Side changes, visit on a Saturday night. Throngs of people crowd the sidewalks sampling new eateries, jazz clubs and night life. To an old-timer it's an unbelievable sight! And it's going to get busier. Joining the **Rex Movie Theater** is **City Theatre's** new home in a restored church at 13th & Bingham. And the fantastic **Beehive Coffee Shop** near 12th really has the area buzzing. The word is out that South Side is Pittsburgh's new Greenwich Village!

Browsing on Carson don't miss **Down to Earth's** beautiful crafts at 1022. . . **Carson St Gallery** at 1102 and **South Bank Gallery,** 1300. Of interest to architectural buffs are the restored Italianate **Antique Gallery** at 1713 and the 110-year-old **Cast Iron Building** at 1737—one of the area's largest intact cast iron facades. At 12th & Bingham off Carson are the rounded arches of the historic Romanesque **South Side Market House**. . . don't miss **Dynasty Crafts** in the Square. Nearby on 18th St. is **Birmingham Loft** gallery. New restaurants continue to spring up, most with a 'no reservations' policy. . . but if you miss one you're within easy walking distance of another.

Where To Eat:

Beehive Coffee House *14th & Carson. Mon-Thur 7-midnite, Fri-Sat til 4 am, Sun 9-11.* **488-4483.**
Coffee/tea dessertery with odd chairs, chess, charm, fabulous brews, sweets; entertainment. Inexp.

Bloomers *27th & Jane. Tues-Thur 5-12, Fri-Sat til 2. MC,V.* **381-1700.**
An unusual cafe with women artists, entertainment, light dining, drinks. Inexp-Mod.

Blue Lou's *1510 E Carson. Tues-Sat 11am-1:30am. AE,DC,MC,V.* **381-7675.**
Barbecued ribs, chicken with lively juke box, waiters sliding down a firehouse pole. Inexp fun.

Brady St Bridge Cafe *2228 E Carson. Mon-Thur 11:30-10, Fri-Sat til 11:30. AE,DC,MC.* **488-1818.** Old Pittsburgh Victorian nostalgia, long antique bar, eclectic menu; outdoor patio. Mod. (See Review)

Cafe Allegro *51 S 12th. Lunch Mon-Fri 11:30-3. Dinner Tues-Thur 4:30-10:30, Fri-Sat til 12, Sun 4:30-9:30. Reser. MC,V.* **481-7788.** Charming two-story restaurant with light Riviera cuisine, espresso bar. Good prices. Mod. (See Review)

Cardillo's Club Cafe *52 S 12th. Tues-Sat 6pm-2am. AE,MC,V.* **381-3777.** Stylish NY cafe with smooth father/son jazz piano duo. Great entertainment, good food. Mod. (See Review)

Chinese on Carson *1506 E Carson. Mon-Thur 11-10, Fri-Sat til 11. Sun 4-10. AE,DC,MC,V.* **431-1717.** A good-looking 2nd floor room with beautiful ambience, affordable menu. Mod.

City Grill *2019 E Carson. Mon-Sat 11-11. AE,DC,MC.V.* **481-6868.** Sizzling hardwood grills—steaks, ribs, chicken, fish. After-theatre favorite. Mod.

Hunan Gourmet *1209 E Carson. Mon-Thur 11:30-10, Fri-Sat til 11. Sun 3-9:30. AE,DC,MC,V.* **488-8100.** Superior Hunan/Mandarin specialities in very pleasant setting. All day Dim-Sum. Inexp-Mod.

J J's *21st & Carson. Tues-Sun 4:30-10:30, Fri-Sat til 11:30. Bar til 2. Sun 4:30-9:30. AE,MC,V.* **481-2900.** Casual, dinner only—steaks, chops, chicken. Rhythm/Blues Fri-Sat; Jazz Sun 9-1. Mod.

Le Pommier *2104 E Carson. Lunch Mon-Fri 11:30-2:30, Dinner Mon-Fri 6-10, Sat 5:30-10:30. AE,DC,MC,V.* **431-1901.** Simple, elegant country French cuisine. A thoroughbred! Mod-Exp. (See Review)

Margaritaville *2200 E Carson. Mon-Sat 11-2am. AE,DC,MC,V.* **431-2200.** South of border menu—enchiladas, burritos, mean margaritas—Inex-Mod.

Mario's *1514 E Carson. Mon-Sat 11-2am. Sun 1-10. AE,DC,MC,V.* **381-5610.** Real Italian from the pasta streamers in the window to good natured noise on the balcony. Inexp. (See Review)

Pgh Steak Co *1924 E Carson. Lunch Mon-Sat 11-4. Dinner Mon-Thur 5-12, Fri-Sat til 1. AE,DC,MC,V.* **381-5505.** Two-level room with steak, grills, sandwiches, pasta. Mod.

Rumors *1828 E Carson. Mon-Thur 11-9:30, Fri-Sat til 12, Bar til 2. Sun 4-10. AE,DC,MC.V.* **431-4500.** Popular upscale tavern with handsome food, decor. Charbroiled gourmet burgers, seafood, deli sandwiches. Mod.

17th St Cafe *75 S 17th. Lunch Mon-Sat 11:30-2. Dinner Mon-Thur 5-10, Fri-Sat til 11. AE,DC,MC,V.* **431-9988.** Casual bar/cafe with good food, entertainment. Mod.

Tambellini's Restaurant/Art Gallery *2302 E Carson. Mon-Sat 7am-midnite. AE,MC,V.* **431-6790.** Relaxed, warm restaurant with owner's art on display; pasta, chicken, fish, homemade soups. Inexp-Mod.

Curry On
South Craig St

Star of India

412 S Craig Street, Oakland. Lunch Mon-Sat 11:30-2:30, Dinner Sun-Thur 5-10, Fri & Sat til 10:30. AE,MC,V. **681-5700.**

One of the city's first good-sized Indian restaurants, this calm room is sending tantalizing whiffs of curry up and down the South Craig Street shopping area. The pleasant glass-fronted room suffices nicely for this venture in cooking from many Indian states—Machan, Biryani, Delhi/Darbar, Bay of Bengal, Punjab, Bahare Murg—exotic names from the East matched to an array of delicious dishes.

When To Go: Lunch, Dinner.

What To Order: There are nearly 60 dishes here with most in the $8-$10 range but it's often difficult to know if what you're ordering will suffice for a whole meal. We suggest you start with a Thali plate—a vegetarian or non-vegetarian assortment of specialty dishes that will give you an idea of the particular Indian tastes that most appeal to you. We found the **Vegetarian Thali** a good full meal for $12.95...and especially liked the crispy Indian bread...**wafer-thin fried papadam**...the spicy lentil soup (dal)...and an unforgettable, herb-seasoned **Muteer Paneer,** a blend of homemade cottage cheese and green peas. Even the dessert, **Gulab Jamun,** a bland-tasting fried cheese ball in syrup, was pleasing.

Indian cooking—a medley of spices unfamiliar to the average palate, often wholly unexpected—can become a favorite with tasting and testing.

Another great dish here is the **Mix-Grill Tandoori**—a selection of shish kabob, boti kabob (lamb), Chicken Tikka (marinated in yogurt), chicken and shrimp with rice & chutney—a good bargain at $9.95. There's also a delicious **Bhartha,** an herb-spiced eggplant for $7.95—not, however, a full dinner for the average diner. One way to order is to augment a vegetarian dish with the tasty, deep fried Pakora and Somasa vegetable appetizers. Then add the delicious **Onion Nan**—a gourmet's version of Indian unleavened bread with moist onions...or the **Poori,** a soft bread with a savory sauce...and of course the papadam, an Indian staple. Dinner for two should come close to $30.

Prices: Lunch $7-$9, Dinner $8-$11.

What To Wear: Casually comfortable.

Recommended: Indian Cuisine.

Great Cuisine In Wilmerding!

Station Brake Cafe

500 Station Street, Wilmerding. 12 mi from Pgh—Parkway East to Rt 130 South, Wilmerding Exit. Lunch Mon-Fri 11-3, Dinner Mon-Sat 5-10, Sun 4:30-9. AE,DC,MC,V. **823-1600.**

What happens when a caterer from a small metropolis tours Europe and comes home frustrated with the food and service in his own hometown? He creates the Station Brake Cafe, of course, right in the commercial heart of town. He hires a European trained chef and sets out to recreate all of the refined food and service he's enjoyed abroad—everything from chilled forks to sorbets, tuxedoed waiters to flambeed desserts. Tom Setz is the restaurateur and fame of his unusual restaurant has spread to the big city—with local diners making the trek to find out what all the excitement's about. Tom was dedicated to giving the average person "a king's dining experience" at rock bottom prices. Prices are now much more haute for the cuisine here but the restaurant's fun. And when you've recovered from the incongruous setting and are sitting in the smoke glassed-in dining room with the fireplace blazing, the street view softens as night descends. Cars sweeping up and down the hill leave streaks of light. . .and yes the magic does happen. . .and diners go away relaxed and happy.

When to Go: We suggest the weekend for a special dinner.

What To Order: We won't give away all of the secrets here but the extras do make a difference—fine china settings—no two alike, chilled salad forks, warm towels, the flurry of waiters attending to your every need, assiduous tableside service, a strolling magician and even monogrammed matches for those with reservations—a wonderful setting for couples or groups out for an evening of pleasure.

An ambitious menu offers very fancy dishes—coq au vin, beef Wellington, tournedos, many versions of veal, Cajun and seafood flown in from Boston. Prices range from $13.95 for Poulet Marengo—chicken with herbs over egg pasta—to as high as $32.95 for Lobster Savannah. We enjoyed the complimentary **Salmon Mousse Pate,** Caesar Salad prepared tableside ($5.95) and Mama Setz's **Wedding Soup**. . .and for entrees—the **Black Angus Filet Mignon with Mushrooms** and the **Coquille Marquery**—shrimp, scallops sauteed with shallots, sherry and garlic. Dinners include soup/salad, vegetable or potato. Dessert flambees i.e. **Cherries Jubilee** ($5.95) are encouraged. . .everyone on the staff gets a chance to perform. . .and there's an award-winning **Chocolate Cordial Cake.**

Prices: Lunch $5-$10, Dinner $13-$28

What To Wear: Formal or casual, you'll feel at home.

Recommended: Continental Cuisine, Night of Romance.

The Shops at Station Square

**Around The World
At Station Square**

The Shops at Station Square

Smithfield & Carson Streets, South Side. Mon-Sat 10-9. Sunday 12-5. Restaurant hours vary. Ten-minute stroll across Smithfield St Bridge or hop the subway to the Square. **261-9911.**

Travel around the world in 65 shops...from Iceland to Ireland to Japan and everywhere in between...all under the high-raftered roof of the restored P&LE Freight House and airy Commerce Court. A triumph of restoration, Pittsburgh's riverfront 'Ghirardelli Square' is a delightful shopping experience and a favorite visitor and tourist stop. And with more than 10 restaurants...good food **and** good taste abounds! Save some time to vist the outdoor Bessemer Court and Transporation Museum.

When To Go: Anytime Sat til 9, Sun 12-5. Most restaurants are open seven days a week.

What To See: Give yourself at least half a day to explore the Shops...beginning with the Freight House world of Pittsburgh memorabilia, modish fashions and furniture, imported coffee and cheeses, books and bears (stuffed). Browse in **World's Treasures** for crystal & Hummels, S W Randall for toys, **Paper Mill, Basquettes** and **Heart to Heart** for unique gifts. Feel the calm elegance of **Maison de Campagne's** French country accessories and enjoy the fashions—wools and laces at **St Brendan's Crossing**, designer labels of **Rodier Paris,** classics by **Carroll Reed, Chaz's** shoes...and young mods at Casual Corner and The Limited. And don't miss the beautiful, handmade designs at the small **Chandree of Beverly Hills** boutique at the far end of the Freight House. Before you move on explore the second level where you can take home a book or souvenir of Pittsburgh from Pgh History & Landmarks' **Cornerstone** shop.

Take a breather at a small table near **Nicholas Coffee Co** or **Likety Split** for your favorite gourmet coffee and/or an ice cream/yogurt treat.

Then on to Commerce Court—one of Pittsburgh's best interiors with its high, airy skylit atrium...an exhilerating upward view by the fountain. Here you'll find more beautiful browsing...lovely fabrics and clothing at **Laura Ashley,** fine Italian fashions at **Antonio da Pescara,** Icelandic woolens at **Constable's of Bermuda,** Etienne Aigner designs at Charlene's and the wonderful wares of **Flying Colors.** Outside, the kids will love exploring Bessemer Court with its 10-ton Bessemer converter and railroad engine and the antique autos of the Transportation Museum open 7 days

The Shops at Station Square

12-8. You can explore for antiques in the unusual Railway Car Express Shops. **Weekends in good weather the whole family can take a horse-drawn surrey ride through Station Square.**

What To Wear: Your casual best.

Where To Eat: **Bobby Rubino's** *Commerce Ct. 7 days. Mon-Thur 11-10:30, Fri-Sat til 12:30, Sun til 9. AE,MC,V.* **642-RIBS.**
Handsome restaurant with a big bar and barbecue—ribs $10-$15, chicken $6.95, burgers, colossal onion ring $2-$5.

Chauncy's *Commerce Court. 7 nights 4:30-2am. Dinner Tues-Sat 6-10. Happy Hour weekdays 5-7. AE,MC,V.* **232-0601.**
Dancing for the sophisticated young, good buffet/dinner $6-$10. Big spacious nightclub atmosphere.

Cheese Cellar Mon-Sat 11:30-1am, bar til 2. Sun Brunch 10:30-2:30, Dinner til 11. AE,DC,MC,V. **471-3355.**
Intimate European rathskeller, outdoor cafe in summer; delicious fondue, cheese & sausage boards, sandwiches, salads. $3-$10.

Houlihan's Old Place *Mon-Thur 11-11, Fri-Sat til 12:45. Sun 10:30-10:30. AE,DC,MC,V.* **232-0302.**
Marvelous 'up' atmosphere amid antique paraphernalia, good food, fun. (See Review)

Jimbo's Hot Dog Company *Mon-Sat 11-9:30, Fri-Sat til 11. Sun 11-6.* **765-1543.**
Hot dogs, kolbassi, fish sandwiches, chili, big selection of beers, tables on the mallway. $1-$2.50.

Kiku's of Japan *Lunch Mon-Sat 11:30-2:30, Dinner Mon-Thur 5-10:30, Fri-Sat til 11:30. Sun 12-10. AE,DC,MC,V.* **765-3200.**
Authentic Japanese cuisine, beautifully served sushi, tempura, a la carte specialties. Lunch $4.50-$11. Dinner $10-$23.

River Cafe *Sun-Thur 11:30-10, Fri-Sat til 11. AE,MC,V.* **765-2795.**
Bar, lofty cafe on second level with airy ambience, seafood, pasta, veal. $5-$14. (See Review)

Sesame Inn *Mon-Thur 11-10, Fri-Sat til 11. Sun 12-9. AE,MC,V.* **281-8282.**
Szechuan/Hunan sesame specialties in serene surroundings. Lunch $4-$6, Dinner $7.95 up.

Tequila Junction *Mon-Thur 11:30-11, Fri-Sat til 12. Sun 12-10. AE,DC,MC,V.* **261-3265.**
Real Mexican atmosphere & cuisine. Wonderful place to relax. (See Review)

Stephen's La Piccola Casa

New Jewel Sparkles In Oakland

Stephen's La Piccola Casa

5100 Baum Blvd, Oakland. Lunch Mon-Fri 11:30-3. Dinner Mon-Thur 5-11, Fri & Sat til 12. Sun 4-10. Reser sugg. AE,DC,MC,V. **682-9446.**

This is a little jewel of a restaurant! The former Win, Place & Show, long a sophisticated sleeper with Oakland urbanites, has been transformed into an exquisite band-box. It's now lighter, airier with a smart NY ambience—banquette seating in subtle shades of beige and burgundy, front windows outlined in sparkling lights. Young owners Stephen Roth and Alan Lape have innovative ideas and with David Ayn, one of Pittsburgh's finest chefs, ensconced in the kitchen, this canopied little spot is making a big bid for recognition. David, known for his superb cuisine at many city restaurants (including the old Fallen Angel and La Tache) has many loyal fans who are following him to his newest mecca.

When To Go: This evening. . .about a quarter to nine.

What To Order: As expected, the creative culinary juices are flowing here with items like Lobster Ravioli with Sun-Dried Tomato Cream Sauce, Veal Stuffed with Deviled Crabmeat topped with chestnut & orange sauce, and more veals, pasta, chicken and beef. Dinner begins with a basket of extraordinary breads—salt sticks, foccaccia and David's wonderful applenut bread with big, juicy yellow raisins. Good bread always bodes well for a good meal and it was followed by a subtle, divine curried butternut squash soup swimming with shrimp, a zestful Caesar salad with sweet roasted peppers and again. . .tender, juicy shrimp. We could happily dine here on bread, wine, soups and appetizers. . .grilled eggplant & mozzarella, steamed mussels, char-roasted peppers. . .from $5-$7. But the **Maryland Crab Cakes with Dijon Mustard Sauce** garnished with delicious mostarda—miniature Italian fruit, apricots & cherries, marinated in sweet mustard oil—is too good to miss at $17. There are also delicious **Veal Chops** either with **glazed apricots in ginger sauce** or with **crushed Parmesan and apple-stuffed prunes in apple/brandy sauce,** both steep at $24.95, but it's a rare pleasure when ambience and fine cuisine blend into a perfect whole!

Lunches at Stephen's are more economical for the same fine cuisine. . .lobster bisque for $3.95, crab cakes at $7.95. . .Angel Hair $5.50, and some good sandwiches for $4.95! Put this place in your date book now!

Prices: Lunch $4.95-$9, Dinner $12-$24. Late Supper $5-$11.

What To Wear: It's a smart, sophisticated crowd.

Recommended: Continental Cuisine, Connoisseur Dining, Fabulous Buys—Lunch, Late Supper.

Strip—Down by the Riverside

**Riverfront Fun
On Boardwalk**

Strip—Down by the Riverside

Boardwalk off Smallman at 16th St. Enter thru parking lot under the bridge at 15th St, turn right. 7 days. **471-2226.**

Pittsburgh's downtown riverfront renaissance begins with this 420-ft floating boardwalk, the first phase of the exciting $50 million entertainment complex on 12 acres between the Veterans and 16th St bridges. Built on three barges moored about 30 feet from the Allegheny shore to accommodate the rise and fall of the river, the Boardwalk houses two restaurants, a disco, banquet hall, a 20 by 50 ft swimming/splash pool, outdoor patio deck and space for boating patrons to dock along three sides. It all spells new Pittsburgh riverfront fun! The Boardwalk is approached by ramp from an esplanade along the landscaped shore, gaily decorated with nautical flags that spell out the letters S T R I P in code.

Within walking distance of downtown, the riverfront complex is expected to attract conventioneers and visitors as well as Pittsburgh natives. A half-mile Riverwalk, lamp lit at night, stretches the length of the project to the 60-slip Downtown Yacht Club marina on the downtown side of the Boardwalk. Long range plans for the 12-acre complex include a huge ESBN Sports Bar, more restaurants, night clubs, a hotel, Omni corporate entertainment center, health spa, performance hall, mini-theatre and other recreational and entertainment facilities.

Where To Party:

Two two-story buildings on either side of the Boardwalk house the following restaurants/facilities (open summer '91).
Crewsers, *1st floor, right.*
Big 250-seat restaurant/150 additional on outdoor patio, with two bars, a nautical theme; glass walls along river slide open for summer breezes. Sandwiches, pasta, grilled fish/steak. Mod.

Patio Deck
Open air deck/bar with umbrellaed tables, lounge chairs around the pool; service from Crewsers. Free live entertainment inc steel bands, will add to Caribbean feel for summertime fun. Boating customers will be able to dock on all three sides of the Boardwalk. Mod.

Donzi's, *1st floor, left.*
Glitzy, neon, upscale Euro-style disco. Dancing to DJs, live bands. Accommodates 500 for cocktails/dancing. Also a private club with sunken bar, couches. Cover varies. Mod-Exp.

Buster's Crab,*2nd floor, right.*
Raw bar/restaurant specializing in fresh seafood with topside view of river scenery. Mod.

Riverwatch, *2nd floor, left.*
Banquet hall with space for 250-300 and an outer deck, a brand new facility for parties, corporate meetings.

**Sights, Smells
Taste of Strip**

Strip District

Penn Avenue and Smallman Street from 17th to 28th.

Saturday at the Strip—Pittsburgh's bustling wholesale food market—is an invigorating adventure into one of the city's most colorful areas. This is the real Pittsburgh melting pot—wholesale center for foodstuffs from all over the world. Beginning at two in the morning the Strip swarms with activity as trucks unload produce, cheeses, meats from Italy, Greece, the Orient, and farms far and near as the city sleeps. Night revelers are catching a bite at the famous late-night eatery, **Primanti's** as workers break for 'lunch' and the city's chefs seek out the day's freshest fare.

But Saturday mornings the Strip belongs to retail buyers—serious cooks and discerning gourmets in search of fresh provender, bargain prices and hard-to-find ingredients. You can plunge into the Strip's exciting sights, smells, and tastes at Penn & 20th—the pungent cheeses, Italian meats, hot sausage, salami, Greek olives at **Pittsburgh Macaroni Company** at 2010 Penn, Shirings Meats at 1812 Penn, Parma Sausage at 1734 Penn, and ten blocks down on Smallman the **Pittsburgh Cheese Terminal.** And for magnificent bread is **Panini's** at 1806 Penn...baskets & baskets of fresh homemade rolls, salt sticks, braided rings, sour dough, Sicilian rye and fragrant **Broccoli Bread**—with sausage, broccoli, onion, garlic & oil baked in Italian bread—a meal in itself.

For fish lovers there are fascinating displays at **Benkovitz Seafoods,** 23rd & Smallman and **Wholey's** at 1711 Penn. And everywhere is sidewalk produce—tomatoes, corn, lettuce, watermelon fresh from the farm. Your food basket runneth over! Other Strip rarities are **Sambok's** at 17th & Penn for Chinese pea pods & paper lanterns, **Penn Avenue Pottery** at 1905 Penn for hand-thrown pieces fired in a kiln in the back room, and **Alioto's** at 2101 Penn with its produce and wicker furniture and baskets. Complete your tour with a break at the Society for Art in Crafts at 2100 Smallman.

Further down Smallman the 100-year-old St Stanislaus Church looms over the cobblestone square with its horizontàl stripes reminiscent of a Florentine basilica and its fantastic stained glass windows...ask about tours.

A great time to sample the Strip is during the annual **May Springfest or fall Oktoberfest** when the whole area rolls out for sidewalk fun, food booths & entertainment. Several small sidewalk cafes also spring up in summer, adding to . the colorful street scene. And at 16th Street Strip—Down by the Riverside brings new riverfront excitement, for the first time extending the Strip all the way to the Allegheny riverbank. (See Review.) You can take a 2-1/2 hr **Tour of the Strip** offered by Allegheny County Cooperative Extension Service the 2nd & 4th Thur of the month starting from St Patrick's

Church on 17th. Call **392-8540**. Customized tours of the area are also offered by Food Consultants (276-0908) who also publish a Strip District guide.

Where To Eat: Many of the Strip eateries keep market hours—open early am and closed in the afternoon. Other restaurants have regular hours.

Benkovitz Seafoods *23rd & Smallman. Mon-Fri 8:30-5:30. Sat 8-5. MC,V.* **263-3016.**
Fish market with beautifully displayed fish, seafood; great fish sandwiches, shrimp, breaded oysters, shrimp bisque. Take-out, counter or snacking by big lobster pool. $2-$7.

Brandy's *2323 Penn. Mon-Thur 11:15-2am, Fri-Sat til 2:30. Sun 3-11. AE,DC,MC,V.* **566-1000.**
First of the area's classy restaurants with good business lunches, breakfast at late hours. Lunch $3-$7, Dinner $10-$14.

De Luca's *2015 Penn. Mon-Sat 6am-4pm. Sun 7-3. No credit cards.* **566-2195.**
Small lunchroom with Italian frittatas and one of best breakfasts in the city. $1.50-$4.

Fat Frank's *Smallman/20th. Mon-Tues 11-8, Wed-Thur til 11, Fri-Sat til 2. No credit cards.* **471-3388.**
Big hot dogs, burgers, kielbasa, sausage sandwiches in casual eatery with baseball theme. $2-$8.75.

Paski's *2533 Penn. Lunch Mon-Fri 11-2, Dinner Mon-Thur 5-10, Fri-Sat til 12. AE,DC,MC,V.* **566-2782.**
Homey restaurant with some great food bargains, ribs on Fri. Lunch $4-$7. Dinner $6-$15.

Primanti's *46 18th St between Penn & Smallman. Mon-Sat 24 hrs. Sun til 5am. No credit cards.* **263-2142**
Hours are in tune with bustling market which comes alive at 2am. Workers, truckers, night owls from all over the city come for famous sandwiches $3.

Roland's *1904 Penn. Mon 6am-4pm, Tues-Sat 6-10. AE,DC MC,V.* **261-3401.**
Hospitable bar/restaurant with New Orlean's feel; seafood, Cajun, old Southern foods. Lunch $4-$6, Dinner $10-$13.

Spaghetti Warehouse *2601 Smallman. Mon-Thur 11:30-10, Fri-Sat til 11. Sun 12-10. AE,CB,DC,MC,V.* **261-6511.**
Big place with big portions of pasta, lasagna, other Italian dishes. Family prices $3-$9.

Wholey's *1711 Penn. Mon-Thur 8-5:30, Fri til 6, Sat til 5. No credit cards.* **391-3737.**
Bustling, big fish market with sandwiches, shrimp in a basket, deviled crab, soup. $2.95 up. Take out, 2nd fl tables.

Suzie's

The Greek Experience

Suzie's

130 Sixth Street, Downtown. Mon-Thur 11-9, Fri & Sat til 11. **261-6443.** *Also 1704 Shady, Squirrel Hill. Mon-Thur 11:30-10, Fri & Sat til 11, Sun 4-9.* **422-8066.** *MC,V. No liquor Downtown.* 🚹

If you knew Suzie's like we do you wouldn't miss an opportunity to visit this little downtown Greek restaurant or its popular new branch in Squirrel Hill—both with wonderful homemade food at great prices. Greek cuisine is one of our favorites—a nostalgic reminder of an idyllic trip to the Aegean islands—wonderful memories of sitting at small cafes on sunny wharves, watching the sun set over the waters, sampling the local wine, the delicious moussaka, Greek salads—tangy olives, feta cheese, sliced tomatoes in a row—and then the thin filo pastries, moist with nuts & honey, washed down with strong Greek coffee. Bringing back all of these memories is the food at Suzie's—and as in Greece—the price is right. And in typical Greek fashion, the Suzie's Downtown spills out into a busy sidewalk cafe in summer.

When To Go: As both restaurants are busy at regular lunch and dinner hours—try late afternoon or after-theatre.

What To Order: All of our favorite Greek dishes are here—cooked by the restaurant's owners Suzie Moraitis Grant and her husband Marc. You can get a sample taste of the various specialties with the **Appetizer Plate** ($9) which includes tarama—delicious Greek caviar of whipped pink fish roe, olive oil and lemon juice . . . fit for the gods—along with tzantziki—a cool mixture of cucumber, garlic, sour cream, grape leaves and hummus. For an entree there's a fine **Moussaka—the eggplant-ground beef casserole with Bechamel sauce** ($8.50) or the **Spanakopita, spinach-cheese pie in filo dough** ($7.50)—both served with rice, vegetable, a mini-Greek salad and delicious homemade bread.

Our dessert favorites are the big bowls of creamy **Rice Pudding** with whipped cream ($1.75) or the delectable **Ekmek**—sponge cake soaked in honey with custard and whipped cream, one of the city's best at $2.75. With Greek coffee at $2 you can bring in dinner at around $20 for 2. You owe it to yourself to try the food at Suzie's and . . . if you have but one trip to make in your life . . . make it the Greek islands for their unearthly beauty and inimitable, earthy cuisine.

Prices: Lunch $3.75-$6, Dinner $7-$13.

What To Wear: Informal, casual.

Recommended: Greek Cuisine, Fabulous Buys, Outdoor Dining, Late Supper.

Pittsburgh Name For Seafood

Tambellini's

860 Saw Mill Run Blvd, Rt 51 just other side of Liberty Tunnels. Mon-Fri 11-11, Sat til 12. AE,DC,MC,V. **481-1118.**

Tambellini's has been a name synonymous with good food & seafood in Pittsburgh for nearly 40 years with Tambellini restaurants all over town. But this is the grand-daddy of them all. Many diners remember the original—a small, crowded room on Mt Washington from which grew Louis Tambellini's dream—this big, opulent restaurant, dedicated to good dining and large enough to accommodate all of the Tambellini fans. There's room for 800 in six rooms! This is the city's largest restaurant and true to its fame it's always crowded.

When To Go: To really savour the seafood we suggest a relaxing late lunch from 2-4.

What To Order: Lunch is a wonderful way to sample delicious house specialties at bargain prices—many from $6-$8 in the generous portions for which this restaurant is noted. There's everything from linguini with mussels for $7.50 to stone crab claws in season for $10. Luncheon menus include **Shrimp or Scallops Louie in garlic sauce with toasted bread crumbs—a dish created by the owner,** Louisiana Redfish Cajun Style, Virginia Spots, Lemon Sole, Broiled Scrod... all served with a wide choice of potatoes, vegetable or salad. And featured all the time is the delicious **Baked Stuffed Imperial Crab** for $14.95.

Scores of entrees are available anytime for lunch or dinner, a vast array of seafood, fish, steaks, chops and pasta for $14-$20. And each night there's a **Seafood Special** with potato, tossed salad, dessert and coffee for $11.75—a price that can't be beat.

For a special dinner try the gargantuan **Seafood Platter— lobster, crab cakes, shrimp, oysters, sole, scallops, a complete dinner for $22.50**—a wonderful buy in itself and even better when shared by two ($2 plate charge). Top off your meal with a half litre of house wine—red or white for $7—and enjoy your seafood feast.

Don't forget this restaurant is also open for after-theatre dining on sandwiches and snacks or a full meal til 11 weeknights, 12 on weekends...a boon for Pittsburgh late diners.

Prices: Lunch $5.50-$8.50, Dinner $12.50-$17.50.

What To Wear: Plain or fancy, eating is the serious business here.

Recommended: American Cuisine, Connoisseur Dining, Executive Dining, Rich Man's Dining, Late Supper.

REVIEWS

Tequila Junction

South of the Border in Pittsburgh, PA

Tequila Junction
Second Level, Freight House, Shops at Station Square. Mon-Thur 11:30-11, Fri & Sat til 12. Sun 12-10. No reser. AE,D,MC,V. **261-3265.** 🛆

If you miss the warmth and romance of Mexican dining, a nice slow visit to Tequila Junction will bring back mellow memories. In an area where pastiche often triumphs, this restaurant has food and atmosphere authentic enough to please the most avid Mex-Amer food buff. Relaxed is the best approach to the Junction so take a right at the door and make the small wooden bar your first stop to savour the stucco walls, red tiled floors, blue & white counters... and the smell of salsa again.

For the strong, there's a Gold Shooter of Jose Cuervo Tequila, $3 & up, with the traditional lemon and salt. There's also Mexican beer for $3.50. But the Junction is most famous for its **oversized Margaritas in giant cocktail goblets** $3.75 regular, strawberry, nine other flavors— guaranteed to have you seeing through rose-colored glasses. As the drink is large and the night long, we suggest you sip and carry it to your table to last through the meal—but not before sampling the bar's **homemade tortilla chips with the house's special piquant salsa**...the best dip in town. When you're sufficiently mellowed it's time to enter the gracious dining room with its candlelit tables, high backed Mexican chairs and veranda overlooking the Shops.

When To Go: Off-hours to savour the atmosphere. Lunch at 2. Dinner after 6 weekdays to avoid weekend lines of fellow sojourners.

What To Order: The *'Tequila Gaceta'* newspaper/menu will put your budget worries at ease. **Prices have barely budged here in years.** Highest item is steak—plain or with relleno sauce—$14.95. Combinations of Tacos, Burritos and Enchiladas with rice & frijoles are from $5-$8.

We recommend the **Chimichanga**—a deep-fried burrito with frijoles and beef or chicken—topped with guacamole, sour cream & tomatoes and served with rice, plenty for dinner at $7.50. Or you can share an order of three of the house's best—a **Ground Beef Taco, Chicken & Cheese Enchilada** and a **Shredded Beef Burrito** with delicious house sauce $3-$4.
If you liked the dip at the bar you'll love the house's **Chili con Queso**—melted cheese with chilies, tomatoes, onions & chips for $2.95. Watch for it on other entrees.

Prices: Lunch/Dinner $6-$10.

What To Wear: Leisurely smile...clothes to match.

Recommended: Mexican-American Cuisine, Fabulous Buys, Late Supper.

The Terrace Room

**Elegant Dining
At Grand Hotel**

The Terrace Room

*The Westin William Penn, Mellon Square, Downtown. Open 7
days 6:30am-11pm. Sun Brunch 10-2. Reser sugg.
AE,DC,MC,V.* **553-5235.**

Dining at this grand hotel is always an exciting occasion...more so since the renovation of the ornate Terrace Room off the lobby. A Pittsburgh landmark, the room has been restored to its 1916 splendor, the beautiful Italianate molded ceiling, crystal chandeliers, huge mirrors, walnut paneling and rose damask walls bringing back wonderful memories from a lavish Pittsburgh era.

The service is excellent—and pleasant—the beef is unexcelled and the warm, comfortable surroundings make this restaurant ideal for a happy celebration...an anniversary, holiday dinner or reunion of old friends.

When To Go: Sunday Dinner or Saturday night for dining (5:30-11) and dancing from 8 to midnight.

What To Order: Dinner dancing in the 'T' has become a tradition for many Pittsburghers who come to enjoy the fine cuisine and the music of the Nick Lomakin Trio. Come early any night to enjoy a cocktail ($4.25) or wine ($3.75) and the piano in the beautiful Palm Court Lobby, a wonderful prelude to dinner. A new menu returns the food to its original Renaissance theme, using the finest local Italian foodstuffs. Entrees, served with soup or salad, include from Veal Ravioli with Lobster Claw Sauce, Broiled Veal with Merlot Butter and the house's rendition of Paella to homemade pastas—Pecorino Romano Tortellini, Spinach and Egg Linguine with Marinated Shrimp—and the ever-popular Filet Mignon and NY Strip.

But we recommend you try the house specialty, **"the finest prime rib in Pittsburgh,"** a juicy 12-oz Crown Cut served with baked potato and vegetable...a hearty dinner for $21. Included is the Terrace Room Salad with crumbled gorgonzola or hot soup of the day from Ray's Kettle. And for dessert...the renowned **William Penn Cheesecake with fresh strawberries** (¢3.25), one of the best anywhere. Lighter and delicious is the Broiled Berries Sabayon, also $3.25. Dinner with house wine and dessert comes to around $60 for 2 for an elegant urban repast.

Prices: Breakfast $5-$12, Lunch $6-$13, Dinner $12.25-$24.

What To Wear: Enjoy your finery in beautiful surroundings.

Recommended: Continental Cuisine, Rich Man's Guide, Executive Dining, Brunch, Pittsburgh After Dark.

Tessaro's

Sizzling Food From The Hardwood Grill

Tessaro's
4601 Liberty Avenue, Bloomfield. Mon-Sat 11-12, Bar til 2. AE,DC,MC,V. **682-6809.**

Long before we visited this eatery, rumors of its fabulous hardwood grills wafted back to us. Ribs, big thick pork chops, sizzling steak at great prices. First impressions of just another neighborhood bar were quickly smothered in the heavenly aromas at the door and helped us through the first long wait for a table. And we found—'tis true, 'tis true! This is real good eatin', some of the best in town. A hungry man/woman's mecca, Tessaro's brims with good cheer. It's a warm, friendly place with eight booths opposite a busy bar decorated with bright lights. Owner Kelly Harrington, a big, mild 'black Irishman' greets you at the door and somehow keeps the long lines moving...no reservations. From the denizens of the booths happily packing away food—many from the shirt & tie crowd—it's obvious something extraordinary is going on here. It's a Pittsburgh resurgence of real down home cookin'.

When To Go: Lines subside some during weekdays—Monday for Mexican, Thursday for ribs. It's a busy place late night weekends.

What To Order: We were lucky enough to taste the ribs first...and they were **delicious, zesty and tender with big flavour seared in by the intense, hardwood flame** $7.95-$8.95. After the ribs we were hardly able to sample our big Grilled Chicken Sandwich ($5)...best we've ever had...with heaps of Mom's potato salad and homemade cole slaw. Fit for a queen. On our next visit the burgers ($4.50-$5.75) came up to their big reputation...the crust charred, tender pink inside...especiallly the gourmet version on a big bun with chunks of melted cheese and mushrooms oozing out over the edge...wow! Then we had to sample the entrees ($10-$14)—for our readers, of course—and were happy to find that salmon and swordfish were perfect from the grill and the fried potatoes were out of sight. So...what was left but to go back Monday for Mexican. It's not billed as authentic but turned out to be the biggest surprise...a delectable homemade recipe, the **Big Bear,** its deliciously melting insides—a union of grilled chicken (or beef), guacamole, sour cream, salsa, lettuce, tomato, cheese—grilled inside a tortilla...crisp around the edges. This was the best. They had to haul the plate away. What can we say... good eating is good eating. Someone waiting for a table told us, "I discovered this place last Friday and I've already been back three times." Now all that remains is to sample . the big steak, the huge chops...the chili...

Prices: $2.50 for soup to $14 for filet mignon.

What To Wear: Something loose and comfortable.

Recommended: American Cuisine, Fabulous Buys, Late Supper.

Tramp's Grand Old Saloon

A Little Of New York

Tramp's Grand Old Saloon

212 Blvd of the Allies (between Market & Wood), Downtown. Hours: Mon-Thur 11:30-10:30, Fri & Sat til 11:30. Bar til 2. Reser sugg. AE,DC,MC,V. **261-1990.**

This is one of downtown's most charming restaurants with small warm rooms, brick walls and Greenwich Village atmosphere. . . its private nooks a great place for a romantic rendezvous. Owners Ed & Bill Zelesko have renovated an old 1860 building—the stained glass transom gives the location as '80 Second St'—which traces its history back to one of Pittsburgh's oldest bar-bordellos. Loaded with atmosphere, Tramp's has candlelit tables, a small back skylight room on the site of a former garden, a venerable old bar and a 200-year-old clock which sometimes chimes on the hour. A recent addition is the outdoor patio off the second floor for rooftop dining—another urban pleasure. And for food and service Tramp's is in the tradition of the small, good New York restaurants.

When To Go: Lunch 11:30-5, Late Supper Fri & Sat til 11:30.

What To Order: Dinners including house specialties—chicken, flounder, fettucini—range from $11-$14 but the pasta and 'Luncheon Ladies' can be had for much less. Entrees named after former 'ladies of the house' are the Adeline—Chicken Breast on a bed of Rice Pilaf, Dotty—Chicken with Shrimp, Snow Peas and Mushrooms, Flossie—the Catch of the Day—all from $7-$9. Three good sandwiches, ham, beefburger and fish $5-$6, are available day & night as are soups, salads and desserts from $3-$6. Drinks are in the $3.25-$3.75 range.

Our choice for lunch is the **Steak Salad, Chicken Breast or Catch of the Day** beautifully prepared with an interesting vegetable-rice pilaf ($7-$8), and a tall glass of house wine $3. With beverage and tax your meal comes to about $25 for 2. For a late snack the **Spinach Salad** at $5.95 or one of the sandwiches with drinks will bring you close to $16 for 2 and the atmosphere's worth it.

Before you leave, climb the long, narrow front staircase to Dolly's Boudoir, a comfortable room and bar. Next door is the Madame's Room complete with fireplace, antiques and adjoining patio. Both are popular spots for private parties.

Prices: Lunch $4.95-$10, Dinner $8.95-$15.

What To Wear: Lovely atmosphere lends itself to dress-up for evening tryst, informal for lunch.

Recommended: American Cuisine, Party Rooms, Late Supper.

Poor Man's Tips
More Ways to Save Money Dining

A La Carte An adventuresome way of ordering—probably what the restaurant staff do on their nights out. Sharing and sampling several dishes can be fun. Some restaurants have a modest plate charge. Ask!

Always Ask If you don't understand a menu item or a foreign language menu, the server is usually glad to assist you. If you question a charge on your check . . don't be shy. They'll respect your alertness. A comfortable, satisfied diner returns.

Hidden Costs If a menu is recited don't hesitate to ask the cost of daily specials. Also watch for hidden costs on extras - i.e. special dressings, appetizers. Ask if they are extra. In some night clubs the price of drinks rises with the entertainment and it pays to order when the band's not playing.

Specials Take advantage of the Early Bird dinners, fabulous buys, bargain brunches in this Guide. Shop around to save.

Wine There's a wise saying about wine by the bottle "If you can afford it you won't like it." House wines by the glass or carafe are often the best buy—many are excellent.

Tips Tips are part of the service worker's salary. What's fair? Regular service, 15%, special service, 20%, so-so service, 10%.

Tipping for the Rich Man's Feast

Pittsburgh restaurants are less formal than many other cities'. Some fine restaurants automatically add a 15% gratuity to your check, continental fashion. But tipping well is still the best insurance that your fabulous feast will be a special night to remember and you'll be greeted warmly on your return. The cast in a fine restaurant usually includes:

The Maitre d' Everything revolves around the maitre d', the gentleman—usually tuxedoed—who greets you at the door. He seats you, gets you a good table and makes sure your dinner is a success—and, most importantly, other staff take their cue from him. Most Pittsburgh restaurants say that tipping head waiters is not necessary except for unusual service. But you can insure a very special evening by slipping him a folded $5, $10—or up.

Wine Steward (Sommelier) Also a very important person in making your evening a success, he can be recognized by the tasting cup and medallion around his neck. He helps you select the right wine and insures it's properly served. For special service tip a minimum of 15%-20% of the cost of the wine.

Waiter Minimum of 15%-20%, a portion of which is shared with the busboys.

Here's a quick guide to downtown restaurants for the convenience of visitors, tourists, shoppers. Eateries are listed geographically by Convention Ctr/Vista... Penn/Liberty Cultural Dist...Gateway/Market...4th Ave/Midtown..Grant/Uptown.

CONVENTION CENTER/ VISTA/STRIP

British Bicycle Club

923 Penn. Downtown. Mon-Fri 10-10. AE,DC,MC,V. **391-9623.**
Good grills, sandwiches, fish & chips in lively pub atmosphere. Mod.

Brandy's

2323 Penn, Strip. Mon-Sat 5-2. Sun 3-11. AE,DC,MC,V. **566-1000.**
First class dining amid romantic greenery. Amer cuisine. Mod. (See Review)

DelFrate's

971 Liberty. Mon-Fri 11-10. AE,DC,MC,V. **391-2294.**
Authentic Italian, veal, pasta in warm surroundings. Inexp-Mod. (See Review)

Emilia Romagna

942 Penn. Lunch Mon-Fri 11:30-2, Dinner Mon-Thur 5-10, Fri-Sat til 11. AE,DC,MC,V. **765-3598.**
Calm upper room with extraordinary North Italian cuisine. Mod. (See Review)

Liang's Hunan

Vista/Liberty Center, Penn & Liberty. Sun-Thur 11:30-10, Fri-Sat til 11. AE,DC,MC,V. **471-1688.**
Outstanding Oriental in splendid decor; gourmet Hunan, Szechwan—smoked duck, pheasant, venison. Hong Kong Dim Sum Sat/Sun 11:30-3. Mod-Exp.

Mahoney's

949 Liberty. Lunch only Mon-Fri 11-2. AE,DC,MC,V. **471-4243.**
Good sandwiches, entrees in handsome decor. Inexp.

Spaghetti Warehouse

2601 Smallman, Strip. Mon-Thur 11:30-10, Fri-Sat til 11. Sun 12-10. AE,CB,DC,MC,V. **261-6511.**
Family prices in big, lively restaurant; popular Italian dishes, spaghetti with 11 sauces, lasagna. Inexp-Mod.

Strip—Down by the Riverside

Boardwalk, 16th/Smallman. Parking lot entrance under 16th St Bridge. **471-2226.**
Crewsers, seafood restaurant with nautical theme, first to open in $5M Allegheny riverfront entertainment complex. Also **Buster's Crab,** 2nd floor seafood/raw bar; **Donzi's** European disco; plus delightful open air **Patio Deck** for eating/drinking. Mod.

Vista—Pittsburgh

Liberty Center, 1000 Penn. AE,D,DC, MC,V. **281-3700.**
Deluxe buffet, Euro-Amer, seafood in beautiful Orchard Cafe. 7 days 6:30-10:30. Mod-Exp. (See Review) Amer Regional/Cont in Edwardian **Harvest Room** Mon-Fri 11:45-10:30, Sat 6:30-10:30. Exp. (See Rich Man) Late bites, music in **Motions** 7 days 4-11. Mod.

PENN/LIBERTY CULTURAL DISTRICT

Bravo! Franco

613 Penn. Mon-Sat Lunch 11:30-4, Dinner 5-11. AE,DC,MC,V. **642-6677.**
Sophisticated before/after-theatre favorite across from Heinz Hall. Italian-Continental. Mod-Exp.

Bravo! Trattoria

134 6th St. 7 days 11:30-11. Closed Mon eve. AE,MC,DC,V. **642-7600.**
Sister to Bravo! Franco; superfine N Ital, informal bistro setting. Great pasta, crab cakes. Mod. (See Review)

Carmassi's

711 Penn. Mon-Sat 11:30-10:30, later & Sun for performances. AE,DC,MC,V. **281-6644.**
Ital seafood, pasta, veal in modern, two-level space. Specialties - grilled swordfish, Maryland crabcakes. (Formerly of North Hills fame.) Mod.

PENN/LIBERTY (cont'd)

Frenchy's
136 6th St. Mon-Sat 11-11. AE,MC,V. **261-6476.**
One of area's oldest; popular room specializing in seafood, pasta. Inexp-Mod.

The Overture
212 6th St. Lunch Mon-Fri 11-3, Dinner Mon-Thur 5-11, Fri & Sat til 12. AE,D,DC,MC,V. **391-0500.**
Multi-level room with theatrical feel, Broadway soundtracks, piano. Ital-Amer steak, seafood, veal, pasta. Mod-Exp.

Richest Restaurant
140 6th St. Mon-Sat 9-9. AE,D,DC,MC,V. **471-7799.**
NY deli/bar, institution since 1936. Kosher corned beef, blintzes. Inexp.

Suzie's
130 6th St. Mon 11-3, Tues-Thur 11-8, Fri, Sat, show nights til 11. MC,V. **261-6443.**
Authentic little Greek cafe, sidewalk tables in summer. Inexp. (See Review)

Tambellini's
139 7th St. Mon-Sat 11:30-11:30. AE,MC,V. **391-1091.**
Busy room with good Italian fare—veal, pasta, fried zucchini. Mod-Exp.

GATEWAY/POINT/MARKET SQ

Avenue of the Cafes
Fifth Avenue Place, 5th/Stanwix. Mon-Sat 10-6, Mon & Thur til 9.
Arcade food court boasts popular eateries on balcony with view of splendid lobby, among them **Sbarro's** Ital food under $3, **Steak Escape** & **Warburton's Bakery**. Inexp.

Froggy's
100 Market. Mon-Thur 11:30-11, Fri-Sat til 12. AE,DC,MC,V. **471-3764.**
Charming, old style bar/diningroom with good beef, big drinks, atmosphere. Mod. (See Review)

Gallagher's
2 Market Place. Mon-Fri. Lunch only 11-2:30, Sat 12-3. Bar/snacks til 2. AE,DC,MC,V. **261-5554.**
Friendly Irish pub with sandwiches, stew, Irish coffee, sing-a-longs. Inexp.

Hana's
#1 Graeme, Market Square. Lunch, Mon-Fri 11:30-3, Dinner 4:30-10. AE,DC,MC,V. **471-9988.**
Japanese/Oriental. Inexp-Mod.

Hilton Hotel
Gateway Center. AE,D,DC,MC,V. **391-4600.**
Bright **Promenade Cafe** on park, patio. 7 days 7am-5. Mod. More formal dinner in **Sterlings** Mon-Sun 5-11:30. Mod-Exp.

Jake's Above the Square
430 Market. Mon-Thur 11:30-11, Fri til 12, Sat 5-12. Sun 4-10. AE,DC,MC,V. **338-0900.**
Upscale cuisine with N Ital, Amer regional, great fish, superior wine list. Dinner piano. Valet parking. Exp.

Jamie's on the Square
435 Market. Mon-Sat 11-11. Sun 11-8. AE,MC,DC,V. **471-1722.**
Popular for casual business lunch. Tangy barbecued ribs, huge steak salad. Mod.

Max & Erma's
Horne's Dept Store, Stanwix. Mon-Thur 11-11, Fri-Sat til 12. AE,DC,MC,V. **471-1140.**
Bright room with electic menu, popular downtown happy hour. Inexp-Mod.

Mick McGuire's
22 Graeme, Market Square. Mon-Sat 8-12. Sun 8-7. AE,DC,MC,V. **642-7526.**
Cozy Irish pub with juicy burgers, Irish stew, corn beef. Enter. Fri. Inex.

1902 Landmark Tavern
24 Market Square. Mon-Sat Lunch 11:30-4, Dinner 5-11. AE,D,DC,MC,V. **471-1902.**
Quaint, restored tavern, marble floors, raw bar, oldtime atmosphere. Inex-Mod.

2

THE DOWNTOWNER

GATEWAY/POINT/MARKET SQ. (cont'd)

Original Oyster House
20 Market Place. Mon-Sat 9-11. No credit cards. **566-7925.**
Historic old saloon with fabulous fish sandwiches, oysters, clams. Inexp.

PPG Food Court
#2 PPG Place. Mon-Sat 11-4:30. Varied eateries in Atrium's grand lower level inc **Grecian Isles, Somma's Pizza,** *British specialties at* **Warburton's** *plus veal, seafood at* **Euro Cafe** Inexp.

Ruth's Chris Steak House
6 PPG Place. Lunch Mon-Fri 11:30-3. Dinner Mon-Sat 5-11. Sun 5-9. AE,DC,MC,V. **391-4800.**
Burnished steak house, part of famous chain with #1 prime steaks, accessories. Exp. (See Review)

Scoglio
500 Liberty. Mon 11:30-2, Tues-Fri til 10. Sat 4:30-10. AE,DC,MC,V. **391-1226.**
Fans swear by this second floor room's N Ital pasta, veal. Mod.

Tramp's
212 Blvd of Allies. Mon-Thur 11:30-10:30, Fri-Sat til 11:30. AE,DC,MC,V. **261-1990.**
Charming restored old bordello/bar with lots of atmosphere, good late supper menu. Inexp-Mod. (See Review)

MIDTOWN 4TH/WOOD

Kason's
Bank Tower, 311 Fourth. Mon-Wed 11:30-11, Thur & Fri til 1. Sat 12-7. AE,D,DC,MC,V. **391-1122.**
A longtime institution in Bank Tower's lower level. Popular lunch, Happy Hour spot. Pre-Pirate/Penguin game 2 for 1 specials. Inexp.

Klein's
330 Fourth. Mon-Thur 11-9:30, Fri til 10. AE,D,DC,MC,V. **232-3311.**
Famous, bustling seafood house, great bouillabaisse, Caesar salad, salt sticks. Mod.

Mandarin Gourmet
YWCA Lobby, 305 Wood. Mon-Sat 11-9. AE,D,DC,MC,V. **261-6151.**
Popular Chinese—lobster, General Tso, chicken specials. Get there early, beat lunch lines. Inexp.

Piccolo, Piccolo
1 Wood. Lunch Mon-Fri 11:30-3, Dinner Mon-Thur 5-10, Fri-Sat til 11. AE,DC,MC,V. **261-7234.**
Popular trattoria with extraordinary antipasto buffet, pastas, sidewalk tables in summer. Mod.

Senor Birds
Bank Tower, 311 Fourth. Mon-Wed 11:30-8, Thur-Fri til 12. AE,D,MC,V. **391-1122.**
Mexican cantina with Pgh twist. Daily fiesta specials, happy hour, Fri nite entertainment. Mexican pizza! Inexp.

Warner Centre Food Court
332 Fifth. Mon-Sat Lunch 11-3. **281-9000.**
Bevy of eateries on Balcony—Tivoli's, Grand Wok, Steak Escape, plus pizza, tacos, gelato. Inexp.

GRANT STREET/UPTOWN

Apollo
429 Forbes. Breakfast/Lunch Mon-Fri 7-3. No credit cards. **471-3033.**
Upscale fast-food with homemade soups & salads, char-grilled sandwiches. Inexp.

Bangkok Taste
428 Forbes. Mon-Fri 11-9, Sat 12-8. AE,M,V. **338-9111.**
Superb Thai cuisine with a gourmet touch. Great noonday buffet 11-2 with varied dishes for $6.95. Inexp-Mod.

The Carlton

1 Mellon Bank Ctr, Grant. Lunch Mon-Fri 11:30-2:30, Dinner Mon-Thur 5-10, Fri-Sat til 11. AE,DC,MC,V. **391-4099.**
Handsome, sophisticated room with prime beef, chops, fresh fish, seafood. Business favorite. Mod-Exp.

Chinatown Inn

522 Third. Lunch Mon-Sat 11-2:30, Dinner til 12. Sun 2-11. AE,D,DC,MC,V. **261-1292.**
Chinese specialties in serene surroundings. Inexp-Mod.

Common Plea

308 Ross. Lunch Mon-Fri 11:30-2:30, Dinner Mon-Sat 5-10:30. AE,DC,MC,V. **281-5140.**
Lawyers' favorite upstairs room with 'courtly' atmosphere, great appetizers, seafood. Mod-Exp.

Dingbat's

One Oxford Centre. Lunch Mon-Sat 11:30-2, Dinner 5-12am. AE,D,DC,MC,V. **392-0350.**
Popular, handsome restaurant with terrace patio in summer, big bar, eclectic menu—dinners, sandwiches, salads. Inexp-Mod. (See Review)

Juno Trattoria

One Oxford Centre. Third Level. Mon-Thur 11:30-10, Fri-Sat til 12. AE,D,DC,MC,V. **392-0225.**
Authentic Ital specialties in sleek balcony setting; great homemade bread, pasta, pizza. Inexp-Mod. (See Review)

Kaufmann's Dept Store

Fifth/Smithfield. Store charge only. **232-2682**
Best coffee shop food in town at 1st fl **Tic-Toc** 11-7, Inexp. Also light fare, desserts in **Edgar's** 11th floor dining-room, Lunch Mon-Fri 11-4, Sat til 3, Dinner Mon & Thur 4-8. Inexp-Mod.

Pietro's

Hyatt Regency Pittsburgh. 7 days 6:30-11. AE,DC,MC,V. **288-9326.**
Modern, spacious, two-level room with fine dining on N Italian cuisine, sumptuous Sunday Brunch; pleasant outdoor patio overlooking city. Mod-Exp.

Ruddy Duck

Bigelow/Sixth. Mon-Thur 6:30am-1, Fri til 10, Sat/Sun 7-12. AE,D,DC,MC,V. **281-3825.**
Warm, brassy room with Amer cuisine, breakfast to supper; good duck, sandwiches. Bargain Sun Buffet $7-$8. Mod.

Top of The Triangle

USX Bldg. Lunch Mon-Fri 11:30-3, Dinner 5:30-10. Sat 12-3, 5:30-12. Sun 4-9. AE,DC,MC,V. **471-4100.**
Fine Amer/Cont dining with spectacular view from 62nd floor. Dancing, bar til 2. Mod-Exp.

Westin William Penn

Mellon Square. AE,DC,MC.V. 7 days 6:30-11. **281-7100.**
Breakfast/lunch/dinner, Continental cuisine in elegant **Terrace Room** off grand lobby. Mod-Exp. Breakfast/lunch in **Garden Deli,** mezzanine, Mon-Fri 6-2. Inexp. Tea, cocktails, piano in relaxing **Palm Court Lobby** 7 days 11-1. Mod. (See Review)

Station Square (See Reviews 1)

Mt Washington (See City Views 7)

Gourmet's Glossary

almondine—garnished with blanched almonds sauteed in butter.

aperitif—a short alcoholic beverage, usually taken as an appetite stimulant; may refer to any pre-dinner drink.

Barsac—sauteed in butter & Sauternes, sprinkled with cheese & bread crumbs.

beef Wellington—marinated filet, topped with mushrooms and baked in a puff pastry crust, garnished with bordelaise— a red wine and marrow sauce.

Bearnaise—Hollandaise sauce with tarragon, shallots, other seasonings & wine.

bechamel—a white cream sauce seasoned with cloves and nutmeg.

bisque—a rich cream soup usually from fish or shellfish; a rich frozen dessert.

Bourguignon, a la—a red wine sauce with mushrooms & onion.

Chateaubriand—thick slice from center cut of beef filet, grilled, usually sliced at tableside and served with Chateaubriand sauce (wine, shallots & butter) or Bearnaise, a creamy wine sauce.

cherries jubilee—stone cherries simmered in syrup, flamed in brandy or liqueur.

coquille St. Jacques—scallops.

crepes Suzette—thin pancakes flamed in a sauce of Curacao & orange juice.

en crute—in a pastry shell.

English trifle—mixture of cake soaked in Madeira or liqueur with rum custard, whipped cream & fruit jam.

escargot—snails, usually served in half shell.

flambe—flamed with brandy or liqueur.

foie gras—specially fattened goose or duck liver.

Hollandaise—thick sauce made with eggs, butter, lemon juice or vinegar.

Madeira—a brown sauce of meat stock and Madeira wine.

medallions—small round or oval pieces o meat, often called tournedos when beef

mousse—a molded, usually cold dish, either a dessert with rich cream ingredients or a gelatin based meat, fish or vegetable mold.

osso buco—veal shank simmered in spiced white wine, treasured for bone marrow.

peach Melba—a dessert of half peach with vanilla ice cream, topped with raspberry sauce & whipped cream.

persillade—chopped parsley topping often mixed with garlic & bread crumbs.

piccata—veal sauteed in lemon, butter, mushrooms and white wine.

provencale, a la—spicy, generally with garlic and tomato.

saltimbocca—veal cutlets stuffed with ham, sage & Mozzarella cheese, sauteed in white wine sauce.

scallopini—thinly sliced meat, usually veal, or fish, flattened and fried in butter or oil.

siciliana—broiled steak, baked with coating of oregano & garlic seasoned bread crumbs.

sorbet—a light fruit ice generally less sweet than sherbet, served between courses to refresh the palate.

souffle—a high, light dessert or savory dish, pureed and thickened with egg yolks and beaten egg whites.

torte—usually dessert, rich layers of cake made with crumbs, eggs, nuts, topped with whipped cream and fruit.

truffles—underground fungus used for flavoring and as a garnish.

3

What makes a fabulous meal? A combination of good food, wine, beautiful surroundings, elegant service...and most especially...the company. Here are some fabulous feasts for those occasions when money's no object.... showcasing the extraordinary cuisine available in the Gr Pittsburgh area.

Plush Dinner for Two
Sweeping View

Chestnut Ridge Inn

Rt 22, Blairsville. Dinner Mon-Thur 5-10, Fri & Sat til 11. Sun Brunch 11-2, Dinner til 9. **459-7191.**

This big inn with a sweeping view of the Chestnut Ridge Golf Course is known for its superior service and superb dining. The upstairs restaurant is an elegant affair—crystal chandeliers, plush blue carpeting, a beautiful stained glass window in the ceiling—a classy, comfortable setting. A pianist adds to dinnertime atmosphere. Lunches and late supper in the downstairs restaurant are a moderate $3-$10 but upstairs dinner entrees climb from $14-$23 for delicacies such as Medallions of Beef stuffed with Swiss Cheese and Lobster, fresh fish, and a new lamb dish with dried prunes, exotic spices & brandy—all served with relish tray and potato or vegetable. For our feast Chestnut Ridge Chef/Owner Felix Melloul presents a Salmon Banquet.

Suggested Feast

Relish Tray: All of the Inn's dinners are preceded by a beautiful tray of crisp vegetables, black Italian olives and pate.
Appetizer: Scalloped Mousse Florentine, Clam Sauce Nouvelle, $6.95.
Soup: Italian Wedding Soup, $1.50.
Salad: Tossed fresh garden greens vinaigrette, $2.95.
Sorbet: Lemon-lime to clear the palate.
Entree: Baby Salmon Filet stuffed with a duxelles (pureed mushroom) and crabmeat, baked in a puff pastry and served with dill Hollandaise, $19.95 accompanied by a vegetable, potato or rice and house-baked French bread.
Dessert: A special Coffee Espresso, $1.50.
Wine: A good dry white Calif Pinot Chardonnay Les Charmes, $13.50.
The Tab: Appetizer $6.95, Soup $1.50, Salad $2.95, Entree $19.95, Dessert Coffee $1.50, Wine $13.50. Total for 2: $79 plus tax and gratuity for a beautiful meal in beautiful surroundings.

The High Life—Feasting
Atop Mt Washington

Christopher's

1411 Grandview Ave, Mt Washington. Mon-Thur 5-11, Fri & Sat til 12. **381-4500.**

One of the best dining experiences in the city is at this restaurant high atop Mt Washington with spectacular views in all directions from its sheer glass walls. An outside elevator whisks diners to the glamorous multi-level rooftop room with dramatic lighting, a top-hat/white-tie feel and innovative use of glass, aluminum and coal—a sophisticated showcase for Pittsburgh products. Everything about this restaurant says Pittsburgh is someplace special. Dinners can be done for less—entrees range from $18-$35, several in the $19-$22 range—but for our feast Owner Christopher Passodelis and Chef Doug Zimmerman have put together a menu to match the spectacular decor. Allow at least four hours for your meal.

Suggested Feast

Appetizer: An exciting beginning—A trio of Caviar—Imperial Beluga, Osetra and Sevruga ($165) served with a bottle of Taittinger champagne ($208).
Salad: Smoked Duck Salad, $5.95.
Entrees: Southern Pheasant coated with cornmeal, sauteed and served over a sauce of pheasant glace with lentils and Swiss chard, $26; and Rack of Lamb Rosemary in a delicate sauce of rosemary, mushrooms and Chartreuse liqueur, $29.
Dessert: Cafe Leigoia—coffee ice cream in a cookie shell with coffee liqueur, garnished with banana slices—and Chocolate Macadamia & Praline Tarts, $4.50 each.
Finishing Touch: Glass of Louis XIII cognac, $95 for 2.
The Tab: Appetizer $165, Salad $5.95, Entree $29, Dessert $4.50, Wine $303. Total: $547 for 2 plus tax and gratuity for your night at the top!

Divine Dinner for Two

Angel's Corner

Atwood at Bates Street, Oakland. Dinner Mon-Sat 5-10. Reser. AE,MC,V. **682-1879.**

This handsome dining room, housed in a former church, has made the most of the high ceilings, stained glass windows and exposed wood to create a warm, intimate, candlelit atmosphere. Entrees range from $15-$23 for fresh seafood, beef, poultry, veal and pork...served with a vegetable and starch and homemade angel rolls—light biscuit dough in the shape of an angel. Over all watches a very attentive staff. The Corner has suggested a divine repast including many of the restaurant's specialties. Before your dinner visit the balcony Choir Loft for cocktails—also a great place for after-theatre desserts and a vast array of armagnacs, cognacs and ports, all available for your grand finale.

Suggested Feast

Appetizer: Angel's Shrimp Florentine—angel hair pasta and cream with baby shrimp and ribbons of fresh spinach, $4.50.

Salad: Romaine lettuce salad with choice of creamy Dijon or homemade Caesar dressing, served with angel rolls.

Entree: Filet Mignon Dijonaise, twin filets with mustard-peppercorn crust, broiled to order and splashed with cognac, $21.95.

Dessert: Homemade dark chocolate truffles—sweet dark chocolate laced with Grand Marnier, rolled in crushed almonds & cocoa, $3.50.

After Dinner Drink: Flaming Angel Coffee, prepared tableside: Tia Maria & Irish Mist flamed, topped with whipped cream and a dash of nutmeg, $6.50. Vintage ports, $10.

Wine: With the meal Moet Chandon White Star Champagne, $52 a bottle.

The Tab: Appetizer $4.50, Entree $21.95, Dessert $3.50, After Dinner Drink $6.50, Port $10, Wine $52. Total: $135 for 2 plus tax & gratuity for a heavenly dinner.

Romantic French Dining— On The Terrace

Cafe Azure

317 S Craig Street, Oakland. Lunch Mon-Sat 11:30-3, Dinner Mon-Thur 6-10, Fri & Sat til 10:30. Reser. AE,DC,MC,V. **681-3533.**

Owner Rob Fleury's restaurant philosophy—attention to every detail of cuisine, ambience and service—have combined to make a winner of this sophisticated Oakland cafe with a suave contemporary decor. Chef Barbara Kuhn's fine French cuisine highlights inspired appetizers—vegetable timbales and rice terrines—and inventive fish, fowl and pasta entrees $6-$12 for lunch and $12-$24 for dinner. In good weather add to your delight by dining on the blue-awninged patio, one of the city's best ambiences. For our feast the house has chosen a Lamb Dinner.

Suggested Feast:

Appetizer: Oriental Crab Cake with tamari garlic butter, $7.

Salad: Warm Asparagus with grilled new potatoes, beets and hard-cooked eggs with a creamy Parmesan-tomato-chive vinaigrette, $6.75.

Entree: Lamb Loin filled with goat cheese, spinach, pine nuts and a fresh tomato-thyme demi-sauce, $23.

Dessert: A Baum Torte, alternating layers of almond pastry and pistachios finished with a butter cream, glazed with chocolate and served on a bed of creme Anglaise, $6.

Wine: Beringer Private Reserve Cabernet Sauvignon 1986, $60.

The Tab: Appetizer $7, Salad $6.75, Entree $23, Dessert $6, Wine $60 for a total of $104 for a delightful dinner.

RICH MAN'S GUIDE

Candlelight Dining in Elizabethan Castle

Hyeholde

190 Hyeholde Drive, Coraopolis, 5 min from Airport. Lunch Mon-Fri 11:30-2. Dinner Mon-Sat 5-10. Reser sugg. **264-3116.**

Perhaps Pittsburgh's most famous restaurant, a legend in and out of the city, Hyeholde is situated on beautiful wooded grounds. Considered one of the 20 finest restaurants in the U.S., it has received every major award including the coveted Mobil Four-Star rating. Every Pittsburgher should dine here at least once to enjoy the hospitality of this warm Elizabethan mansion with its flagstone floors, big fireplaces and hanging tapestries. More casual lunches are now $5.50-$9.50 and romantic dinner by candlelight is a reasonable $12.50-$19.75 for gourmet entrees—Chicken Hyeholde stuffed with apples & chestnuts, veal, Virginia spots, steak and grilled swordfish. Our Rich Man's feast stars Hyeholde's most renowned specialties—Rack of Lamb.

Suggested Feast

Entree: Rack of Lamb Persillade, lamb rolled in parslied bread crumbs, roasted and served with Dijon mustard sauce, $19.75. Dinner includes sorbets, between courses, crisp vegetables al dente or potato, and freshly baked bread.
Appetizer: The house's famous Sherry Bisque from a 'secret recipe', $2.50.
Salad: Choice of Emperor's Salad, romaine with garlic croutons ($3.50) or fresh vegetables on romaine with mint dressing ($3).
Dessert: From a beautiful dessert tray—Coeur a la Creme, a creamy concoction of dark chocolate in a flaky crust topped with pastry cream and strawberries, $4.50.
Wine: To complement your dinner an Alexander Valley '87 Cabernet Sauvignon $33, or Clos Dubois '88 Merlot, $29.
The Tab: Entree $19.75, Appetizer $2.50, Salad $3.50, Dessert $4.50, $60 for 2; plus Wine $33. Total: $93 for 2 plus tax & gratuity. For a romantic repast.

American Feast in Edwardian Elegance

The Harvest

Pittsburgh Vista Hotel, Liberty Center at Penn Avenue, Downtown. Lunch Mon-Fri 11:30-2:30, Dinner Mon-Sat 5:30-10:30. AE,D,DC,MC,V. **281-8160.**

This warm, elegant room has an Edwardian flavour—glass, brass, a genial, comfortable bar and paintings of the harvest bounty. The cuisine, the finest of American/continental with a 4-Star Mobil rating, features a changing menu of regional favorites—Poached Chinook Salmon, Sea Trout, Loin of Venison, Rack of Lamb, house made fettuccine and authentic American desserts i.e. Dutch Apple and Black Bottom pies. Entrees range from $10-$17 for lunch, $14-$24.50 for dinner with special pre-theatre dinners on performance nights—a wonderful time to sample the cuisine and matchless service of a European-trained staff. Chef extraordinaire Willi Nuenlist has included several regional favorites in his feast.

Suggested Feast

Aperitif: A refreshing beginning, Chambord liqueur with French champagne, $6.50 glass.
Cold Appetizer: Beef Carpaccio with truffles, freshly grated Parmesan on seasonal greens, $6.75.
Hot Appetizer: Crisfield Crab Cakes with roasted bell pepper sauce, $7.75.
Soup: Clear Duck Consomme, $3.25.
Entree: Pan Fried Tenderloin of Veal—medallions of prime veal loin with Pa mushrooms sauteed with Merlot wine and sage, in a cream sauce; served with seasonal vegetable and croquette potatoes, $20.
Wine: Chateau St Michel Merlot, å Washington state red burgundy, $26.
Dessert: Black Bottom Pie, the Harvest's signature dessert—dark and light chocolate mousse in a chocolate crumb crust, $4.50.
The Tab: Aperitif $6.50, Appetizers $14.50, Soup $3.25, Entree $20, Dessert $4.50, Wine $39. Total: $136.50 for 2 plus tax & gratuity for a unique banquet.

Roman Banquet in Hills of Pittsburgh CCCXLIV for Two

D'Imperio's

3412 William Penn Hwy, Wilkins Twp.
Dinner Tues-Sun 5-11. Reser. **823-4800.**
D'Imperio's, a mecca for serious diners, has earned a reputation as one of the best restaurants in Western Pa for the grace of its continental cuisine and service. The famous $35 six-course dinners include choice of 18 entrees, i.e. trout stuffed with escargot, lemon sole, baked shrimp with Roquefort, six veals, beef Wellington, steak—all served with hot & cold appetizers, soup, salad, fresh fruit and delicious desserts. A three-course version is available to budget diners for $15-$25. For our *Guide* Owner Tony D'Imperio drew on some of the restaurant's most famous dishes for a fabulous 'once in a lifetime' Roman banquet, a feast fit for a Pittsburgh king.

Italian Feast

Aperitif: Punt e Mes, an aperitif of herbs & spices served on ice, $3.50
Appetizer: Grilled Swordfish with Coconut, $6.95.
Pasta: Spinach Spaghettini with Pesto Genovese, $3.95.
Entree: Red Snapper Filet in thin pastry with spinach, minced oysters and Galliano, potted asparagus with Hollandaise, $18.75.
Salad: Hearts of Endive & Escarole Vinaigrette, $3.
Intermezzo: A sorbet of grapefruit ice generously drenched with Polish Wyborowa (vodka), $5.
After Dinner: A final touch—Ghiottini, hard, crunchy almond cookies with espresso, $3.
Wines: With Appetizer & Pasta: Vernaccia di San Gimignano, a crisp dry white wine, the oldest of Italian wines. . . made as far back as the 13th Century, $25; with Entree: California Chardonnay from Farniente Winery, $65; with Dessert: 1/2 bottle Trockenbeerenauslese, a German dessert wine from individually selected late harvest berries, $90. Then a glass of King Louis XIII, the world's oldest known French cognac, an ounce $75 for 2, ($910 a bottle). Is it any wonder the ancient Romans reclined on couches while dining!
The Tab: Aperitif $3.50, Appetizer $6.95, Pasta $3.95, Entree $18.75, Salad $3, Intermezzo $5, Cookies & Espresso $3. **Total:** Food $88.30 for 2 plus $255 for wine for a total of $344 for your wonderful epicurean feast for 2 plus tax & gratuity. As the Romans do!

Extraordinary Steak Dinner

The Colony

Greentree & Cochran Roads, South Hills.
Mon-Thur 5:30-10:30, Fri-Sat til 11.
Reser sugg. **561-2060.**
A warm restaurant with an informal atmosphere around an open brick grill, this is where many Pittsburgh executives go to relax and enjoy what is indubitably one of, if not the best, steaks in town (*Travel/Holiday* & local awards). And now there's nightly entertainment and music in the lounge til 12. The menu boasts grilled swordfish, lemon sole, lamb chops, lobster, veal ($20-$26), but it's the steak you'll want. P.S. You can now take home some of the house's famous steak sauce.

Suggested Feast:

Appetizer: House specialty Shrimp Scampi in garlic sauce, $7.50, a wonderful prelude to dinner.
Entree: Sirloin Steak (13-14 oz) sizzling from the charcoal grill, basted with special 'Colony Sauce', $26. With a salad and baked potato/pasta, vegetables, sour cream, chives, bacon toppings.
Dessert: Fresh fruit or selection from the pastry tray is included with dinner.
The Wine: A Robert Mondavi Cabernet Sauvignon $28.
The Tab: Appetizer $7.50, Steak $26, Wine $28. Total: $95 for 2 plus tax and gratuity for a 'king of steaks' dinner.

Gourmet's Lamb Feast at Laforet

Laforet

5701 Bryant St, Highland Park. Dinner Tues-Thur 6-10, Fri & Sat 5:30-11. **665-9000.**
The exquisite cuisine from this restaurant has piqued serious interest from city's gourmets. Inventive cuisine, flawlessly presented, is the hallmark of this little Victorian town house with lots of polished charm. Epicurean delights, mousses, refined vegetables, delectable desserts grace the dinner menu ranging from $18-$24. Husband-wife Owner/Chefs Michael and Candace Urrichio have chosen a lamb feast with wines for a romantic dinner at Laforet.

Suggested Feast:

Appetizer: Smoked duck & garlic sausage, served with duck comfit and puff pastry, $5.75. With '85 Gewurztraminer Trimbac Cuvee $44.
Salad: Exotic greens topped with baked chevre and fresh herbs, $5.25. With an '86 Pouilly Fume Blondelet, 1/2 bottle $19.
Fish: Grilled Norwegian Salmon served with a smoked salmon butter sauce, $7.50. With an '85 Meursault Les Perrieres Ampeau, $65.
Grapefruit Granita: A forked ice.
Meat: Lamb chops stuffed with foie gras, pan roasted with morels and julienne of yellow squash glazed with a port sauce, $22.50. 1/2 bottle 1983 Cote Roti Guigal, $25.
Dessert: A medley of ten desserts on one plate splashed with purees and sauces and served with a Sauterne Chateau Filhot 1983, $25.
The Tab: Appetizer $5.75, Salad $5.25, Fish $7.50, Meat $22.50, Dessert $25 for 2, Wines $178 for a total of $285 plus tax and gratuity for a great gourmet meal.

> *" Among the great whom Heaven has made to shine, How few have learned the art of arts—to dine."*
> *Oliver Wendell Holmes*

> *"A man's reach should exceed his grasp else what's a heaven for."*
> *Browning*

Fabulous Fish Dinner

Piccolo Mondo

Foster Plaza Bldg 7, Greentree, off Holiday Inn Drive. Lunch Mon-Fri 11:30-2:30, Dinner 5-10, Fri & Sat til 11. Reser sugg six or more. AE,D,DC,MC,V. **922-0920.**
One of the city's most beautiful restaurants, this chandeliered, carpeted room, warmed with multi-hues of mauve, rose and green is now the elegant home of new owner Rico Lorenzini of Rico's fame. He returns, with son David, to the South Hills where he began his restaurant career. Piccolo is noted for its splendid cuisine, continental service and the relaxing atmosphere of the spacious hilltop room with a sweeping view of Greentree's woodland. Dining here, a gastronomic celebration, is surprisingly reasonable...lunch for $5.25-$10 and dinner from $12-$26 up. The menu encompasses lobster, veal, pasta and the best fish in town—Dover sole, lemon sole, salmon—all served with a French/Italian flair. Our menu is a Fish Feast for a special occasion.

Suggested Feast

Appetizer: "Half & Half", two homemade pasta dishes—Rotolo Milanese with pink marinara, and Stuffed Agnolotti in white cream sauce, $7.25.
Salad: Caprice Salad—sliced tomatoes, Buffalo mozzarella, $4.95.
Entree: Grouper sauteed with almonds, mushrooms in a brown butter sauce served with vegetable or potato, $19.
Dessert: Tiramisu, an Italian delicacy with mascarpone served with a blend of chocolate/espresso coffee, $4.
Wine: Terre di Tufo Teruzzi & Puthod, a Tuscan white wine $41.
The Tab: Appetizer $14.50, Salad $9.90, Entree $38, Dessert $8, Wine $41. Total: $112 for 2 plus tax and gratuity for a wonderful dinner.

Banquet In French Manor House Setting

Jacqueline's

Webster Hall, 4415 Fifth Avenue, Oakland. Mon-Thur 6-10, Fri & Sat til 11. **683-4525.**
This imperial room with its French blue walls, draped windows and shining silver service is a perfect "liaison dangereuse" setting for a French manor house banquet. New York Chef Steve Cortez is creating some extraordinary cuisine at this new restaurant on the site of former La Normande in Webster Hall. You can enter from the handsome, canopied entrance on Fifth Avenue or from the building lobby. The menu, ranging from $12-$26, offers classical versions of duck, lamb, guinea hen, filet mignon, veal and fish with some exquisite sauces. There's also a beautifully presented Salade Riche with lobster, foie gras, truffles and walnut truffle sauce for those who prefer gourmet 'light.' As expected, the service matches the cuisine. The house has chosen a Dover Sole banquet for an elegant candlelight feast.

Suggested Feast

Appetizer: Ragout de Champignon Sauvage Morels—sauteed wild portobelos & shitaki mushrooms with a Madeira demiglace, served over fragrant herb bread, $8.25.
Soup: Soupe de Longots et Faisan, white bean & pheasant soup, $5.95.
Salad: Salade du Saumon Marinee—sauteed salmon served over baby lettuces, dressed with a light vinaigrette, $6.50.
Entree: Goujonet De Sole Marie—thin, tender strips of dover sole sauteed and served with a saffron cream sauce, $25.95.
Dessert: Crepes Jacqueline with glazed apples and applesauce, prepared tableside, $5.95.
Wine: half bottle of Gevry Chambertin 1982, $28, and a Mersault Mommesin 1986, $59.
The Tab: Appetizer $8.25, Soup $5.95, Entree $25.95, Dessert $5.95, Wine $87. Dinner for 2: $190 plus tax and gratuity.

What a Weekend At World Class Spa!

An hour from Pittsburgh is Nemacolin, a world class spa, rated one of the top five in the country. Featured on TV's "Life Styles of the Rich & Famous," the scenic mountain resort is located in Farmington, Rt 40 East in the Laurel Mountains. The 550-acre resort/conference center has beautiful grounds, three lakes, a 200-seat amphitheatre, 18-hole PGA golf course, a stable and its own private air strip.

You can take off pounds in this posh setting and enjoy regular cuisine at the four-star Golden Trout Restaurant or healthy spa fare at Allures restaurant. (The resort also has a 10,000 bottle wine cellar.)

Housed in a separate building, the spa boasts a Jr Olympic-size pool, sauna, steam room, whirlpool, exercise equipment and treatment facilities. **Overnight Discovery Package:** two days, one night including meals and eight spa treatments—custom facial, body polish, Swedish massage, manicure, pedicure, make-up application (women), reflexology (men), aroma therapy scalp treatment and hair styling. **The Tab:** $394 per person/double occupancy including all gratuities and access to all resort facilities. **Contact:** Spa Director Susan Brewer— **800-422-2736** or **412-329-6772.**

Romantic Everyman's Feast $70 A Couple

Redwood

87 Castner Street, Donora, 45 minutes from Pgh on Route 51. By reser only. AE,DC,MC,V. 379-6540.
Every man can be a rich man for a night and enjoy a delectable dinner at this small restaurant which has received laurels from *Travel, Holiday* and *Fortune* magazines for its cuisine and unique personal service. Dinner is surprisingly affordable at this intimate eight-table 'living room,' with consummate attention to detail—alabaster lamps, roses on the tables, beautiful settings creating a romantic atmosphere for an unforgettable evening. Entrees—rack of lamb, stuffed lobster tail, veal Francaise, NY sirloin ($16-$23) arrive with many extra touches. Before or after dinner you can relax with cocktails in the flagstone courtyard of the grape arbor behind the restaurant.

Suggested Feast

Appetizer: Dinner begins with three delicious hors d'oeuvres—Cheese & Pate, Hot Crab Coquille and Shrimp Feurtine...all for $15 a couple.
Entree: House specialty Beef Braccia-lette, medallions of filet mignon simmered in a light wine sauce with rosemary, $18.50. Included are a salad with tarragon from the restaurant's herb garden, stuffed baked potato, freshly baked rolls and Parmesan cheese bread.
Dessert: Your choice of Bavarian Chocolate Cream Torte, Bananas Foster or Cherries Jubilee from $2.50-$4.50.
Wine: There are more than 75 wines in the cellar but one of the best is the house light, dry rose, $10.50 a bottle.
The Tab: Appetizer $15 for 2, Entree $18.50, Dessert $4.50, Wine: $10.50. Total: $71.50 for 2 plus tax and gratuity for an unforgettable everyman's feast.

"A man hath no better thing under the sun, than to eat, and to drink, and to be merry."
Ecclesiastes 8:15

Gracious Dining in Hilltop House

Rico's

Park Place off Babcock Blvd, N Hills. Lunch Mon-Sat 11:45-2:30, Dinner Mon-Thur 4-10:30, Fri & Sat til 11:30. Reser for eight or more. AE,DC,MC,V. 931-1989.
This beautiful restaurant, set in a quaint old house on a hilltop, has a sterling reputation for its fine North Italian cuisine and quality fish, steaks and seafood. Six rooms provide for warm, intimate dining. Not all entrees here are in the Rich Man's bracket. You can lunch for $5.50-$9 and dine for $9.75-$28.50 with the graciousness of fine service. But for our 'dream dinner', Rico's has put together a fine Italian feast—a Veal and Seafood Platter with the best of wines. And as all of the ingredients are always at hand, the meal can be served with very little notice.

Suggested Feast

Appetizer: Lump Crabmeat Hoelzel, $9.50 with a white wine, Girard Chenin Blanc, $19.
Salad: Hearts of palm with house Italian dressing with Roquefort, $3.50.
Pasta: 1/2 order of Farfalle—bowtie shaped pasta with Beluga caviar in a pink cream sauce—and l/2 order of Angel Hair in a light cream sauce topped with roasted pignola nuts, $12.50 for 2. With a 1979 Mersault white wine, $53.
Entree: A Veal and Seafood assortment for 2—three different types of veal, fresh fish and seafood served with a sauteed Spinach Aglio con Olio—garlic with oil, $29.95. Continue with the Mersault or a soft red Barbarossa, $43.
Dessert: Sauteed Strawberries a la Don flambeed with Grand Marnier over French vanilla ice cream, $5.75 person. With a 150-year old Cuvee Grand Marnier, 1-1/2-oz glass, $16 each.
The Tab: Appetizer $9.50, Salad $3.50, Pasta $12.50 for 2, Entree $29.95, Dessert $5.75, Wines $147. Total $256.90 for 2, plus tax & gratuity.

Serious Steak Lovers Feast

Ruth's Chris Steak House

6 PPG Place, Downtown. Lunch Mon-Fri 11:30-3. Dinner Mon-Sat 5-11, Sun 4-8. Free indoor parking. Reser sugg. AE,DC,MC,V. **391-4800.**
This burnished restaurant in PPG Plaza is an impressive steak house—the 19th of the famous Ruth's Chris chain. A warm, comfortable room with lots of rich cherry wood and glass, it's a gracious setting for a very special sizzling steak. It also has excellent grilled chicken, veal and lamb chops plus seafood, fresh Maine lobster, beautifully done vegetables and potatoes prepared seven different ways. Lunches range from $5.95 for a 1/3 lb hamburger to $15 for veal chops. Dinners are from $15-$42.

Suggested Feast

Appetizer: Mushrooms stuffed with Crabmeat or Shrimp Remoulade—a spicy, garlicky beginning for your steak lover's feast, each $6.95.
Salad: To clear your palate, the special house Italian Salad—a bed of fresh greens with tomatoes, artichoke hearts, chopped eggs, onions, celery, olives, topped with Parmesan cheese and anchovies, $4.
Entree: Feast on an aged US Prime NY Strip, cut and broiled to your specifications and served in sizzling butter, $21. (For a non-beef entree try the Chicken California—a marinated, herb-seasoned grilled double breast $15, or 2-5 lb Maine Lobster at market price.)
Vegetable: A house special—Creamed Spinach, $3.50.
Dessert: Finish with a warm, fragrant Bread Pudding with Whiskey Sauce $3, or Pecan Pie a la Mode, $4.
Wine: Duckhorn Merlot, a light-bodied, full-tasting California red, $60 bottle.
The Tab: Appetizer $6.95, Salad $4, Entree $21, Vegetable $3.50, Dessert $3, Wine $60. Total: $210 for 2 plus beverage, tax and gratuity for a super steak dinner.

Stellar Seafood Banquet For Two

Tambellini's

860 Saw Mill Run Blvd, Rt 51, just beyond Liberty Tunnels. Mon-Fri 11-11, Sat til 12. AE,DC,MC,V. **481-1118.**
Pittsburgh's premiere name in seafood, this big, elegant restaurant grew from the first small Tambellini's on Mt Washington. Now the largest in the city, it's still serving stellar seafood and Italian cuisine in five rooms that seat 800 . . . and there's been no compromise with quality. This is the place for that special seafood feast when eating well in convivial surroundings is the main object. Let yourself go on the specialties here—Lobster, Shrimp or Scallops Louie, Scrod, Louisiana Redfish, Crab Imperial and a host of fresh seasonal items flown in daily—plus delicious pastas and antipastos. This is a seafood lover's paradise. For our feast Chef Andrew Tambellini has chosen a Seafood Platter banquet.

Suggested Feast

Appetizer: Antipasto for 2—a big, zesty array of Italian meats, peppers, olives, cheeses, $8.50.
Entree: Assorted Seafood Platter a la Louie—lemon sole, lobster tail, sea scallops, jumbo shrimp, baked fresh oysters, small deviled crab—broiled in garlic butter with seasoned bread crumbs, originated by Louis Tambellini himself, $22.50.
Pasta: Angel Hair with cream sauce & pignola nuts, $7.50 for 2.
Dessert: A cool finish with spumoni $2.50, or rich Black Forest Cheesecake, $2.75.
Wine: Santa Margherita Pinot Grigio, a white Italian wine, $26.
The Tab: Appetizer $8.50 for 2, Entrees $22.50, Pasta $7 for 2, Dessert $5.25, Wine $26. Total: $97 for 2 plus tax and gratuity for a seafood night to remember.

3

A Nostalgic Night In Elegant Terrace Room

The Terrace Room

Westin William Penn, Downtown. 7 days. Breakfast 6:30-11, Lunch 11-2, Dinner 5:30-11. AE,DC,MC,V. **553-5235.**
The hotel's beautiful grand lobby sets the stage for a feast in this elegantly restored Edwardian dining room—a page from a more lavish era. The crystal chandeliers and ornate ceilings are a perfect setting for continental dining from $12-$24 for Veal Rib Chops, New York Steak, Filet Mignon, Swordfish and new menu items in keeping with the room's original Italian Renaissance theme, and of course the restaurant's specialty—the best prime rib in the city. Stay on for dancing Saturday night til 12. Our dinner here is a beautifully designed Roast Loin of Veal.

Suggested Feast

Appetizer: Fried Calamari with Lemon Horseradish Aioli, $3.95.
Soup: Seafood Gumbo with spicy andouille sausage, $4.50.
Entree: Roast Loin of Veal filled with prosciutto, provolone, spinach and sausage, $23.95.
Dessert: Pizzele Cone with seasonal fruit and Marsala Zabaglione, $3.50.
Wine: A 1985 B & G Graves, a heavy French Bordeaux, $28.
The Tab: Appetizer $3.95, Soup $4.50, Entree $23.95, Dessert $3.50, Wine $28. Total: Just $100 for 2 (plus tax and gratuity) for a nostalgic night in this beautiful room.

Fireworks at the Angel

Tin Angel

1204 Grandview Avenue, Mt Washington. Mon-Thur 5-9:30, Fri & Sat til 10. Reser. **381-1919.**
The first restaurant atop Mt Washington, now an elegant two-tiered room, the Angel is still one of the most glamorous and romantic spots in town. With its sweeping view of the city, it's a wondrous place from which to view July 4th fireworks at the Point. The verbal menu, with entrees from $23.75 to $36.50, includes filet, NY strip, medallions of beef, sole almondine, South African lobster and combination Surf 'n Turf chosen for our dinner here.

Suggested Feast

Entree: Your Steak and Lobster dinner comes complete with appetizer, vegetable, a delicious rice pilaf and dessert, $36.50.
Appetizer: Fresh Fruit Cocktail followed by an unforgettable hors d'oeuvres platter—grape leaves, huge olives and exotic marinated items—best appetizer in town.
Dessert: Try the Tin Angel Parfait or the Pecan Ball with chocolate sauce. Then refreshing minty pineapple with creme de menthe to finish in a mellow mood as you watch the city lights.
Wine: Rutherford Hill Chardonnay or a red Robert Mondavi Pinot Noir, both at $27.
The Tab: Surf 'n Turf Dinner $36.50, Wine $27. Total: $100 for 2 plus tax and gratuity for a heavenly night atop the town.

Before the Symphony Dine As Mozart Did

Pgh Symphony season subscribers can now partake of dinner two hours before performances in the damask-walled, crystal-chandeliered Mozart Room. A doorman awaits at the Hoezel entrance to Heinz Hall (to the right of the main 6th Street entrance) to check your coats, which you need not retrieve til after the performance. Then on to dinner with choice of four entrees—poultry, beef, seafood, veal/lamb ($18-$22) complete with vegetable, salad, sorbet and pre-dinner hors d'oeuvres...drinks and dessert cart extra. Only one seating and 15 tables for dinner so be sure to reserve. Then you step directly into the Heinz Hall lobby, returning to exit from the restaurant entrance. A most convenient way to dine and beat pre-performance traffic...wonderful in cold weather. Reservations only. Call **392-4887.**

Fine Wine And Dine
At Wooden Angel

Wooden Angel

Sharon Road & Leopard Lane, Bridge-water, Beaver Valley. (45 min from Pgh, 20 min from Airport.) Tues-Fri 11:30-11. Sat 5-midnite. Reser. **774-7880.**
The fame of this restaurant's owner, Alex Sebastian, has spread near and far for his wine wizardry and passion for American vintages. People drive for miles to savour the restaurant's cuisine and explore its huge cellars of American wines—more than 500 from all over the U.S. . . California, New York, Washington State, Oregon. The restaurant's wine list, lauded in '87 as one of the Top 10 in the World by *Wine Spectator Magazine*, has also garnered several *Holiday* and *Mobil* awards. Your host will graciously take you on a tour of the cellars after your dinner in this warm, comfortable restaurant with lots of brick and rough-hewn wood. Lunch is a reasonable $4.50-$10 with dinners $14-$30 for steak, lobster, lamb and fish. For our Rich Man's Feast, Sebastian has put together a feast matching fine American wines to American cuisine—a dinner with four sharing the food and rare vintages at a fixe prix of $272 for 4, $64 a person.

Fine Wine Feast

Appetizer: Cherry & Apple Smoked Duck Breast with roasted vegetables and NY State goat cheese. **Wine:** An Eberle Chardonnay.
Pasta: Saffron Fettucini with mussels, chives, bacon and heavy cream. **Wine:** Firestone Johannisberg Riesling from California.
Fish: Sauteed Red Snapper in olive oil with port wine sauce.
Wine: Knudsen Erath '85 Pinot Noir, Oregon.
Sorbet: Lemon Sorbet
Entree: Roast Rack of Lamb with rosemary and black pepper, served with wild mushrooms. **Wine:** Storybook Zinfindel, California.
Salad: Tomatoes with fresh Mozzarella, fresh basil and balsamic vinegar.
Cheese & Fruit
Dessert: Amaretto Cake with apricot glaze, topped with fresh raspberries & whipped cream. Wine: Santino "Lisa Marie."
The Tab: $272 for dinner for 4 including tax & gratuity—for a night of American wining and dining to remember.

3

Your Carriage Awaits

Stretch out. . . settle back. . . relax. . . your carriage will glide to the door of your destination for that very special night on the town. You can rent anything from a Lincoln stretch limo to luxury sedans, vans or busses for getting visiting VIPs to and from the Airport, a night on the town, weddings, proms or any special event from a plethora of local companies including **Allegheny Limo—Carey of Pittsburgh, Premiere, Carriage Services, Pittsburgh Limo and Reimer's.**
Definitely a Rich Man's pleasure is **Star Limo's** 30-ft white Lincoln which seats 10 and includes twin moon roofs,

two TVs, stereo, CD player, VCR, an electronic bar and special interior lighting. $100 a hour, 3-hour minimum. AE,DC. Call **461-9088.**

Or travel in style in the ultimate in rag tops, **Vintage Limo's** 1936 White open-air touring car with oak floors and panels, a carved oak dash, brass trimmings, stereo, three bars, air conditioning and a top that folds back to open the roof to the sky. Ideal for groups up to 14. $85 an hour includes chauffeur. Reserve far ahead with John Damratoski. **793-2131.**

Gourmet Wining/Dining Clubs... Special Dinners

La Chaine de Rotisseurs

For the serious gourmet—enthusiasts, chefs, food professionals—this chapter of the international, Paris-based society meets every three months at prominent restaurants. The object—to enjoy good food, wine and fellowship. There are 30-40 members—by invitation—with a $175 membership fee, and dinners at about $100 a person. Black tie is required at club dinners. If you're interested call Pete Hanowich, **486-3946.**

Les Amis du Vin

The Pittsburgh chapter of this international society has received the Chapter of the Year award for its ambitious activities here. About 500 members—wine lovers all—meet twice monthly for tastings, dinners and wine classes at the Pittsburgh Vista Hotel and various city locations. Tastings run about $20-$40 an event. Dinners, with a selection of fine wines, range from $75-$125. Wine lovers can apply to Ray Szymanski, **655-2852.**

Les Dames du Vin

The only women's wine tasters' group outside California, Les Dames' 35-40 members meet thrice monthly at members' homes or restaurants to sample the fruit of the vine. They share the cost of wine and purchase their own dinners—or a hostess provides cheese & crackers. Membership in this nine-year-old group is a modest $5. Male guests are invited to four annual events including a Wine Dinner, Bastille Day tasting and a Belgium Beer tasting. The occasional male guest at regular meetings must come bearing champagne. Distaff tasters can call Sharryn Donn Campbell at **661-4810.**

Jacqueline's Country Dinners

Jacqueline's in Webster Hall at 4415 Fifth Avenue offers a series of Special Country Dinners with rare recipes—Irish, Portuguese with wines to match. Set price for the dinners, including wine, is about $50-$65 a person. For info call **683-4525.**

Le Pommier Regional Dinners

This country French restaurant at 2104 E Carson Street, South Side, offers monthly dinners on occasional Wednesdays starting at 7:30, highlighting provinces and regions of France or French-influenced cuisines i.e. Cajun, Moroccan. They're fun and affordable at a set price of $24.95 for four courses inc tax. You buy your own wine. Le Pommier also offers cooking classes on the third Tuesday of each month with a demonstration, lunch, wine and service for only $27.50 per person, popular with local gourmet cooks. Call **431-1901** to register.

March of Dimes Gourmet Gala

Local celebrites and business leaders join renowned chefs to create their own recipes for charity at an annual May dinner at the Pittsburgh Hilton. $125 person. **391-3193.**

Children's Hospital Gourmet Dinner

Famous chefs come to town each fall for one of the biggest dinners of the year, the Children's Hospital/Pgh Press Gourmet Dinner, traditionally at Le Mont Restaurant on Mt Washington. Donations are around $500 a couple for a worthy cause. **263-1421.**

Taste of Nation

Every spring more than 40 Pittsburgh chefs showcase their best for the benefit of the Greater Pgh Food Bank. Only $35 a person for some first-class cuisine. **672-4949.**

PITTSBURGH

AFTER DARK

Welcome to Pittsburgh's exciting new night life---from Happy Hours at dusk to the wee hours of the morning in 24-Hour Pittsburgh. New night life in the South Side, the Strip and Mt Washington is adding excitement to Pgh After Dark. For many Pittsburghers the day begins at sundown!

Happy Hours

If you want to take a short ride in the fast lane you can move around to the city's weekday Happy Hours... a lively hub of the local social scene where you can unwind, relax and find people driving on the same track. You may find a niche you visit ritually or speed up to make a variety of stops between 5-7 Monday thru Friday. And, with the emphasis on Happy Hour food, in the doing you can snack your way to dinner on a selection of buffets for a happy, hungry hour. **Drinks: Inexpensive —under $2.75; Moderate—under $3.75; Expensive—$3.75 & up.**

DOWNTOWN AREA

Carlton
One Mellon Bank Center, Downtown.
Food: Varies—wing-dings, eggrolls, sometimes turkey, roast beef.
Crowd: Bankers—suit & tie.
Atmosphere: Professional.
Drinks: Expensive.

Chauncy's
Commerce Court, Station Square.
Food: Hot & cold buffet, wing-dings, veggies, stuffed mushrooms. Super Friday buffet—ham, beef, multi-salads.
Crowd: Yuppie mania. You'll have to fight your way in.
Atmosphere: Crowded fun.
Drinks: Moderate.

Dingbat's City-Tavern
Oxford Centre, Downtown.
Food: Varies—barbecue beef, tacos, wing-dings.
Crowd: Yuppies—young, loud & lively.
Atmosphere: Great! Outdoor patio in summer.
Drinks: Inexpensive.

Froggy's
100 Market St, Downtown.
Food: Munchies, Nachos/Cheese.
Crowd: Seasoned—reporters/sports writers.
Atmosphere: Intellectually exciting.
Drinks: Moderate—for largest shot in town.

Gandy Dancer
Landmark Bldg, Station Square.
Food: Varies from mussels to stuffed Sicilian pepperada, poor man's pizza rolls, smelts, BBQ chicken. The best!
Crowd: A great mix. Everyone fits in.
Atmosphere: Crowded, relaxed fun.
Music: Piano.
Drinks: Inexpensive.

Hilton Hotel Lobby
Gateway Center, Downtown.
Food: Super hors d'oeuvres, finger foods.
Atmosphere: Elegantly relaxing, spills outside to terrace in good weather.
Music: Mellow piano.
Drinks: Expensive—worth the setting.

Holiday Inn, University
100 Lytton Ave.
Food: $1 buys medley hot/cold items.
Atmosphere: University, professionals.
Music: Background.
Drinks: Expensive.

Houlihan's
Freight House, Station Square.
Food: 1/2 off on appetizers—zucchini, skewered chicken, Cajun shrimp.
Crowd: Young professionals.
Atmosphere: Very laid back.
Drinks: Inexpensive.

Kason's
Bank Tower, 31 Fourth, Downtown.
Food: Munchies, 1/2 off on hors d'oeuvres Mon-Thur.
Crowd: Fun young professionals.
Atmosphere: Lively, DJ dancing.
Drinks: Moderate

Happy Hours

Motions
Pittsburgh Vista Hotel, Downtown.
Food: Buffet Mon-Fri, drink specials.
Crowd: Young downtown professionals.
Atmosphere: Sophisticated, lively.
Drinks: Expensive.

Maggie Mae's Sportin' House
110 Federal Street, North Side. Food:
Munchies, chips.
Crowd: Hard working variety.
Atmosphere: Noisy but fun.
Drinks: Inexpensive.

Max & Erma's
Horne's Dept Store, Stanwix St.
Food: Egg rolls, munchies.
Crowd: Interesting corporate types, brokers, computer buffs.
Atmosphere: Spirited, friendly.
Drinks: Inexpensive.

Ruddy Duck
Ramada, Bigelow Blvd, Downtown.
Food: Hot hors d'oeuvres never run out.
Crowd: Sophisticated professionals.
Atmosphere: Classy, quiet, laid back.
Drinks: Moderate.

Senor Birds
Bank Tower, 311 Fourth, Downtown.
Food: No specials.
Crowd: Young fun lovers.
Atmosphere: Boisterous fiesta mood.
Drinks: Moderate.

Top of the Triangle
USX Tower, Grant St, Downtown.
Food: Cheese, veggies, hot item; discounts on appetizers.
Crowd: Downtown business.
Atmosphere: A cut above the rest, view of the city from 62nd floor.
Drinks: Moderate-Expensive.

Waterfall Terrace
Sheraton Station Square.
Food: Hot & cold hors d'oeuvres.
Crowd: Sophisticated.
Atmosphere: Beautiful riverfront views.
Drinks: Moderate.

Wine Lovers Take Note

Le Pommier's Wine Bar is drawing a connoisseur crowd Fridays 5-7 to taste three wines each week and partake of hors d'oeuvres, $14 a tasting. A good change of pace. Noted for its country French cuisine, the restaurant is located at 2104 E Carson Street, South Side. **431-1901.**

SUBURBS

Cahoots
Marriott Hotel, Greentree.
Food: Hungry man's mecca. 99¢ buys you great nightly specials—miniature pizzas, wing-dings, ravioli, potato skins/zucchini. Thur Steak Dinner 5-11 for $1.99!
Crowd: Professional, sales, corp types.
Atmosphere: Classy, upscale, laid back.
Drinks: Inexpensive.

Colony Lounge
Greentree & Cochran Rds, Scott Twp.
Food: Cheese, shrimp, bacon-wraps.
Crowd: Business/professional.
Atmosphere: Congenial, low-key.
Drinks: Expensive.

Cousin's
7 Parkway Center, Greentree.
Food: 6-foot hoagies, taco salad, wings.
Crowd: Mixed blue/white collar.
Atmosphere: Friendly, casual.
Drinks: Inexpensive-Moderate.

Dingbat's
Waterworks Shopping Center, Fox Chapel & Robinson Township.
Food: Good variety of munchies.
Crowd: Young professionals & all ages.
Atmosphere: Friendly, good noise level.
Drinks: Moderate.

4

Happy Hours/Late Supper

Greenery
Holiday Inn, Greentree.
Food: Plentiful munchies.
Crowd: Young, corporate, prosperous.
Atmosphere: Airy & spacious amid the greenery.
Drinks: Moderate.

Houlihan's
300 Mall Boulevard, Monroeville.
Food: Veggies, chips, one hot item. Fri great fish sandwiches, shrimp $1-$1.50.
Crowd: Business & shoppers—21 & up.
Atmosphere: Comfortable & relaxed.
Drinks: Inexpensive.

Pittsburgh Sports Garden
1 Carson Street, Station Square.
Food: Hot wings, pizza, zucchini strips, more for $1.95 plate.
Crowd: Young, upscale.
Atmosphere: Sporty, DJ music.
Drinks: Mod-Exp.

TGI Friday's *240 Mall Boulevard, Monroeville.*
Food: Hot snacks—tacos, wing-dings.
Crowd: Local business crowd—25-35.
Atmosphere: Casual, informal.
Drinks: Moderate.

Valentine's
Howard Johnson's, Monroeville
Food: Great buffet spread hot & cold.
Crowd: Exec set, 30 something & plus.
Atmosphere: Jumpin' up crowd. DJ Friday.
Drinks: Moderate.

LATE SUPPER

(See also Oriental/Asian restaurants 13)

Allegheny Brewery & Pub
Troy Hill Rd, North Side. Tues-Sat til 12am. AE,MC,V. **237-9402.**
Wonderful German beer, cuisine, fun, full menu til closing. Music Wed-Sat. Inexp.

Aussie's
4617 Liberty Ave, Bloomfield. Sun-Thur til 11, Fri-Sat til 12am.
Atmospheric Australian bar; everything from lobster to wings; "Aussie Burgers" with pineapple & BBQ sauce ($3-$20). Australian beer on tap. Drinks: Mod.

Bangkok House
3233 W Liberty, Dormont. Sat til 11:30. AE,MC,V. **338-9111.**
Rare Thai specialties in serene, romantic room. Good end to an eve. Inexp-Mod.

Billy's Bistro
1720 Lowrie, N Side. Fri-Sat til 11. AE,DC,MC,V. **231-9277.**
Lobster, ribs, steak, sandwiches ($2-$11) in lively bar. Drinks: Inexp-Mod

Bobby Rubino's
Commerce Court, Station Sq. Fri-Sat til 12:30. AE,MC,V. **642-RIBS.**
Popular handsome room, long bar; ribs, burgers, snacks ($4-$16). Drinks: Mod.

Brady St Bridge Cafe
2228 E Carson St, South Side. Fri-Sat til 11:30. AE,MC,V. **488-1818.**
Atmosphere in restored Victorian setting. Full menu Fri-Sat—chicken, shrimp, blackened meats plus sandwiches, salads ($4-18). Drinks: Mod.

Brandy's
2323 Penn, Strip. Mon-Thur til 2. Fri-Sat til 2:30. AE,DC,MC,V. **566-1000.**
Romantic hanging gardens, skylight roof. Entrees ($10-$14) burgers, dessert, breakfast ($3.50-$6). Drinks: Mod.

Late Supper

Bravo! Franco
613 Penn, Downtown. Mon-Sat til 11. Reser sugg. AE,DC,MC,V. **642-6677.**
Ideal before/after theatre dining in spiffy decor. Late dinner—osso buco, fish, seafood, great appetizers, desserts $5-$18. Drinks: Exp.

Bravo! Trattoria
134 6th Ave, Downtown. Tues-Sun til 11. AE,DC,MC,V. **642-7600.**
More casual bistro setting for same fine cuisine as Franco's; dinners, appetizers/desserts $5-$16. Drinks: Mod.

Cafe Allegro
51 S 12th St, South Side. Fri-Sat til 12. MC,V. **481-7788.**
Inventive Ital/French "riviera" cuisine in charming atmosphere, one of city's best. Dinners, appetizers, small pastas ($6-$19). Drinks: Mod.

Cafe 401
401 Shady Ave, Shadyside. Mon-Sat til 12. AE,MC,V. **361-1900.**
Stylish, casual Italian fare, big continental patio with umbrellaed tables in summer. New gathering place. Dinners, snacks ($3-$18). Drinks: Mod.

Caffe Giovanni
Hartwell Bldg, Walnut/Aiken, Shadyside. Wed-Sat til 11. AE,DC,MC,V. **621-8881.**
First class Italian dining complements beautifully designed space. Entrees, appetizers/desserts. ($7-$20.)

Cafe Sam
5242 Baum Blvd, Oakland. Wed-Thur til 11, Fri-Sat til 12. Reser sugg. AE,MC,V. **621-2000.**
Ideal late dining from inventive gourmet kitchen. Amer-Cont dinners, snacks $5.25-$15). Roof patio. Drinks: Mod.

Cheese Cellar
Shops at Station Sq. Mon-Sat til 1, Sun til 11. AE,DC,MC,V. **471-3355.**
Intimate booths, crowded lively bar. Entrees and delicious fondues, cheese/sausage boards, salads, luscious desserts ($3-$11). Drinks: Mod.

City Grill
2019 E Carson, South Side. Mon-Sat til 11. AE,DC,MC,V. **481-6868.**
Crowds come for great hardwood grills, snacks in urbane setting ($4.50-$12). After-theatre favorite. Drinks: Mod.

Clark Bar & Grill
503 Martindale St. Mon-Sat til 2. AE,D,MC,V. **231-5720.**
Lively bar in old Clark Candy Bldg near Stadium; grills, chicken, ribs, pasta $5-$16. Drinks: Mod.

Dingbat's City Tavern
Oxford Centre, Downtown. Mon-Thur til 11:30, Fri-Sat til 1. AE,DC,MC,V. **392-0350.**
Burnished room with convivial bar, good day/night menu; char-broiled seafood, steak, pizza, sandwiches, dessert ($4.75-$13). Drinks: Mod.

Elbow Room
5744 Ellsworth Avenue, Shadyside. Mon-Thur til 12, Fri-Sat til 1am, Sun til 11. AE,MC,V. **441-5222.**
Popular Shadyside bar/eatery with good dinners, burgers, sandwiches, patio. ($1.50-$6). Drinks: Inexp-Mod.

Emilia Romagna
942 Penn Ave, Downtown. Fri-Sat til 11. AE,DC,MC,V. **765-3598.**
Wonderful N Ital cuisine in upper room, great veal, Tuscan bread, frittatas appetizers ($6-$15). Drinks: Mod.

Frenchy's
136 Sixth St, Downtown. Mon-Fri til 11, Sat til 12. AE,MC,V. **261-6476.**
Full dinners plus sandwiches, salads, cold buffet ($3.50-$20). Casual, fast pre-theatre meals. Drinks: Mod.

Gandy Dancer
Station Square. Mon-Thur til 1am, Fri-Sat til 2. AE,D,DC,MC,V. **261-1717.**
Wonderful atmosphere, fun, great buys on seafood ($2-$14).

4

Late Supper

Great Scot *413 S Craig, Oakland. Mon-Thur til 11, Fri-Sat til 12. AE,MC,V.* **683-1450.**
Great late night menu, friendly bar/restaurant. Inventive entrees, burgers, snacks ($2.50-$15). Drinks: Mod-Exp.

Gullifty's
1922 Murray, Squirrel Hill. Sun-Thur til 12, Fri-Sat til 1. AE,D,DC,MC,V. **521-8222.**
Big menu in informal, deli-like atmosphere. Entrees, sandwiches, pizza, famed desserts ($2-$12). Drinks: Inexp.

Harris Grill
5747 Ellsworth Avenue, Shadyside. 7 days til 2. AE,MC,V. **363-0833.**
Popular 'taverna' with good Greek specialties—gyros, moussaka, salad— and good conversation, outdoors in summer ($2-$8). Imported beer. Drinks: Inexp-Mod.

Houlihan's
Station Square. Mon-Thur til 11, Fri-Sat til 12:45. AE,DC,MC,V. **232-0302.**
Lively menu, colorful pub paraphernalia. Entrees, intriguing snacks, DJ Dancing nightly. Drinks: Mod-Exp.

Jacqie's/Jacqueline's *Webster Hall, 4415 5th Ave, Oakland. Fri-Sat til 11. AE,DC,MC,V.* **683-4344.**
Jacqie's Stylish room, piano nightly; Ital entrees, appetizers ($3-$26). Drinks: Mod. **Jacqueline's** Formal French cuisine, decor ($23-$27) Drinks: Exp.

Jake's Above the Square
430 Market, Downtown. Mon-Thur til 11, Fri-Sat til 12. AE,DC,MC,V. **338-0900.**
Elegant 2nd floor room with great view of Square, upscale N Ital/Amer entrees, appetizers ($8-$33). Drinks: Mod-Exp.

Khalil's
4757 Baum Blvd, Oakland Tues-Sat til 11:30. AE,DC,MC,V. **683-4757.**
Late dinners/appetizers every night on two floors in this Mid-East eatery. Grape leaves to shish kabob ($3-$10.90). Drinks: Mod.

Maggie Mae's Sportin' House
110 Federal Street, North Side. Mon-Sat til 11. AE,MC,V. **231-8181.**
Colorful atmosphere, lively bar; entrees, appetizers sandwiches, desserts ($1.35-$12). Drinks: Mod.

Margaritaville
2200 E Carson, S Side. Mon-Thur til 11, Fri-Sat til 12. AE,DC,MC,V. **431-2200.**
Mex-Amer cuisine, platters/munchies ($2.50-$10), 12 kinds of margaritas. Drinks: Mod.

Mario's South Side Saloon
1514 E Carson Street, South Side. Mon-Sat til 2. AE,DC,MC,V. **381-5610.**
Lively Italian eatery with excellent, pasta, meats, seafood ($3-$12). Crowded fun. Drinks: Inexp.

Max & Erma's
Downtown, Horne's Dept Store, Stanwix St, **471-1140.** *Shadyside: 5533 Walnut,* **681-5775.** *Mon-Thur til 11, Fri-Sat til 12. AE,D,DC,MC,V.*
Up atmosphere for dinners—pasta, fish—sandwiches, appetizers, desserts, $2.50-$13. Drinks: Mod.

Max's Allegheny Tavern
Middle/Suismon St, N Side. Mon-Thur til 11, Fri-Sat til 1. AE,DC,MC,V. **231-1899.**
Real old time atmosphere, German wursts, beer, sandwiches, salads ($2-$12). DJ Wed-Sat in Rathskeller. Drinks: Mod.

The 1902 Landmark Tavern
24 Market St, Downtown. Mon-Sat til 12. AE,DC,MC,V. **471-1902.**
Restored old tavern with big bar, tile walls, ceiling fan. Dinners, sandwiches, raw bar ($3-19). Drinks: Mod.

Pasta Piatto
736 Bellefonte, Shadyside. Wed, Fri, Sat til 11. MC,V. **621-5547.**
Pgh's favorite Italian, wonderful homemade pastas, desserts, appetizers ($5-$20).

Late Supper

Per Favore
Royal York, 3955 Bigelow Blvd, Oakland. Fri & Sat til 11. Reser sugg. AE,DC,MC,V. **681-9147.**
Popular Italian in gracious decor, pasta, meats, gourmet pizzas, snacks ($5-$22). Drinks: Mod.

Pietro's
Hyatt Regency Pittsburgh. 7 nights til 11. AE,DC,MC,V. **471-1234.**
Fine Ital dinners, appetizers, sandwiches in glass-walled room, patio overlooking city ($5-$22). Drinks: Mod-Exp.

River Cafe
Station Square. Fri-Sat til 11:30. AE,DC,MC. **765-2795.**
Outstanding Amer/Cajun food amid colorful stained glass. Dinners, appetizers, desserts. ($5.75-$13). Drinks: Mod.

Ruth's Chris Steak House
6 PPG Place, Downtown. Mon-Sat til 11. Reser sugg. AE,DC,MC,V. **391-4800.**
Polished setting for premiere steaks, seafood in one of famous chain ($17-$35). Drinks: Exp.

Samreny's
4808 Baum Blvd, Oakland. Tues-Sat til 12. No credit cards. **682-1212.**
Lebanese favorites in homey atmosphere, cozy bar. Dinners, appetizers ($2-$14). Drinks: Mod.

Stephen's La Piccola Casa
5100 Baum Blvd, Oakland. Mon-Thur til 11, Fri-Sat til 12. AE,DC,MC,V. **682-9446.**
Little jewel of a NY restaurant with wonderful cuisine from Chef David Ayn. Better make reservations ($12-$18).

Suzie's
Downtown: 130 6th, **261-6443.** *Squirrel Hill: 1704 Shady,* **422-8066.** *Fri-Sat til 11. MC,V.* Authentic Greek food in simple room. Great dinners, wonderful appetizers ($4-$13). Drinks: Mod.

Strip—Down by the Riverside
Boardwalk on the Allegheny at 16th/Smallman. Enter thru parking lot at 15th St. AE,DC,MC,V. **471-2226.**
Two nautical restaurants with seafood/raw bar—**Crewsers** and **Buster's Crab**—on 420-ft floating boardwalk; plus food/fun on riverside **Patio Deck.** Mod.

Sweet Basil's
5882 Forbes Avenue, Squirrel Hill. Tues-Sat til 11. MC,V. **421-9958.**
Popular, informal, with charming, clean-cut look, back-to-basic dinners, snacks. ($3-$13). Drinks: Inexp-Mod.

Tambellini's
860 Saw Mill Run, Rt 51. Mon-Fri til 11, Sat til 12. AE,DC,MC,V. **471-1118.**
Famous Pittsburgh name for great seafood, pasta. Dinners, a la carte ($8-$17.50). Drinks: Mod.

Tequila Junction
Station Square. Mon-Thur til 11, Fri-Sat til 12. AE,DC,MC,V. **261-3265.**
Romantic setting, full Mex-Amer menu til closing ($3-$10). Tiled bar with tequila shooters, big margaritas. Drinks: Mod.

Tessaro's
4601 Liberty, Bloomfield. Mon-Sat til 12, bar til 2. AE,DC,MC,V. **682-6809.**
Cozy neighborhood bar, great dinners, sandwiches from hardwood grill ($5-$14). Worth the wait! Drinks: Inexp-Mod.

Tramp's
212 Blvd Allies, Downtown. Fri-Sat til 11:30. Bar til 2. AE,DC,MC,V. **261-1990.**
Oldtime bar-bordello, brick walls, candlelit tables. Dinners, a la carte ($5-$14). Drinks: Mod.

Waterfall Terrace
Sheraton, Station Sq. Sun-Thur til 12, Fri-Sat til 2. AE,DC,MC,V. **261-2000.**
Dinner, appetizers ($4-$23) in pretty cafe along riverfront. Drinks in adjoining **Atrium Lounge** Mod.

4

PITTSBURGH AFTER DARK

Piano Bars/Jazz Rooms

PIANO BARS

Chats
Marriott, Greentree. Fri-Sat til midnite. AE,DC,MC,V. **922-8400.**
Quiet, sophisticated lounge, unique zig-zag bar, relaxing top 40s piano. Food next door til 12. Drinks: Mod.

Froggy's
100 Market Street at First Avenue, Downtown. Mon-Sat til 2. AE,DC,MC,V. **471-3764.**
Lively bar with jazz piano Fri-Sat til closing, full menu til 11. Great grills, sandwiches ($4-$18), 'biggest drinks in town' 3-1/2 oz—$3.50. Drinks: Mod.

Gallagher's Pub
2 Market Place, Downtown. Mon-Sat til 1:30. AE,DC,MC,V. **261-5554.**
Sing-a-long fans love this warm Irish saloon with Joe Salamon's piano from 9 on. Lively sentimental crowd. Irish beer. No food eves. Drinks: Mod.

Gandy Dancer
Landmarks Bldg, Station Square. Mon-Thur til 11, Fri-Sat til 1. AE,DC,MC,V. **261-1717.**
Rollicking crowds & nightly fun in famous bar off Grand Concourse with Reid Jaynes on piano til 8:30, Larry Beile til 1. Full menu Mon-Thur til 11, Fri-Sat til 1; great prices on seafood, pasta $3-$10. Drinks: Mod.

Hilton Hotel Lobby
Gateway Center, Downtown. Mon-Sat 4:30-12am. AE,MC,DC,V. **391-4600.**
Plush relaxing most nights in **Scenes,** elegant lobby lounge, patio in good weather. Hors d'oeuvres (complimentary during Happy Hour). Drinks: Exp.

More
Bayard & Craig, Oakland. Wed-Fri til 12, Sat til 1. AE,DC,MC,V. **621-2700.**
Classy "neighborhood bar" with piano Wed-Sat from 7 til closing. Regulars occasionally break into song—some solo. First class dining, late nite menu Sat only til 11, $6-$22. Drinks: Mod.

Palm Court Lobby
Westin William Penn, Downtown. Mon-Sat til 1, Sun til 12am. AE,DC,MC,V. **281-7100.**
Piano in grand, chandeliered lobby early evening til 11 nightly. Dim Sum—Chinese hors d'oeuvres—$4.75 til closing. Elegant ambience. Drinks: Exp.

Shiloh Inn
123 Shiloh Street, Mt Washington. Mon-Sat til 2. AE,DC,MC,V. **431-4000.**
Convivial crowd at charming bar atop the Mount with piano music nightly 7:30-1:30. Dinner ($10-$18) Fri-Sat til 11:30 in antique drawing rooms. City's best pousse cafe—15 layers of liqueur poured in 4 minutes by colorful owner-barkeeper. Drinks: Mod.

JAZZ ROOMS

Cardillo's Club Cafe
56 S 12th Street, South Side. Tues-Thur 8:30-12:30 Fri-Sat 7:30-1. AE,MC,V. **381-3777.**
Some of city's best jazz in this sophisticated cafe with Bobby & Harry Cardillo father/son piano duo & guest artists on weekends. Great eatin' too. Weekend $2 cover waived with dinner $11-15; sandwiches/appetizers $4-$9. (See Review)

Crawford Grill
2141 Wylie Avenue, Hill District. Fri 5:30-9:30. No credit cards. **471-1565.**
Jazz Fridays only 5:30-9:30. No food. Drinks: Inexp.

Hemingway's
3911 Forbes Avenue, Oakland. 7 days 11-2. AE,DC,MC,V. **621-4100.**
Weekend jazz Fri-Sat til 1:30 at this popular campus hang-out. Tuesday Poetry Readings 8:30-10:30 in the back room. Full menu weekends til 12, $4-$12.50. Drinks: Inexp-Mod.

Holiday Inn, University
100 Lytton Ave (across from Syria Mosque). Fri-Sat 9:30-1:30. AE,DC,MC,V. **682-6200.**
Comfortable, couched lounge off dining-room with top local jazz bands Fri-Sat and Pgh Jazz Society bands & artists Sun 7-11. Sandwiches & appetizers $5-$8. You can join the Jazz Society at the door & get 10% off drinks, 20% off food. Drinks: Mod-Exp.

J J 's
21st & Carson Sts, South Side. Fri-Sun 1:30. AE,DC,MC,V. **481-2900.**
Dancing to blues bands Fri, jazz bands Sat-Sun with Spider Rondinelli, Kenny Blake. Snacks, dinners ($3-$12). Drinks: Mod.

James St Pub
422 Foreland & James, North Side. Mon-Thur til 1, Fri-Sat til 2. AE,DC,MC.V. **323-2222.**
Casual, restaurant/bar with live jazz talent Fri-Sat 9-1. Dinners, good late night menu til 12 weekends ($10-$13); Good time crowd. Drinks: Mod.

Shadyside Balcony
5520 Walnut Street, Shadyside. Mon-Sat til 2. AE,DC,V. **687-0110.**
Where it's at on local jazz scene—six nights a week in this lively cafe/restaurant with the best jazz/fusion bands in town. Listen while dining or join the crowd at very busy bar. Late bites in lounge/restaurant with cuisine as creative as music—quiche, càshew chicken, chili, pizza $5 up. Drinks: Mod.

Zebra Room
(Eileen's) 708 N Dallas Ave near Frankstown, Homewood. Thur & Sat til 2. No food. (Take green carpeted ramp to right of Eileen's Bar.) **361-9503.**
On again, off again weekend jazz in a long, elegant smoke-glass room. Worth checking out. Drinks: Inexp.

Jazz in the Afternoon
Saturday afternoon jam sessions are becoming popular around the city. You can catch them at **Frankie's,** 1822 S Braddock in Swissvale, the **Blue Note Cafe,** 19th/Carson in South Side, a long-time Saturday happening, and at the **Too Sweet Lounge** at Frankstown & N Lang in Homewood. Local musicians have standing invitations to sit in. Sessions usually run from 4-8.

4

TOP 40s/OLDIES

Cousin's
7 Parkway Ctr, Greentree. Tues-Thur til 1, Fri-Sat til 2. AE,DC,MC,V. **928-0700.**
Casual lounge draws crowd for listening/dancing; DJ Fri, live bands Sat. Snacks Fri-Sat til 11 $2-$6. Drinks: Mod.

Cahoots
Marriott Hotel, Greentree. 7 nites til 2. AE,DC,MC,V. **922-8400.**
Plush lounge with stylish 25-40 crowd. Live bands, two shows Fri-Sat. $5 cover. Karaoke sing-a-long Thur 9-12. $5 cover. Dinner/snacks til 12am at hotel restaurants. Drinks: Mod-Exp.

Houlihan's
Freight House, Station Sq & Monroeville Mall. Mon-Thur til 11, Fri-Sat til 12:30, Bar til 2. AE,DC,MC,V. **232-0302.**
DJ nightly in small, cozy lounge off the bar. Dinner/snacks $5-$13. Drinks: Mod.

Motions
Pittsburgh Vista Hotel, Liberty Center. 7 days til 2am. AE,DC,MC,V. **281-8164.**
Intimate, sophisticated lounge with top 40s listening/dancing, DJ Fri-Sat, occasional live entertainment. Late menu til 12 $4-$8. Drinks: Mod-Exp.

Mr C's
Sheraton, Station Square. Fri-Sat til 2. AE,DC,MC,V. **261-2000.**
Listening/dancing to live top 40s bands in modern, sophisticated lounge. Food at Waterfall Terrace til 12. Drinks: Mod.

Rock/R&B

ROCK/R & B

Anthony's Southside
1306 E Carson Street, South Side. Wed-Sat til 2. No credit cards. **431-8960.**
A jumpin' club with get-down jam sessions Wed 9-1. Reggae Thur, jazz bands Fri-Sat, $3 cover. Burgers, sandwiches, $2.50-$3.50. Drinks: Mod.

The Backroom
1117 E Carson Street, South Side. Tues-Sun 6-2am. No credit cards. **431-7484.**
Variety of live music for all tastes. Blues/rock jam sessions Tues, Country Jam Thur, open to all musicians. Imported beer, drink specials, snacks. Cover $1-$3. Drinks: Inexp.

Cafe Renaissance
217 Shiloh Street, Mt Washington. Mon-Sat til 2. No credit cards. **431-7848.**
Live rock Tues, Joey G & the House-rockers! Sat nite all ages; great food. Two blocks from scenic overlook & Mon Incline. Cover $2. Drinks: Mod.

The Decade
223 Atwood Street, Oakland. Sun-Sat til 2. No credit cards. **682-1211.**
Legend in its own time—popular singles spot with hottest rock action in town, live bands nightly. Cover $1-$4, natl bands $5-$6. Drinks: Inexp.

Electric Banana
3887 Bigelow Blvd, Oakland. Tues-Sat 8-2. **682-8296.**
On the cutting edge of rock—alternative, new age, new wave, thrash metal, psychedelic, plus original Pgh music and occasional stellar attraction. Tues-Sat 8-2, cover $3 up; All Ages show Sun 8-11, cover $7 & up. Pizza, burgers, Drinks: Inexp-Mod.

Pittsburgh Music Shows
Three local music shows to watch for are the *In Pittsburgh* Music Awards—spotlighting local musicians from rock to classical, the annual **IC Light Rock Challenge** an annual rock event at Graffiti, and **WDVE's Charity Jam,** highlighting local & national stars.

Excuses Bar/Grill
2526 E Carson St, South Side. Thur-Sat til 2. No credit cards. **431-9847.**
All ages on hand for live blues/R&B/rock Thur-Sat til 2. Great wings! Cover $2-$3. Drinks: Inexp.

Frankie's
1822 S Braddock Avenue, Swissvale. 7 days til 2 am. AE,V. **351-8000.**
R&B/reggae/rock weekends, Wed Sing-a-Long. Sat afternoon jazz 4-8. Bar food, gourmet sandwiches; good age mix. Drinks: Inexp.

The Loop
8 Brilliant Avenue, Aspinwall. 7 days til 2. No credit cards. **771-1166.**
Lively center for 20-30's crowd. DJ Thur-Fri, live blues/rock Sat. Wings/draft special Mon. Weekend cover $2, guest artists, $5. Drinks: Inexp.

Moondogs
378 Freeport Rd, Blawnox. Mon-Sat 9:30-2. No credit cards. **828-2040.**
Live blues, reggae, comedy Wed-Sat. All ages, snacks. Cover $1-$4. Drinks: Inexp.

Zelda's Greenhouse
117 Bouquet Street, Oakland. Mon-Sat til 2. No credit cards. **681-3971.**
Popular young singles spot goes on forever! High voltage music, sing-a-longs amid hanging greenery. Cover Tues, Thurs & Fri. Drink discounts Tues-Fri. Snacks. Drinks: Inexp.

Country Western/Comedy

COUNTRY/WESTERN

Crystal Lounge
1216 Woods Run Avenue, North Side. Sat til 2am. No credit cards. **766-9255.**
Urban cowboy band Sat til 2am on 'largest dance floor in Pgh.' Sometimes rock. Bring your dancin' shoes! Drinks: Inexp.

Foggy Bottom
4021 Homestead Duquesne Road, W Mifflin. No credit cards. **462-4777.**
Live country weekends. $1-$2. Drinks: Inexp.

Holiday Inn, McKnight Road
N Hills. AE,DC,MC,V. **366-5200.**
Live local country Sun night. No cover. Drinks: Mod-Exp.

Horseshoe Bar/Lounge
2500 E Carson Street, South Side. Sat til 2. No credit cards. **431-8332.**
Live country music every Sat with Bobby Bee til 2am. No cover. Drinks: Inexp.

Howard Johnson
2750 Mosside Blvd, Monroeville. AE,DC,MC,V. **372-1022.**
Mostly country Thur-Sat. Cover varies with band. Mod-Exp.

Irongate Lounge
Howard Johnson Pgh Airport. AE,DC, MC,V. **923-2244.**
Dancing to live country bands Fri & Sat 9:30-1. Snacks 24 hrs.

Country Line
To find out who's playing where call WDSY Weekend Country Line **333-9563.**

Comedy Anyone?

Funny Bone, Station Square
7 days. AE,MC,V. 281-3130.
National/local talent at area's #1 comedy club. *Mon/Tues Open Stage 8:30, $3 cover; Wed/Thur/Sun 8:30, $5; Fri 8:30 & 10:30, $8; Sat 7:15, 9:30, 11:30, $8.* 2 beverage min every nite. No food. Drinks: Mod-Exp.

Funny Bone East, Radisson Monroeville
Thur-Sat. AE,DC,MC,V. Reser. **856-7888.**
Thur 8:30, $5 cover; Fri-Sat 8:30 & 10:30, $8. 2 beverage min. Munchies, pizza $2-$8. Drinks: Mod-Exp.

Juicy's Lounge
4968 Library Road, Bethel. Tues-Sat 9-2. No credit cards. **835-9915.**
Country every night. Live bands Wed, Fri & Sat, Cover $1. No cover Tues & Thur. Snacks. Drinks: Inexp.

Nashville North
7824 Saltzburg Road, Plum Township. MC,V. Fri-Sat 10-1:30. **795-8000.**
Dancing/listening to big name live bands. Sandwiches, dinners $3-$6. Cover $2. Drinks: Inexp-Mod.

Nightscape
Holiday Inn, RIDC Park, Blawnox off Rt 28. 7 days til 12-1. AE,DC,MC,V. **963-0600.**
Country music/dancing Sun from 8-12 in casual surroundings; live jazz Sat. Sandwiches, snacks til 11. No cover. Drinks: Inexp-Mod.

4

Mostly Dancing

MOSTLY DANCING

Bootleggers on the Water
10 Washington Avenue, Oakmont. Tues-Sat til 2. AE,D,MC,V. **826-8666.**
Join spirited young crowd for DJ dancing in booming room along the river—oldies to rock, live country; nightly entertainment inc karaoke sing-a-longs. Cover varies. Drinks: Mod.

Brother Olive's Lounge
Mon-Sat til 2. No credit cards. **281-7670.**
Dancing to live rhythm/blues Thur-Sat til 2. Cover $3. Ladies Wed night. Drinks: Mod.

Chauncy's
Commerce Court, Station Square, 7 nights 8-2. AE,MC,V. **232-0601.**
An over-25 Yuppie haunt with a classy, spacious ballroom atmosphere, crowded every night. Tues—Oldies; Mon/Wed/Thur/Sun Top 40s; Fri-Sat 70s/80s. Dinner 6-10, appetizers til 2. ($5-$12). Drinks: Mod-Exp.

Confetti
1165 McKinney Lane, Parkway Center Mall. Tues-Sat til 2am. AE,MC,V. **921-3388.**
Beautiful celebration atmosphere for dancing to Top 40s Tues-Sat; All ages from 20-40. Free buffet Tues-Fri til 8. Cover Tues-Thur $1; Fri after 7pm and Sat $5. Drinks: Mod.

Illusions
Fulton Bldg. 107 6th Street, Downtown. Wed-Fri 9-2. Sat 8-12. AE,DC,MC,V. **281-0349.**
Frenetic, far-out disco in ultra mod setting. Two big bars and video screens in marbled rotunda. Cover varies. Drinks: Mod.

Greenery
Holiday Inn, Greentree. 7 nights 9-2. AE,DC,MC,V. **922-8100.**
Non-stop DJ dancing in big, bouncy disco with romantic greenery, glass walls. An energetic young crowd. No food after 10. No cover. Drinks: Mod.

Dancing in the Dark

Fox Chapel Yacht Club
1366 Old Freeport Rd, Fox Chapel. AE,MC,V. **963-8881.**
Dancing to live music under the stars Fri-Sat on a romantic outdoor deck bar along the Allegheny. No cover. Drinks: Mod.

Kason's
Bank Tower, 411 Fourth Ave, Downtown. Mon-Wed til 11, Thur & Fri til 1. AE,DC,DS,V. **391-1122.**
Popular after-work spot with dancing every night, packed for live DJ Fri. Munchies, appetizers & dinners ($3-$11). Pirate/Penguin game specials on eats. Drinks: Mod.

Metropol
1600 Smallman, Strip District. Wed-Sat 8-2. AE,MC,V. **261-2221.**
Pittsburgh's hottest, an exciting high-tech club with nightly DJ, live bands Wed, top recording artists weekdays and room for 1000 revelers. Creative industrial decor with exposed pylons, gusts of steam, catwalks linking multi-levels, Strobes create high intensity atmosphere for dancing or watching from balconies. You'll see everything from jeans to stretch limousines. Cover Weekdays $2, Fri-Sat $5, Sun $3. Free buffet at Fri Happy Hour & sometimes thru week. **Coffee House** next door for more serious revelers. Drinks: Mod.

Roadster Cafe
130 N Negley at Penn Ave, East Liberty. 7 days til 2am. AE,V. **391-9606.**
DJ dancing Wed-Thur, live reggae Tues, live rock & roll Fri-Sat. 10¢ wings, 99¢ gyros; all you can eat fish Fri $4.95. Cover. Drinks: Inexp.

Dining/Dancing/Dinner Theater

Upstage
3609 Forbes Avenue, Oakland.
Mon, Wed-Sun til 2. No credit cards.
681-9777.
Young crowd for live bands from art-pop to rockabilly, progressive dance music Wed, Fri-Sun. DJ dancing Mon & Thur, all ages dance party Sun from 7. No food. Cover varies. Drinks. Inexp.

Valentine's
Howard Johnson's, Mosside Blvd, Monroeville. 7 nights 9-2. **372-1022.**
Top 40s DJ Disco Wed, Fri, Sat; country band Sun in fashionable young room. Sandwiches/platters $5. Drinks: Mod.

DINING/DANCING

Costanza's
240 Fourth Avenue, Downtown. Mon-Sat til 2. AE,DC,MC,V. Reser. **232-0706.**
Dining/dancing Fri-Sat to live top 40s bands in night club atmosphere. Dinner til 11 ($7-$10) good Italian, burgers—til 2. Drinks: Inexp-Mod.

Harley Hotel
Off Rodi Road, Penn Hills. 7 nights til 2am. AE,DC,MC,V. **244-1600.**
Elegant evening—dining in romantic Three Rivers room with live band dancing in the lounge Fri-Sat 9:30-1:30. Dinner $5-$16. Drinks: Mod.

Hyeholde Cabaret
190 Hyeholde Drive, Coraopolis. 5 min from Airport. Fri-Sat 7-2am. AE,DC,MC,V. **264-3116.**
Enjoy Hyeholde's award-winning cuisine and stay on for a romantic evening at the Cabaret. Live bands, soft jazz, name entertainment. Cover for national artists. Dinner $12.50-$19.75 or appetizers/desserts in the Cabaret $5-$8. Good place to fall in love again. Drinks: Exp.

Joe's Jazz Lounge
D'Imperio's, 3412 Wm Penn Highway, Wilkins Twp. Tues-Sat til 2. Reser sugg. AE,MC,V. **823-4800.**
Follow a delectable dinner at D'Imperio's, one of city's finest, with mellow music in the warm, romantic lounge. Dancing to live combo Fri-Sat. You can dine in restaurant or the more intimate lounge $15-$26, great appetizers $4-7. Drinks: Mod-Exp.

The Living Room
1778 N Highland Road, Upper St Clair. Mon-Sat til 2. AE,DC,MC,V. **835-9772.**
Informal supper club with mellow music, dancing to live bands Wed, Fri-Sat 9-11. Class act. Dinner, Italian specialties $11-$19. Drinks: Mod.

Top of the Triangle
USX Tower, 600 Grant Street. Tues-Thur til 12, Fri-Sat til 1. AE,DC,MC,V. **471-4100.**
Dancing & requests to pianist/vocalist in glamorous 62nd floor lounge with breathtaking view of the city. Late supper Sat til 12. Drinks: Mod-Exp.

DINNER THEATRE

Holiday Inn
4859 McKnight Road, Ross Township. Thur-Sat. AE,DC,MC,V. **366-5200.**
Musical revues Apr-Jun and Sept-Nov. Thurs/Sat Night Package—dinner at 6, show at 8, $24.95. Show only $13. Drinks: Mod.

Marriott Hotel
Greentree. Thur-Sat April 15-Oct. AE,DC,MC,V. **922- 8400.**
Musical comedy revue "Forbidden Pittsburgh", topical material by Pgh's perennial favorites Brockett & Barbara in the circus tent on putting green. Buffet Dinner/Show package at 7pm, $37.

4

VARIETY/SHOWCASE/MISC

Allegheny Brewery & Pub
Troy Hill Road, North Side (across 16th St Bridge.) Tues-Sat til midnite.
AE,MC,V. **237-9402.**
German beer garden authentic down to the high windows, wooden tables, glass wall view of beer-making. Food, fun, live music Wed-Sat 7-11:30. German bands i.e. The Mad Bavarian, zany Five Guys Named Moe & R & B in Louis Jordan tradition. Hearty food $4-$10. Inexp-Mod.

Artery
5847 Ellsworth, Shadyside. Tues-Sat til 1, Sun til 12. AE,MC,V. **362-9111.**
Dinner plus eclectic entertainment in restaurant/club/gallery with very hip modern music, art, dancing, performance. Reggae every Thur. Dinner Tues-Sat 5-11, Sun 5-10 ($5-$10). Drinks: Mod.

Beehive Coffee House
14th & Carson. Mon-Thur 7 am-3am, Fri-Sat 24 hours. No credit cards. **488-4483**
Crazy, one-of-a-kind coffee house with psychodelic tables, chairs, walls by local artists. Fabulous gourmet coffee/teas, cheesecakes/desserts under $3. Parchesi, chess, conversation, poetry, acoustic entertainment. "No alcohol" a welcome change.

Bloomers
27th & Jane, S Side. Wed-Thur 5-12, Fri-Sat til 2. MC,V. **381-1700.**
Unique restaurant with women entertainers—rock, folk, art, performance. Cover varies. Food til 10. Drinks: Mod.

Second Beehive For Oakland

The King's Court Theatre on Forbes will be the home of a second Beehive Coffee House. Same imported coffee, desserts, conversation plus a study "hall" and movies from 7pm to 12. Owners hope to keep it open around the clock.

Fun on the Boardwalk
Strip—Down By Riverside
Off Smallman at 16th St Bridge, enter from parking lot under bridge at 15th St. Major credit cards. **471-2226.**
Exciting nightlife on Pittsburgh's rivers begins with this 420-ft floating boardwalk, phase one of a multi-million, 12-acre recreational complex on the Allegheny. It includes:
Patio Deck/Bar: Riverside fun on big deck the length of the Boardwalk with tables, lounge chairs for relaxing around splash pool; drinks, music i.e. steel bands, great river view, boat docking.
Donzi's: Big glitzy, ultra modern, Euro-style disco. DJ's/Live bands. Cover/Drinks Mod-Exp.
Food on **Patio Deck** and inside at **Crewsers** and **Buster's Crab.** Seafood, snacks, light dinners. Mod. Drinks: Mod.

Blarney Stone
30 Grant Avenue, Etna, Rts 8/28. AE,DC,MC,V. **781-1666.**
City's unofficial Irish center with imports and souvenirs. Irish folk & balladeers, sing-a-longs, popular guest artists. Live entertainment Fri-Sat from 9:30. Cover for guest artists $2-$3, periodic concerts $15-$22. Dinner from 5-9 ($9-$15). Drinks: Mod.

Graffiti
4615 Baum Boulevard, Oakland. Wed-Sat 4-2. MC,V. **682-4210.**
Unique second floor loft showcasing headliners from hard rock to country with everything in between—comedy, Irish singers, reggae and Open Stage on Thur. Club "areas" include balconied dance hall, a smaller video-screened lounge, restaurant—and interesting spaces in between. Some of the hottest acts playing Pgh plus annual Pgh Rock Challenge with local bands. Dinner til 10, burgers, nachos til 12 ($7-$11). Cover varies. Drinks: Mod.

Variety/Showcase/Sports Bars

Grandview Saloon

1212 Grandview Ave, next to Duquesne Incline, Mt Washington, Sun-Thur til 12, Fir-Sat til 1, Bar til 2. AE,DC,DC,V. **431-1400.**
After-sundown fun with a wonderful view of city from wide outdoor decks in five cantilevered levels. Bar/music, great mingling for young upscale crowd. Burgers, salads, light dinners $5-$10. Drinks: Mod.

Liberty Belle

2204 E Carson, South Side. Weekends, other hours vary. No credit cards. **431-0850.**
Home of Frankie Capri, zany one-man band with a crowd-participation act. Patrons put on animal hats, dance around and let it all hang out. Also bands, dancing Sat night. $2 cover when Frankie performs. Drinks: Inexp-Mod.

Club Wet

Sandcastle on the Mon

W Homestead, Rt 837 bet Hi-Level and Glenwood Bridges. Pkw Exit 8 Sq Hill/Homestead, cross Hi-Level bridge, right onto Rt 837, follow blue signs. Wed-Sat 6pm-1am Jun-Labor Day. M,V. **462-6666**
When the sun goes down you can join the fun at this huge water-slide park. There's a picturesque jetty with trees and trails along the Mon, boat docking and nooks for private conversation. Hot tubs, dancing—to DJ's Wed, Fri-Sat—in River City area along the shore. Sing-a-longs and piano music up on the boardwalk. Burgers, grilled sandwiches, pizza, kolbassi $2.50-$5 to eat at riverside patio tables with drinks from Coconut Bob's Bar. Inexp. It's out of this world and it's Pittsburgh! Admission Wed-Thur after 4, $1, Fri-Sat $4.

Metropol Coffee House

2600 Smallman. Sun-Tues 7am-2am, Wed til 3 am, Thur til 4, Fri-Sat til 6 am. **261-2221.**
Large, inviting space adjacent to famous nightclub with state-of-art lighting and stage facilities for art/civic/cultural events. Free flow environment for gourmet coffees, teas, desserts, juices, bar drinks, low-key conversation ($1.50-$3.50). Cover for special events/entertainment. Drinks: Mod.

Penn Cafe

4104 Penn Avenue, Bloomfield. Mon-Sat til 2. AE,DC,MC,V. **621-9449.**
Upstairs/downstairs stages, sometimes two different bands. Blues, ethnic, folk, Irish, rock & roll—and clogging! Good mixed crowd—young professionals & neighborhood. Wings, steak, sandwiches, dinners Fri-Sat til 12 ($2-$5). Drinks: Inexp.

SPORTS BARS

Callahan's Pub & Parlor

505 Walnut, 2nd level. Mon-Sat 11-2. Sun 1-12. AE,MC,V. **687-9212.**
Second floor pool hall with lots of polish, wood & brass. Billiards $5 hour & up. Darts 50¢ & up. Munchies, pizza, burgers, peel 'n eat shrimp 75¢-$5.

Pittsburgh Sports Garden

1 Carson Street, Station Square. Mon-Fri 4pm-2am, Sat 12-2am, Sun 12-midnite. AE,MC,V. **281-1511.**
The sports bar craze is alive and well at this $2 million, 53,000 sq-ft play-ground for fans complete with 40 TVs and a giant scoreboard. Patrons can shoot basketballs, pitch baseballs, hurl darts, play golf, pool, video, pinball machines . . . and dance in a real boxing ring. Or they can bend their elbows at four bars and examine Pgh sports memorabilia. Young, fast-paced, gregarious crowd. Sandwiches, pizza $1.75-$5.50. Cover $1, weekends $4. Drinks: Mod-Exp.

4

Sports Bars/Open All Night

Hi-Tops
4515 William Penn Hwy, Monroeville. Mon-Fri 11-2, Sat & Sun 12-2. AE,MC,V. **856-0441.**
Satellite dishes, 22 televisions let sports fans watch any game they please. Arcade with videos, pool tables, air hockey, dart boards. DJ Wed-Sat, Oldies Tues. Burgers, ribs, steaks, munchies $4.25-$12. Drinks: Inexp.

Zagnut's
503 Martingdale (old Clark Candy Bldg), North Side. Open 3 hrs before Stadium events til 2 am. AE,DC,MC,V. **231-5720.**
Basketball, baseball, video games; DJ dancing weekends. Informal picnic tables, limited menu—calzones, meatball/sausage sandwiches, nachos up to $5. Drinks: Inexp-Mod.

Silky's
1731 Murray Ave, Sq Hill. Mon-Sat til 2. Sun til 12. MC,V. **421-9222.**
You can catch every sports game on TV at this fun, lively neighborhood bar; burgers, munchies, full dinners i.e. pasta, chicken ($3-$11). Get there before game time. Drinks: Inexp-Mod.

Karaoke
(ka-ro-ke)

So you want to be a singing sensation but just need that big break. Why not try Karaoke, the latest craze sweeping taverns across W Pa. Originating in Japan 12 years ago, Karaoke offers pub patrons a shot at the big time as they take microphone in hand and belt out their favorite tunes to recorded music accompaniment for over 800 songs. If you're game you can find Karaoke at **Yesterday's** in S Baldwin Plaza, at the **Greentree Marriott,** at **Bootleggers** in Oakmont, **Ryan's Pub** in Regent Square and **Dynasty** in McKeesport. Call ahead for days & times.

OPEN ALL NIGHT

Beehive Coffee Shop
14th/Carson, South Side. Fri-Sat 24 hours. Mon-Thur 7am-3am. **488-4483.**
Wacky coffee house with art walls, odd chairs, interesting denizens and non-stop coffee for 66 hours on weekends; tea, desserts, entertainment. ($1.50-$5.)

Del-Kid
5536 Steubenville Pike, Robinson Twp. Mon-Sat 24 hours. **787-9945.**
Specialists in breakfasts at all hours $3.50-$13 inc six-egg omelet for $4. Burgers, sandwiches, house special cheese/bacon burger $1.50-$4. Dinners inc good homemade meatloaf $4.25-$13.

Dick's Diner
Rt 22, Murrysville. Fri-Sat 24 hrs. No credit cards. **327-4566.**
A institution for late-nighters. Big array of food at great prices, famous hot roast beef sandwiches, homemade pies. $1-$7.

King's Family Restaurants
7 days 24 hours—Bridgeville, Cranberry Twp, Fox Chapel, Penn Hills, Steubenville Pike, Versailles. 24 hrs weekends only—Monroeville, Plum Borough.
Hearty food, one of best breakfasts in city all night long, $4-$6.

Norwin Diner
Rt 30 7 mi past McKeesport. 7 days 24 hours. MC,V. **863-2941.**
Another famous local diner/restaurant with great chicken, homemade pie $2-$7.

Primanti's
46 18th St between Penn & Smallman. Mon-Sat 24 hours, Sun from 11 pm. **263-2142.**
A legend for spectacular sandwiches in the wee hours for produce workers, college revelers while city sleeps. Hot sausage, kolbassi with fries & slaw on the sandwich $2.75-$3.50. Big breakfast $3.50. Drinks $2-$2.50. Bordertown barroom.

Open All Night

All Night Long

Fast Food: All Denny's restaurants, most Eat'n Parks, Wendy's (drive-in), 5422 Baum Blvd.
Convenience Stores: 7-Elevens, AM/PM and Gulf Stores. Supermarkets: Giant Eagles in East Liberty, Squirrel Hill, South Side, Parkway Center, Monroeville, North Hills, Greentree—Cochran Road, Village Square, Caste Village and Fox Chapel Waterworks.
Pharmacies: Giant Eagle—East Liberty: Shakespeare Street. **361-5248.** Thrift Drug—Miracle Mile, Monroeville **372-5288.**
Animal Emergencies: Allegheny Veterinary Emergency Clinic. **323-9770.** Weekdays 7:30pm-7:30am, Sat 1:30pm-7:30 am Mon. Holidays 24 hours.

Ritter's Diner
5221 Baum Blvd, Oakland. 7 days-24 hours. No credit cards. **682-4852.**
Pittsburgh's favorite at 3 o'clock in the morning. All day menu—spaghetti to NY strip—$3.25-$10. Breakfast bargains (bacon/ham/sausage, eggs, potatoes $2.50) plus hot dogs, sandwiches.

Scotty's Diner
7619 Penn Avenue, Wilkinsburg. 7 days-24 hours. Also Wm Penn Hwy, Monrv. No credit cards. **241-9506.**
Pgh's original "Diner," scene of many an after-date rap session. Coffee, burgers, day/nite breakfast, entrees—pasta to T-Bone steak $1.25 up.

South Shore Diner
17th & Carson. 7 days 24 hours. **431-9292.**
Typical diner fare—breakfast, burgers, daily special, $2-$5.

White Tower
7 days 24 hours. Craig & Centre, Oakland, Chestnut & 16th St, North Side.
Only two left now—the familiar black & white turrets a friendly beacon to city's night people, cops, cabbies. Breakfast, 95¢ burgers, 40¢ coffee, stool-to-stool conversation til dawn.

FOOD IN THE WEE HOURS

Brandy's
Penn & 24th St, Strip Dist. Mon-Sat til 2am, Fri, Sat til 2:30. **566-1000.**
Late night restaurant with romantic greenery, atmosphere. Late snacks—burgers, dessert concoctions, Hungry Man's Breakfasts $3.75-$7.

Mike's Lunch
200 Brownsville Rd, Mt Oliver. Mon-Sat 6am-3:30am. No credit cards.
Breakfast around the clock with strawberry/whipped cream pancakes, french toast; sandwiches, burgers, homemade soups $3-$5.

Original Hot Dog Shop
Forbes & Bouquet. Sun-Thur til 4:30am, Fri-Sat til 6. **621-7388.**
Native Pittsburghers have been known to travel back home for famous "foot long hot dog" now 7-1/2 inches but still the best in town—$1.98 with everything! Burgers, hoagies, pizza $3-$3.50; Ribs $6.88-$9; imported beers for take out.

OPEN EARLY AM

Lindos
947 Western Ave, North Side. Mon-Fri 5am-3pm, Sat 6am-3. **231-0110.**
Small, homey diner with big breakfasts for early workers and night owls $2-$3; homemade soup 95¢, famous gyros, platters up to $3.75.

50 THINGS TO DO

Pittsburgh is a warm, wonderful town with places to go, things to see - and unexpected beauty. And sometimes the best things in town are free! Here's an updated list of some of the city's best old and new attractions. Check the *I Love Pittsburgh!* Pull-Out section in this *Guide* and the *Pittsburgh Pleasures Events Calendar* to keep busy year 'round in America's best city!

Romantic/Unusual Things To Do

1. Spend a Saturday morning shopping at the produce market in the **Strip District.** Explore the fascinating area, lunch at one of the little outdoor cafes.

2. **Take a walking tour** of downtown Pittsburgh's architecture & new Renaissance buildings using the "I Love Pittsburgh! Sightseeing Guide."

3. Spend a wonderful day on the giant slides, Boardwalk at the fabulous water park **Sandcastle on the Mon**...linger for music, dancing, eats, great night views of the river.

4. **View moon, planets** thru big 31" refractor telescope at Allegheny Observatory's once-a-year Open House in September.

5. **Take an incline** to Mt Washington...watch the sun go down...have cocktails/dinner on the outdoor decks of new Grandview Saloon or indoors at Christopher's piano bar or Shiloh Inn.

6. Visit the exciting new **Strip—Down by the Riverside,** watch the boats come into the floating Boardwalk, have dinner/drinks on the Patio Deck.

7. Lunch/tea at **Carnegie's Museum Cafe,** tour beautiful Hall of Minerals and Gems, visit outdoor Sculpture Garden.

8. Visit the fabulous new **Carnegie Science Center** on the North Shore...tour the **USS Requin submarine** moored out front.

9. Join the Saturday night crowds in **South Side**...Pittsburgh's new village...jazz at **Cardillo's,** zany **Beehive Coffee Shop** for fabulous coffee, desserts.

10. Become a member of **The Carnegie**...attend openings...visit behind-the-scenes at Member's Night...attend Silent Auction.

11. Take your own tour of the **Mexican War Streets** or join the annual House Tour in Sept. Visit unique **Chatham Village** housing atop Mt Washington.

12. Take holiday (or daily) **tea at elegant Westin William Penn Hotel**...romantic cocktails in Palm Court lobby lounge.

13. Enjoy a concert under the stars at vast new **Star Lake Ampitheatre.** Order a box lunch ahead or picnic there.

14. **Meet a friend at Station Square**...browse...eat at one of the great restaurants, visit the outdoor museum and Railway Car Shops.

15. **Ride Pittsburgh's subway** back & forth to Station Square, stopping to enjoy the art at Wood Street & Gateway Stations.

16. Have weekend **Dim-Sum** (Chinese Brunch) or get together eight friends for a duck banquet at one of the city's fine Oriental eateries.

17. **Walk the beautiful Trillium Trail** in bloom late April/May on Squaw Run Road, Fox Chapel.

18. Take part in inspiring Christmas "**Messiah Sing-A-Long**" at Heinz Hall which heralds opening of the holiday season.

19. Spend a whole day at **Oxford Centre**...enjoy the architectural atmosphere...delightful browsing in sleek shops. Finish the day on the patio at Dingbat's.

20. **Browse at Craig Street Shops**—lunch outdoors at Kane's Courtyard or on the lovely terrace of Cafe Azure.

21. Make a lunchtime visit at **Trinity Cathedral's** 200-year-old burial ground on Sixth Avenue in the heart of town.

22. Enjoy the real thing—**formal British tea** at Cathy's Windsor Tea Room in Sewickley. Browse in unique shops.

23. Get a **riverside view of Pittsburgh** from the North Shore—outdoors in summer. Walk down to Allegheny Landing through the colorful forms of the outdoor Sculpture Court.

24. Watch the **fun-filled buggy races** in Schenley Park at CMU's Spring Carnival in April...or the Vintage Grand Prix auto races in July.

25. Check out the fun—reggae night...or any night at unique **Graffiti**...catch the mod dancing scene at **Metropol** or art/cultural scene at Metropol's new coffee house.

5

Romantic/Unusual Things To Do

26. Don't miss the **thrilling Grand Prix Formula I speedboat races** at Three Rivers Regatta. Linger thru dusk, visit the hundreds of boats docked at the Point . . . their colored lights flickering in the waters—a romantic night in Pittsburgh.

27. **Take a Gray Line Tour** and learn something about the city. Watch for Architects Assn Tour . . . Executive Suite Tour, Pgh History & Landmarks' intriguing neighborhood tours.

28. **Spend a day in Shadyside**—dine at Pasta Piatto, browse in avenue shops, lunch/tea or dinner at Le Petit Cafe, finish the night with fine jazz at the Balcony.

29. **Visit Pitt Nationality Rooms** . . . roam through the cavernous first floor Commons Room. Discover the beautiful stained glass windows in Heinz Chapel.

30. Visit the unique **underground Twilight Zoo** . . . take a child to the delightful Children's Zoo . . . ride the little railroad.

31. Take out a **gourmet picnic** (see Gourmet to Go) . . . eat it by your fireside . . . or at Roberto Clemente Park along the river.

32. **Watch Pittsburgh's Marathon** in Shadyside, Oakland or a neighborhood of your choice. Enjoy the outdoor cafes, cheering crowds & camaraderie.

33. Don't miss the **Pgh Children's Museum** —borrow a child—in the Old Post Office Building on the North Side.

34. Spend a day at **Kennywood Park.** Ride the new Steel Phantom, the world's fastest roller coaster—80 miles per hour!

35. Don't miss the flowers/food at the city's most delightful fete—the annual **May Market** at Pittsburgh Civic Garden Center.

36. Dance, sing, eat ethnic at the **Pittsburgh Folk Festival** in May . . . at Greek Church festivals . . . and neighborhood festivals all around town May-August.

37. Try **afternoon cocktails for two** on Froggy's hideaway roof patio with its unique view of downtown rooftops.

38. Enjoy bagpipes, sheep herding, beautiful scenery at **Highland Fling** in Ligonier . . . plan a weekend camping party at Lynn Run State Park.

39. Visit remarkable **Old Economy Village in Ambridge** . . . try to catch their annual Kuntsfest . . . or Ambridge Nationality Days.

40. Watch the unique sight of **Royal Regiment's Fife & Drum Corps** parading at historic Point Park on summer Sunday afternoons.

41. Picnic on beautiful grounds at **Hartwood** . . . tour the Tudor Mansion . . . stay for music, theatre-on-the-green.

42. Watch the **July 4th fireworks** . . . something special in Pittsburgh . . . a marvel from close range at the Point's Symphony concert . . . from on high in Mt Washington for a panoramic view . . . or from a Gateway Clipper cruise midst the reflections in the water.

43. Take one of the **riverwalks** along the shores (See Boaters/Outdoor Eateries). Take a boat out on the waters . . . the best way to understand Pittsburgh's history, geography.

44. Listen to the strains of Sousa at Amer Waterways Wind Orchestra's riverside **Marches Concert.**

45. Take in the pomp and a play at **Shakespeare Festival** in Foster Theatre on the Pitt campus.

46. Attend July's **Feis/Dance Competition** at Irish Center in Squirrel Hill.

47. **Go strawberry pickin'** in June at Simmons, Trax, Schramm Farms in nearby countryside.

48. Take your own **tour of North Side's streets** . . . up the steep hills for unique views of the city. Have a fun dinner at Max's Allegheny Tavern o the new Allegheny Brewery & Restaurant on Troy Hill Road.

49. Start off the holiday season amid the beautiful wares of **Pgh Center for Arts Annual Christmas Sale.**

50. Meet a friend for **Light-Up Night** . . see PPG luminaria, Oxford Centre USX holiday decorations at close range . . . discover beautiful Pittsburgh!

6

Here are "Pittsburgh Originals," dishes indigenous to the city, some famous throughout the world. Pittsburgh is also noted for its unique ethnic cuisine....here's where to find it....and enjoy it year round at local food fests. Phil Isaly, grandson of the stores' founder, poses with a famous Klondike at an old-time Isaly's on Perry Highway.

FAMOUS PITTSBURGH FOODS

Pittsburgh Originals

The Isaly's Story...

Chipped Ham

By far one of Pittsburgh's most famous foods, this spicy lunch meat made its debut in 1933 on the slicing machines of Isaly's, a locally-based family chain of dairy stores (1929-1972). Generally made from pressed chopped ham sliced wafer-thin, it can be found at almost any local deli counter. You're not a real Pittsburgher until you bite into soft mounds of chipped ham on white bread or bun...with plain mustard or mayonnaise. It's so missed by former natives that Pittsburgh clubs around the country often truck or fly it in to their celebrations. No longer family-owned, there are about nine Isaly's stores in the Pittsburgh area, all of them still selling chipped ham and Klondikes.

...Klondikes

This is another Isaly's specialty—a vanilla ice-cream bar dipped in pure chocolate and packaged in a familiar silver wrapper. Invented in 1929 by Sam Isaly, Klondikes were made with vanilla ice cream. (If you got one with a pink center you got a free Klondike.) Now sold nationally, they're available in vanilla or chocolate, plain or crispy, singly or by the dozen. Used to be a nickel...now 70¢.

and Skyscraper Cones

Isaly's unique 9-inch skyscraper ice cream cones are part of every old Pittsburgher's childhood. Phil Isaly, grandson of founder Henry Isaly, still has 12 of the original steel sky-scraper scoops. Remember White House (vanilla with big red maraschino cherries) and the old rainbow flavour—a medley of orange, lime, raspberry and lemon. You can still get rainbow at local Isaly's but you'll have to settle for regular scoops—one scoop 80¢, 2 scoops $1.30.

FOODS THAT STARTED HERE

Chiodo's Mystery Sandwich

This sandwich is made at one of the 'burgh's most famous bars, Joe Chiodo's in Homestead. It's a basic mixture of steak, pepperoni, kielbasa, sauerkraut, American/provolone cheese, tomato sauce (and whatever mystery ingredient happens to be on hand) all served on an Italian bun. Chiodo's Bar is also another Pittsburgh institution.

Corned Beef on the Heel

There's a claim this sandwich originated in Pittsburgh using the ends or heels of the bread generally discarded. You cut the heel off a loaf of Kosher rye, slice it horizontally like a bun, pile it with corned beef/meat combination. It was served this way at the old **S & B** (Blvd of Allies & Craft) famed for its corned beef sandwiches. You can still ask for it "on-the-heel" at **Richest Deli,** 6th Ave, Downtown (serving it since '36), and at **Rhoda's** and **Catz N Kids** in Squirrel Hill.

Clark Bar

One of the most popular candy bars in the U.S. was made on the North Side for over 100 years, and is still being made in O'Hara Township (since '86). The big Clark Bar sign on the roof of the old plant near the Stadium advertises the crunchy peanut, chocolate, taffy creation in its familiar orange-red wrapper. It was the product of David Lytle Clark who opened his first candy factory in 1880 on East Ohio Street and started the Clark Company in 1887. Some people remember sending in the wrappers for free Clark chewing gum.

Crabmeat Hoelzel

This is a popular Pittsburgh appetizer—Maryland crabmeat with oil, tarragon/cider vinegar and black pepper served in a terrapin dish to hold the dressing. Created at the Duquesne Club in the late 40s, it was named for club member John P (Jack) Hoelzel, president of the former Pittsburgh Screw & Bolt Company. It's still on the Club's menu and menus all over the country.

Pittsburgh Originals

Devonshire Sandwich

This open-face sandwich—originally chicken (now usually turkey) with a blanket of cheddar cheese sauce and crisp bacon—was invented here by Frank Blandi, owner of Le Mont restaurant and the old Park Schenley. He concocted it in 1936 at his first restaurant, the Stratford at the corner of Centre & Millvale in Oakland across from Devonshire Street...and that's how the sandwich got its name! There are many recipes for the Devonshire but here's the real thing from Blandi himself: For the sauce, start with a roux of flour and butter, add hot milk, a little sharp cheddar, a tbl of chicken base (or 2 to 3 bouillon cubes) and a splash of Worcestershire. Layer the breast of chicken, crisp bacon, then the sauce over toast. Top with paprika & grated Parmesan cheese, dot with a little butter and oven brown (about 15 minutes) for a crispy top. A popular Pittsburgh menu item, the Devonshire has spread to other cities. A staple at Blandi's much-missed Park Schenley, long one of the city's finest, it's on the menu at Per Favore, the restaurant's successor, where Blandi is serving as consultant.

Heinz Ketchup

A world-famous name in food, H J Heinz Company makes its Pittsburgh home on Progress St at the 16th St Bridge on the North Side. Founded in 1869 in Sharpsburg by H. J. (Henry) Heinz and famous for its 57 varieties, it now has more than 3000 products in 150 countries on every continent. Pittsburgh still uses more Heinz ketchup than any other U.S. city and while the bottling's done elsewhere, ketchup is still being made and packaged at the North Side plant for single-serve packets. Heinz babyfood and 80% of its private label soups are also made here. Famous for its pickles, gravy, relish and sauces, Heinz' newest success is its Weight Watchers label.

A Cosmopolitan City

Visitors to Pittsburgh are entranced with the variety of its ethnic foods. One of the city's strengths has always been the richness of its cultural traditions—it has one of the highest percentages of ethnic groups in the U.S. The old-country recipes of the families who came here to make iron and steel have been proudly passed on from generation to generation. And through the years new populations of Mid-Eastern and Asian peoples have added their own special cuisines. This has given the city's food infinite variety...a variety that Pittsburghers take for granted but that makes visitors and business travelers sit up and take notice.

Yesterday's ethnic town is today's cosmopolitan city...ready to make visitors welcome with a taste of their own cuisine—a bit of home away from home.

In turn Pittsburgh has invented a number of dishes on its own and exported them to other cities. Here are some of the foods that Pittsburgh made famous—and the ethnic dishes that made it strong.

Iron City Beer

A Pittsburgh trademark. "Pumpin' Iron" has been a favorite Pittsburgh pastime since 1861. The city's home brews, Iron City & IC Light, are on tap almost everywhere. Pittsburgh Brewing Company can claim the world's first snap-top can, the first canned draft, twist-off bottle tops, first beer cooler (Hop 'n Gator in 1970) and the first holiday beer, Olde Frothingslosh—"the pale, stale ale with the foam on the bottom." Free tours of the brewery end with a taste of the beer in the Ober Brau Haus, the brewery's taproom at 3340 Liberty Ave, Lawrenceville (682-7400).

Pittsburgh Originals

Lemon Blennd

This popular lemon drink, one of the first fruit concentrates, was created about 50 years ago at the old Reymer's Confectionaries in Downtown & East Liberty. It's now sold all over the U.S. Philip Reymer opened his first store at Wood & old Water Street downtown in 1846. Lemon Blennd came along in 1932.

Maurice Salad

This salad was created by the Variety Club kitchen in the William Penn Hotel for band leader Phil Spitalny. Hotel officials say it was originally called the Spitalny Salad and then the Phil Salad—neither of which caught on—and ended up named for Phil's band leader brother Maurice. It's had a long run— it's been on the hotel's Terrace Room menu since 1945. The salad consists of julienne turkey, Swiss cheese and ham over iceberg and bibb lettuce already mixed with a spicy mayonnaise, red peppers & relish. It's served on a plate (rather than in a bowl) with three tomato wedges and black olives. Variations can be found on many Pittsburgh menus.

Original Hot Dogs

Pittsburgh's famous "foot-long hot dog" was a staple at the old Original Famous Sandwich Shop at Larimer & Station Sts in East Liberty, started by "Big Sam" in 1928. Now you can get a 7″ dog at the 'new' Original Hot Dog Shops, the "Big O" at Forbes/Bouquet in Oakland— opened in 1960 by Syd Simon who worked 15 years at the old Famous. Roasted in its skin for flavour, the big dog is 75% beef, 25% pork. Former Pittsburghers have been known to make a trip home just to taste an Original again! (The "Big O" also does a prodigious business in french fries...40,000 lbs—18 ton—of Idahoes are trucked in each week to be peeled and sliced here.

Original Oyster House Fish Sandwich

This jumbo sandwich, breaded cod on a plain bun, is the city's most famous. To get the real thing you have to go to the 120-yr-old Original Oyster House, an historic Market Square landmark (1870), stand at the bar and have a beer—or a buttermilk—with your sandwich & enjoy the "sawdust atmosphere." Real Pittsburgh!

Pecan Ball

Another creation by Pittsburgh restaurateur Frank Blandi...a dessert everyone loves...a scoop of vanilla ice cream rolled in syrupy pecans. In the original recipe a butter rum sauce was poured over the pecans. The Pecan Ball was another staple at the old Park Schenley and the fondly-remembered Pittsburgh Playhouse Restaurant.

Penn Pilsner

This local beer is now being made at the Allegheny Brewery & Pub (in North Side's old Eberhardt & Ober Brewery on Troy Hill), the first 'tied house'— restaurant attached to a brewery—in Pennsylvania since Prohibition. It's pure German beer without additives, made by a German breumeister. While you eat at the recreated German pub you can watch the brewing in shiny copper kettles through a glass wall.

Pittsburgh Steak

This NY strip, delicately charred on the outside and blood-rare on the inside (cooked less than 1 minute) was named for Pittsburgh by a NY chef. The smoke created when the cold steak hit the sizzling skillet reminded him of his hometown in the old Pittsburgh mill days. You can get it now at **Tramps** on the Blvd of the Allies, Downtown. You'll see this steak on menus in other cities.

Pittsburgh Originals/Ethnic Foods

Primanti's Sandwiches

This sandwich has been reviewed in *Newsweek, Penthouse* and Calvin Trillin's book *Third Helpings.* Its claim to fame—to the basic grilled beef patty and cheese on thick Italian bread, french fries and cole slaw are added right **in** the sandwich. Night owls & Strip workers can get them 24 hours a day at Primanti's 18th St site and into the wee hours at 3803 Forbes in Oakland.

Sarah's

The fame of Sarah Evosevich's homemade Yugoslavian meals has spread near and far. For over 50 years Sarah has been cooking in her 1850 'town house' in South Side...ethnic dishes such as Chorba—Serbian vegetable barley soup, Podvarak—turkey with sauerkraut, plus homemade bread and apple strudel. Visiting VIPs are often brought here to show off Pittsburgh's unique ethnic flavour.

White Tower Hamburgers

These old-time flat-grilled burgers, wrapped in the wonderful aroma of grease and frying onions from the grill, are, many swear, still the best in town. They're served on special buns with sour pickles...and hash browns if you want 'em. Originally a nickel, they're still a bargain at 99¢. White Tower burger stands were once beacons all over Pittsburgh. Of the original 14, now only two remain—Centre and Craig in Oakland, and at the 16th St Bridge on the North Side.

William Penn Cheesecake

From one of the most regal kitchens in the city came one of Pittsburgh's most famous desserts, William Penn Cheesecake—a rich, rich recipe, usually topped with strawberry sauce...and still a favorite on the hotel's menu. It dates back to 1921, to two German chefs, brothers Oscar and Hans Joerg, who worked at the William Penn shortly after it opened in 1916. At one time it was exported worldwide.

Pittsburgh Ethnics... Where to Get 'Em

Bagels

The best are in Squirrel Hill at **Bagel-and** which makes them for most of the restaurants in the city. They come in 17 varieties from raisin to onion, blueberry to baby bagels.

Breads

Pittsburgh breads can be summed up in three names: **Panini's** in the Strip for braided rings, Sicilian rye and broccoli bread (sausage, broccoli, onion & garlic); **Susan Bakes & Cooks** for some of the best French, brown breads & baked goods in the city; and **Breadworks,** a favorite restaurant supplier with wonderful breads including focaccia. For Italian, **Mancini's** is the big name with **Barsotti's** a close second. Good bakeries abound in Pittsburgh, among them **Prantl's** in Shadyside and **Jenny Lee's** all over town. There are some great restaurant breads too, among them Pizza Bread from the **Grand Concourse,** olive oil-touched Tuscan bread at **Emilia Romagna**, and David Ayn's applesauce bread at **Stephen's La Piccola Casa.**

British

You can get authentic British "high tea" with pasties (meat pies) at **Cathy's Windsor Tearoom** in Sewickley. You can also get savouries—puffed pastries with meat/cheese fillings—at downtown's **Warburton's British Bakeries.** For formal tea in the **William Penn Lobby** and at other local rooms (See Teas 17.) The best modern tea sandwiches are at **Kaufmann's Tic-Toc** Coffee Shop, great with their unique coffee ice cream soda. P.S. Yorkshire pudding is served with prime rib at the Westin William Penn. And **Aussie's,** a Bloomfield pub, has authentic Australian food/atmosphere.

6

Strip District

Pittsburgh's United Nations of food is the Strip wholesale marketplace where you can find foodstuffs for every cuisine. (See Review)

Ethnic Foods

French

Pittsburgh French cuisine came of age in the last decade. Thanks to the pioneer work of **La Normande,** the city's first world-class French restaurant (which passed the tri-color to **Jacqueline's** in Webster Hall), Gallic connoisseurs are growing in number here. While many ingredients are still flown in from France and NY, the French gourmet shop **La Charcuterie** in Ellsworth Plaza is making gastronomic rarities available to local cooks i.e. truffles, foie gras, hard-to-get herbs. It's run by the chefs of **Laforet,** another fine French restaurant in East Liberty. The city also boasts Country French **Le Pommier,** South Side, **Le Petit Cafe** in Shadyside, **Cafe Azure** in Oakland—and for the economy gourmet—**Simply French** in Oakland.

German

You can enjoy German food, fun at scores of local Octoberfests. For restaurants there's **Max's Allegheny Tavern,** an old German eatery in the heart of North Side, with some of the best wursts, beers & atmosphere. Up on Troy Hill Road **Allegheny Brewery and Pub** is serving some great German food and Penn Pilsner beer in a fun atmosphere with German bands and an outdoor rathskeller. There are also **Otto's** in Dormont and **Kleiner Deutschmann** in Springdale. Best beer is at **Hampton Inn** in Allison Park, **Max's Allegheny Tavern** and **Park House**, North Side & **Chiodo's** in Homestead. (Most eateries make their own wursts or send to Milwaukee!)

Wednesday Greek Lunches

Everybody's welcome at the "Wednesday Lunches" from 11-1:30 at **Holy Trinity Greek Orthodox Church,** 302 W North, N Side for Greek-style chicken, baked fish, meatballs in wine, cheese/spinach pies, braised lamb shank. Loukumades (honey balls) 1st & 3rd Wed. **321-9282.**

Croatian Sunday Picnics

Every Sun from Memorial to Labor Day you can get janjetina (slowly roasted lamb), prasetina (suckling pig), barbecued lamb & pork at **The Croatian Center** picnics at Schnitzen Park Road in Ross. Everyone welcome. Polka band. Adm. $2. **821-9902.**

Greek

You can get all of the makings for Greek/Syrian dinner at **Stamoolis Bros** on Penn Ave in the Strip. **Salim's**, Centre Ave, Oakland has Greek/Lebanese foodstuffs and take-out. Best local Greek eateries are at **Suzie's**, Downtown/Squirrel Hill, **Harris Grill** in Shadyside and **Klay's**, Banksville Rd, South Hills. For gyros it's **Salonika**, 6th St, Downtown. You can get Greek foods at church and community festivals thru the year and at Wed lunch at North Side's Holy Trinity Greek Church.

Indian

Center for Pittsburgh's sizeable Indian population is the **Bombay Emporium** on Craft Avenue in Oakland for foodstuffs & delicate spices. You can also get saffron, coriander, cumin, hard-to-get Indian foods at **Indian Grocery,** 4141 Old Wm Penn Hwy, Monroeville. It's near the Sri Venkateswara Hindu Temple in Penn Hills which serves Indian food Sundays and at festivals. Two strictly Indian restaurants are **Darbar** and **Star of India** in Oakland. Many Oriental eateries serve Indian items. (See Oriental 13)

Irish Food

The city's unofficial Irish headquarters is Tom O'Donoghue's **Blarney Stone** in Etna with Irish food, Irish coffee, Irish entertainment and an Irish pastry chef. You can also get sing-a-longs at **Gallagher's Pub** in Market Sq. Green beer flows throughout the city at St Patrick's Day celebrations after the big parade. For music/dancing there's the annual **Irish Centre Feis** in Squirrel Hill.

Ethnic Foods

Italian Hot Sausage

Pittsburgh is also the "home of Italian." Some of the best hot sausage in the area is at **Merante's,** Bates/McKee in Oakland...southern style, pungent with spices and at **Parma Sausage** and **Sunseri's** in the Strip. Specializing in hot sausage sandwiches are **Primanti's,** Strip & Oakland and **Frankie's** at 3535 Butler Street. P.S. You can get wonderful Italian cheeses in the Strip at **Pgh Cheese Terminal** and **Pittsburgh Macaroni Company.** Sunseri's has some of best provolone in the city.

Italian Groceries

Best of show are **Groceria Merante** on Bates, **Pennsylvana Macaroni Co** & **Sunseri** in the Strip. Also good are **F Donatelli & Son** (since '32) and **Groceria Italiano** both in Bloomfield, **Labriola's,** E Hills and Aspinwall, **DeLallo's** in Pleasant Hills...and **That Italian Place** in Upper St Clair. And it's hard to beat the Italian pastries at **Moio's** in Monroeville. Pittsburgh has more Italian restaurants than other kind...many of them the city's finest i.e. **D'Imperio's** in Wilkins Twp with Ital/Cont, **Pasta Piatto** in Shadyside & the **Bravos!** Downtown.

Kielbasa

You haven't lived ethnic until you've tasted this spicy Slavic sausage a.k.a. kielbassa, kolbassi, kolbassa, kolbasi, kohlbasa depending on your ethnic origin. A big Pittsburgh item, the best can be found at the **Mission Market** and other South Side markets and at many Strip outlets including **Stamoolis.** The **McGinnis Sisters** in South Hills & Monroeville also have good homemade kielbasa. **Primanti's** have it all the time.

Farmer's Markets

Pittsburgh ethnic specialties—kielbasa, homemade breads/pies, hot dogs & sauerkraut—can be found at local Farmers' Markets Jun-Nov on North Side, South Side, Highland Park, Carrick and Wilkinsburg.

Polish Tuesday

Tuesday is Polish day at the Bloomfield Bridge Tavern, 4412 Liberty Ave. You can get kielbasa, pierogi, haluski, golabki (pigs in the blanket—stuffed cabbage), kluski (noodles & cottage cheese) and imported beers. 11am-1am or til the food runs out! $4.99. AE,DC,MC,V. **682-8611.**

Kosher/Jewish Food

Murray Avenue in Squirrel Hill is the city's center for Kosher & Jewish foods. You can get kosher meat & deli at **Kosher Mart** & **Prime Kosher Food of Pittsburgh.** For restaurants there are **King David** Kosher/Chinese & **Yakov's** Kosher/vegetarian. **Pastries Unlimited,** one of best bakeries in the city, is strictly Kosher. Up the street is another great Jewish bakery, **Rosenbloom's.** Jewish-style delis are **Catz N Kids** and **Rhoda's** with everything—latke (potato pancakes), matzo balls, chicken soup, noodle kugel, pickled herring. **Adler's Deli/Catering** has the best lox in the city & **Marvin's Meats** on Forward Avenue can't be beat! Best Reuben sandwich is at the **Richest Deli** downtown. All these good foods come out at Squirrel Hill's annual **Jewish Food Festival.**

Latin American

It's **Reyna Foods** 2023 Penn Ave in the Strip for hard-to-find ingredients for Mexican, Cuban, Puerto Rican and Latin American menus—plus pinatas for a Latin American fiesta. **Mejico** brand tortilla chips are made right here in Etna. Best little Mexican places are **Jose & Toni's,** famous for their Mt Lebanon take-out, **Chili's** in N. Hills, **Fajita Grill** in Pleasant Hills, **Margaritaville** in South Side, **Poncho's** in Ambridge and fast-food **Chi Chi's** all over. Two of the biggest are Station Sq's **Tequila Junction** with the biggest margueritas in town and **Sante Fe** in Upper St Clair.

Ethnic Foods

The Pierogi Parade — Where To Get 'Em

You don't have to be Polish—or even Slavic—to enjoy Pittsburgh pierogi. You can get them homemade by ladies of local ethnic churches (see below) or at **Clara's Pittsburgh Pierogies** *at 2717 Library Road, Castle Shannon (882-3555) in a plain concrete building with some of the best pierogi in town . . . and a drive-thru window! Pierogi (also known as pirogi, perogi, pirohi, pirohy), tender triangles of dough with various fillings, are an East European staple. They can be purchased, along with haluski (fried noodles & sweet cabbage) and other Slavic dishes at the following churches:*

Byzantine Church of Resurrection 455 Center Rd, Monroeville. 3rd Fri Jun-Aug. Order day before. Pierogi— potato, lekvar (prune), cottage cheese, sauerkraut, $3 doz. **372-9415.**

Holy Ghost Byzantine 225 Olivia, McKees Rocks. Fri 8-2. Advance orders. Potato/sauerkraut/cottage cheese, $2.50-$2.75 doz. **331-5155.**

St Anthony's Lyceum, 108 North Ave, Troy Hill. Fri 12-6, Sat 10-12. All kinds inc onion pierogi, $3 doz. **821-9825.**

St Gregory's Russian Orth Church 214 E 15th St, Homestead. Fri 9-4. Halushki & fish sandwiches—Father Shuga fries the fish himself. **462-8256.**

St Elias Byzantine 4200 Homestead/Duquesne Rd, Munhall. Thur-Fri 11-3. Potato & cheese/cottage cheese/ kraut, $3 doz; all kinds of noodles inc haluski & leschky $2 lb. **461-1712.**

St George Ukrainian 3455 California Ave, Brighton Heights. Thur-Fri 10am-5. Cheese/potato/sauerkraut, $2.25-$2.50 doz; sauteed onions 25¢. **766-8800.**

St John Baptist Cathedral 913 Dickson, Munhall. Fri 9-5 Sept-May. Potato/cottage cheese/lekvar/sauerkraut, $3 doz; also haluski, bean & lentil soup, cheregi (donut-like cakes). **461-6882.**

St John Baptist Ukrainian 204 Olivia, McKees Rocks. Thur 3-6, Fri 7-3. Potato/potato & sauerkraut/cottage cheese. $2.40-$2.90 doz. **331-5605.**

St Mary's RC Church Lower Lyceum, 45th St, Lawrenceville. Tues-Fri 9-2. Sauerkraut & bacon, potato, cheese $3 doz. **682-4760.**

St Nicholas Orthodox 6th/Marne, Monongahela. 1st/3rd Fri, every Fri in Lent 11-2. Advance orders. Potato & sauerkraut/lekvar, $2.50-$3. **258-5072.**

St Vladimir Ukrainian Orthodox, 1810 Sidney, S Side. Pierogi Thur Oct-Jul. Potato/kraut/cheese. $2.90 doz. **431-9758**

Oriental

Some of the city's most popular cuisines. Biggest food store is **New Sam Bok** 1735 Penn Ave, Strip, for hard-to-get exotic Chinese/Japanese/Korean items i.e. cuttlefish, banana leaves, burdock root, dried mushrooms. Also in the Strip is **Pgh Oriental Food Mart** with Oriental/ Thai/Philippine/Latin American foods and **P & S Oriental** Thai/Cambodian/ Vietnamese/Chinese. There's also a big selection at **Young's Oriental Grocery,** Forward Ave, Squirrel Hill.

Kim-do's, 3400 Fifth, Oakland, specializes in Chinese/Vietnamese/Caribbean/African. **Tokyo Japanese Food Store** in Ellsworth Plaza, Shadyside, has the city's best sushi, exotic fish, and wide selection of foodstuffs. You can get the makings for 7 Asian cuisines including Japanese, Thai, Korean, Philippine at **East Oriental Food Store,** Wm Penn Hwy, Monroeville. (See Oriental/Asian 13 for more info on 50 area Asian eateries.)

Ethnic Foods/Festivals

Mid-Eastern

There's a big selection of Mid-Eastern foodstuffs at **Chahine's Mediterranean Bakery** in Squirrel Hill. Pittsburgh abounds with mid-Eastern eateries— everything from fine cuisine at **Ali Baba, Sanremy's, Khalil's, Sahara** in Oakland to **Amel's** in Dormont and **Klay's** on Banksville Rd. You can get gyros at **Little Athens** in Squirrel Hill and at **Salonika Gyros** 6th St, Downtown.

Pizza

Two of city's best pizzas are made in Squirrel Hill...**Mineo's** and **Aiello's,** a short block apart on Murray Ave. Many swear by their local **Pizza Hut** or **Pizzeria Uno** in Monroeville. For gourmet pizza **Shadyside Balcony** can't be beat.

Soul/African Food

Headquarters for Pittsburgh soul food is Homewood's **Southern Platter** with down-home, sit-down dinners. **Wilson's** (N Side/E Liberty) is a tradition for tangy ribs with big flavour...a close second is **House of Sauce,** Centre Avenue, Oakland. Newest top entry is **Mr P & P Ribbs,** 5th Ave, Uptown & Homestead with wonderful greens, black-eyed peas, corn bread & biscuits. And many are in love with **Margarie's** "grits breakfasts" at 1534 Brighton Road near West Park. Check them all out at the annual **Harambee Black Arts Festival** in Homewood where native African dishes are also featured. A lot of Oriental food stores have African foodstuffs.

Sweet Potato Pie

Tops are **Leonard & Dorothy Washington's** homemade pies at Hoagie Castle, Homewood & Hamilton, (they also come from all over for the steak hoagies here)...and **Aunt Cheryl's** and **Steve's** at Giant Eagles and other locations.

We're sure we've missed some great Pittsburgh ethnic foods. Give us a call at 681-8528 and tell us your favorite. Must be authentic!

FOOD FESTIVALS
Spring

Pa Maple Festival Meyersdale. Apr. 5 days. Freshly tapped maple syrup, hot cakes/sausage. **814-634-0213.**

St Nicholas Greek Cathedral Fest 419 S Dithridge, Oakland. 1st full wk May. Spanakopeta, mousaka, rice pilaf, lamb, pastries. bouzouki music. **682-3866.**

Strip District Festivals May Springfest & Octoberfest. Taste of every nation from Strip food purveyors. Hot sausage, pierogis, gyros, music, **281-8077.**

Ambridge Nationality Days 3rd wknd May. 22 ethnic food booths. Dancing, **266-3040.**

Polka Parties Seven Springs. Memorial wknd & Oct. **800-452-2223.**

Latin American Festival Univ of Pgh. Spring. Foods from Latin countries — Mexican tacos, burritos; Brazilian seijoda (pork, beans & rice). **648-7392.**

May Market Pgh Civic Garden Ctr, Fifth/Shady. May. Flower market with grilled mushroom sandwiches, strawberries in fondant, funnel cake. **441-4442.**

Summer

Jewish Food Fest Temple Sinai, Squirrel Hill. Early Jun. 3-day fest with all the Jewish specialties. **421-9715.**

Gr Uniontown Ethnic Fest 1st wknd Jun. Hungarian, Polish, Italian, Greek, African; music, dancing. **430-2909.**

Mon-Yough Ethnic Nights McKeesport Riverfront Park. Saturdays Jun-Aug. Ethnic dinners, free concerts. **678-1727.**

6

Pittsburgh Folk Festival

Ethnic foods are featured year round at scores of Pittsburgh area festivals. You can sample all at the famed **Pittsburgh Folk Festival** Memorial Day weekend at Lawrence Convention Center when thousands join more than 20 ethnic groups for continuous music, dancing, food booths. **565-4680.**

FAMOUS PITTSBURGH FOODS
Ethnic Foods/Festivals

Monessen Heritage Festival 3rd wk Jun. One of biggest, 19 nationalities, food, entertainment. **684-3200.**

Holy Dormition Greek Fest Oakmont. Last wknd Jun. Mousaka, pastitso, spanakopeta (spinach pie), stuffed grape leaves; dancing. **828-4144.**

Armstrong Heritage Days Ford City. 5 days nr July 4. Haluski, halupki (stuffed cabbage), also Italian. **548-3226.**

Intl Food/Art Fest Weirton, W Va. Wknd Jul 4. 50 booths, ethnic/Amer food, art, music. **304-797-6969.**

Old Economy Village Fests Ambridge. Kunstfest (Mid-Jul wknd) and Erntefest (Oct). Sauerkraut, dumplings, wursts; crafts, minstrel, tours. **266-1803.**

South Side Summer Spectacular Wk in Jul. Ethnic food booths—hot sausage, kielbasa, entertainment. **481-0651.**

Slovene Fest Lawrence Co. Wknd July. Kolbasi, pierogi, apple dumplings, 20 polka bands. **336-5180.**

Bavarian Fun Fest Sharon. Last wknd Jul & 1st wknd Aug. Wursts, halupki, gyros, music, dancing. **981-3123.**

Harambee Black Arts Fest Homewood. Aug. Soul/Southern—BBQ ribs, Creole, Cajun, native African dishes; arts, music. **362-8217.**

Fayette Co Italian Fest Uniontown. 2nd wknd Aug. One of biggest; homemade pasta, calzone, stromboli. **438-5561.**

Yugoslav Festival Herminie. 3rd Sun Aug. Slavic foods, kolbasi & haluski, Serbian cevapcici (spicy rolled meat), polka/kolo/tambura. **373-0888**

Dankfest Harmony. 4th wknd Aug. German sausage, strudels, homemade ice cream, root beer. Hay rides. **452-7341.**

McKeesport Intl Village last wk Aug. One of oldest fests; 17 ethnic groups—Croatian, Serbian, Irish, African, music, dancing. **675-5033.**

Fall
Allegheny County Rib Cook-Off South Pk Fairgrounds. Labor Day wknd. Natl ribmakers compete with locals. **678-1727.**

Holy Trinity Greek Church Festival 302 W North, N Side. Sept. All the Greek specialties. **321-9282.**

Penn's Colony Fest Prospect. Wknds in Sept. "Pioneer" food, apple fritters, smoked ham, beef on spit. Crafts, entertainment. **241-8006.**

Scottdale Coke/Heritage Fest 2nd/3rd wknd Sept. 30 ethnic booths, Greek/Ital/Slavic food, music. **887-5700.**

German Amer Octoberfest Station Sq 3rd week Sept. Potato pancakes, wienerschnitzel, strudel, music. **561-3354.**

Octoberfest Alleg Brewery & Pub, Troy Hill Rd. Last 2 wknds Sept. Old time German food, bands. **237-9402.**

Covered Bridge Fest Greene/Wash Co. 3rd wknd Sept. Ethnic home/country food at 8 covered bridges. **222-8130.**

Three Rivers Indian Pow-Wow Dorseyville. Last wknd Sept. Amer-Indian food—creamed/fried maize, buffalo meat. Dances/demos. **782-4457.**

Ukrainian Festival Univ of Pgh. Last wknd Sept. Potato dumplings, borscht, kolbassa/sauerkraut, nalysnyky (crepes); music/dancing. **279-3458.**

Sri Venkateswara Hindu Temple Festivals Penn Hills. Indian delicacies Sun and at Jan Thanksgiving Festival & Oct Festival of Lights. **373-3380.**

Ohiopyle Buckwheat Festival 2nd wknd Oct. Pancakes, applesauce, baked goods. **329-1444.**

Mars Apple Festival 2nd Sat Oct. Homemade apple butter, cider, dumplings, pies and cakes. **625-3571.**

Winter
Chinese New Year Banquet Jan-Feb, Sat nearest Chinese New Year. 10-courses, exotic dishes from various cuisines; dancing, music. **833-2339.**

St Patrick's Day Celebration Blarney Stone, Etna. Month of Mar. Area's biggest, Irish food, beers. **781-1666.**

Polishfest Soldier's/Sailor's Hall. 2nd Sun Nov. Polish foods, polka bands. **486-3819.**

7

A city of rolling hills and rivers, Pittsburgh is famous for its spectacular views ...from the top of Mt Washington...from Downtown...from new riverfront vantage points. Here are the best places to view the city - wonderful by day - breathtaking by night - perfect entertainment for both natives & visitors.

FROM MT WASHINGTON

Christopher's
1411 Grandview. Dinner Mon-Thur 5-11, Fri-Sat til 12. Reser. AE,DC,MC,V. **381-4500.**
Exciting three-sided view of city from glass walls of glamorous rooftop restaurant. Dancing Fri in Lounge. $12-$35. Drinks: Exp. A must for out-of-towners. (See Review)

City Market & Deli
1216 Grandview. 7 days 10-6. No credit cards. **481-8585.**
Informal deli near Duquesne Incline with sandwiches, soups, salads, great view of city. $1-$4.50.

Cliffside
1208 Grandview. Dinner, lounge 7 days 5-11. AE,DC,MC,V. **431-6996.**
Spectacular view in sleek, modern decor. Nightly piano from 7. Inventive Amer menu & appetizers. $4-$20. Drinks: Mod.

Georgetowne Inn
1230 Grandview. Lunch, Dinner, Late Snacks Mon-Thur 11-12, Fri-Sat til 1. Sun 4-10. AE,D,DC,MC,V. **481-4424.**
Great view, best bet on limited budget. Entrees inc seafood $13-$26; late snacks, desserts, cheeseboards $3-$7. Drinks: Mod.

Grandview Saloon
1212 Grandview, next to Duquesne Incline. Sun-Thur 11-12, Fri-Sat til 1. Bar til 2. AE,V. **431-1400.**
Spectacular view of Point from Mt Washington's first casual eatery with two outdoor decks, young/family place. Lite dining, sandwiches $3-$10. Drinks Mod-Exp. (See Boaters/Outdoor 8)

LeMont
1114 Grandview. Dinner Mon-Fri 5-10:30, Sat til 11:30, Sun 4-9:30. Lounge til closing. Reser. AE,DC,MC,V. **431-3100.**
Superb view of Golden Triangle from banquettes; continental dining in posh surroundings. $17-30. Drinks: Mod-Exp.

Tin Angel
1204 Grandview. Dinner Mon-Thur 5:30-9:30, Fri-Sat til 10. Reser. AE,DC,MC,V. **381-1919.**
Top-of-town favorite for beautiful view, intimate ambience, music. . . 'most romantic place in town.' Dinners $21-$32. Drinks: Exp. (See Rich Man's Guide)

DOWNTOWN

Top of the Triangle
USX Tower, 600 Grant. Lunch Mon-Fri 11:30-3, Sat 12-3. Dinner Mon-Fri 5:30-10, Sat til 12. Sun 4-9. Parking free in bldg after 4:30. Reser sugg. AE,DC,MC,V. **471-4100.**
Breathtaking view from 62nd floor with city at your feet—great tourist spot. Amer menu $15 up. Piano bar, DJ dancing Mon-Sat til 2. Drinks: Mod-Exp.

FROM THE RIVERFRONT

Carnegie Science Center
North Shore, next to Three Rivers Stadium. **237-3400.**
'Three Rivers view' of Point from exciting new Science Center's glass-walled restaurant seating 200, outdoor terrace; Lunch/Dinner. Mod. **237-3400.** (Open Oct '91)

River Room, Grand Concourse
Landmarks Bldg, Station Sq. Mon-Fri 11:30-11, Sat 4:30-11, Sun Brunch 10-2:30, Dinner 4:30-9. AE,DC,MC,V. **261-1717.**
It's worth the wait for a seat in the River Room for splendid sunset views in Pgh's most elegant restaurant; seafood, steak. Lunch $7-$10, Dinner $17-$30; Great break on daily Early Bird dinners $10-$15. (See Review)

Waterfall Terrace
Sheraton Hotel, Station Square. 7 days 6am-midnite. AE,D,DC,MC,V. **261-2000.**
Indoor cafe with close-up views of downtown across the river; dinners, light fare, sandwiches, late supper $3-$25. Sunday Brunch 10-3 in **Reflections** diningroom with sunny river view.

8

Pittsburgh now boasts an amazing number - 56 marina, riverfront and outdoor eateries - thanks to the city's riverside Renaissance! Whether you choose to eat with a river view or at one of the city's charming new patios/sidewalk cafes...it's a good way to mingle with other city dwellers and enjoy the greatest of urban pleasures - dining al fresco.

Riverfront Restaurants

Allegheny River Boat Club

314 Arch St, Verona. Mon-Fri 3pm-2am. Sat-Sun 12-2am. AE,DC,MC,V. **828-7775.** Casual pub—soup/sandwiches $2-$6, picnic packs to go. Courtyard for large parties for clean-up fee.
Docking: Free for patrons.

Back Porch

114 Speers St, Lower Speers near Belle Vernon Bridge. (Exit 17 off I-70) Lunch Tues-Fri 11:30-4. Dinner Tues-Sat 5-10, Sun 4-9. AE,MC,V. **483-4500.** Charming 1806 Colonial home tucked away in tiny, riverside community near the Mon. Amer cuisine, garden dining on the veranda. Lunch $4-$7, Dinner $13-$19. More casual dining downstairs at English-pub **Side Door.**
Docking: Public launch ramp/trailer parking across street.

Bootleggers on the Water

10 Washington Avenue, Oakmont. Dinner Tues-Sat 4-10. Late menu til 12. AE,D,MC,V. **826-8666.** Friendly, casual. Boaters welcomed to stop and grab a bite after a day out on the water. One of best scenic views on Allegheny from glass-walled bar with spacious deck seating 80. Dress super casual but shoes/tops please. Dinners $9 up. Music weekdays.
Docking: 100ft space free to patrons.

Dublin's Pub

Rt 88, Millsboro, Wash/Greene Co border. (50 mi south of Pgh) Tues-Sun 11-12am. No credit cards. **377-1379.** Roofed outdoor restaurant/bar right on the Mon; full menu, good steak salads. Entertainment weekends/holidays. Shoes/shirt required.
Docking: Free docking for patrons at Green Cove Yacht Club, Ten Mile Ck.

Riverside Shops

127 Speers St, Lower Speers. (Exit 17 off I-70). **483-4668.** Boaters can take advantage of this collection of specialty shops—antiques, crafts, boutiques—with a quaint Victorian motif.

Terrace Dining At New Science Center

Carnegie Science Center's restaurant will have an outdoor terrace fronting the Allegheny on North Shore with a great view of the Point. A family restaurant seating 200, it will be open during Center hours for lunch/dinner Mon-Wed til 5, Thur & Sun til 9:30, Fri-Sat til 10:30. (Oct '91) **237-3400.**

Fox Chapel Yacht Club

1366 Old Freeport Rd, Fox Chapel. Lunch Mon-Sat 11-3. Dinner Mon-Sat 5-9 (summer til 11). Sun Brunch 10-2. AE,MC,V. **963-8881.** Fine dining on Allegheny shore with a majestic view of some of Pgh's most impressive pleasure craft. The name may sound exclusive but the restaurant's open to the public. American cuisine. Lunch $5-$8, Dinner $15-$20. Live music Fri-Sat in dining room and dancing on romantic outdoor deck/bar to live bands in summer. Shorts, casual dress acceptable if coming off river. Mod.
Docking: Members only, free for dining patrons. Reservations please.

Marina One

Mile Post 32.5 on the Mon, RD #3, Riverway East, Monongahela. Sun-Thur 11-10, Fri & Sat til 11. AE,MC,V. **258-2300.** Big deck, space to dock and swim; everything from sandwiches to crab legs, lobster $5-$22. DJ Dancing Thur-Sat. **Docking:** Guest Dock available.

Silkys Crow's Nest

19th & River Rd, Sharpsburg. MC,V. Mon-Sat 11:30-2am, Sun 12-8. **782-3701.** New Allegheny eating/meeting place. Casually elegant, glass-walled, multi-level room seating 150 with great view of the river. Dinners—pasta, steak, seafood $6-$15. Grand piano, entertainment. Also dinner, sandwiches, late snacks in **Boaters Bar** on lower level with outside decks.
Docking: Docking free for patrons.

Riverfront Restaurants

Smitty's
119 River Rd, Lower Speers, near Belle Vernon Bridge. (Exit 17 off I-70) 7 days 11-2am. AE,DC,MC,V. **483-6900.**
One of the most famous eating spots on the Mon, popular seafood restaurant with nautical theme and a big, awninged outdoor deck. Chicken, pasta plus food to go for boaters. $4-$16. **Docking:** Nearby public ramp/trailer parking; docking free to patrons at Boat World Marina if space available.

Speers St Grill
Lower Speers, near Belle Vernon Bridge. (Exit 17 off of I-70). 7 days 11:30-10. MC,V. **483-1911.**
Old Victorian home next door to the **Back Porch.** Great place to enjoy a cool lemonade and homemade ice cream on small outdoor patio with a view of the river. Casual with ribs, chicken, sandwiches, munchies. $4.50-$9. **Docking:** Public ramp/trailer parking.

Strip—Down by the Riverside
Floating Boardwalk on Allegheny between Veterans and 16th St bridges. Enter off Smallman at parking lot at 15th St under bridge. **471-2226.**
Lots of wonderful vistas to choose from in this exciting new riverside recreation center. On a 420-ft floating Boardwalk, moored 30 feet from shore are:
Crewser's Big seafood house, nautical theme, also snacks, two bars. Mod.
Buster's Crab Baltimore-style raw bar with a topside view of waters. Mod.
Patio/Deck Swimming/splash pool with bar/restaurant service, Summertime entertainment. Mod.
Donzi's World-class Euro-style, neon disco. Cover. Mod-Exp.
Docking: 50 slips free to patrons. (Downtown Yacht Club next door.)

Captain's Dinner
Dine under the stars on the decks of the **Gateway Clipper** at the Captain's Dinner or on 265-foot **Majestic,** sailing most days 7-10, May-Dec. The $23-$29 tab includes buffet, dancing, beautiful city view—a truly moving feast. **355-7980.**

Pgh's Spectacular New Water Park

Sandcastle on the Mon
W Homestead, Rt 387 bet Homestead & Glenwood Bridges. (Parkway: Squirrel Hill/Hmstd Exit, across Hi-Level Bridge, right to 387, follow blue signs.) June-Labor Day. 7 days 11-6, Fri-Sat til 7. Evenings Wed-Sat 6-1am. MC,V. **462-6666.**
Everybody loves this fabulous new water park along the Mon. The 30-acre water wonderland has 15 major slides (some of tallest in world—85 ft) 3 kiddie slides, a 1400-ft "lazy river" for floaters, 2 pools, volleyball, and a charming, old-fashioned 1000-ft boardwalk...second only to Atlantic City's. At night the fun goes on—two dance floors, huge hot tubs along the river, sing-a-longs on the Boardwalk. Young, old love it! Picnic food—pizza, burgers, hot dogs/sauerkraut $3-$5. Adm $12.95, after 3 pm $6.95. Eve: Wed-Thur $1, Fri-Sat $4. **Docking:** 50 slips, free to patrons with admission price.

RIVER VIEWS

River's Edge
4616 Alleg River Blvd, Verona. Lunch Mon-Fri 11-4, Dinner Mon-Sat 4-11. AE,DC,MC,V. **793-6167.**
This venerable, Verona haunt has a striking view of Allegheny from glass-enclosed diningroom. Italian. $7-$14.

Paule's Lookout
2627 Skyline Dr, W Mifflin. Tues-Sat 11-9. Sun 12-7:30. AE,DC,MC,V. **466-4500.**
Family restaurant on hilltop with a panoramic view of Mon & Youghiogheny. Seafood, lobster & prime rib. $3-$11.

Veltri's
Rt 907 & Coxcomb Hill, Plum Boro. Dinner Mon-Thur 5-10, Fri-Sat til 11. Reser. AE,DC,MC,V. **335-4474.**
Beautiful view of the the Allegheny, romantic atmosphere; Ital-Amer cuisine. DJ Wed-Sat. $7-$21.

8

Marinas

DOCKING ON THE RIVER

ALLEGHENY

Allegheny Marina *One 62nd Street, Lawrenceville. 7 days 24 hrs.* **782-3113.** Service, supplies, facilities, showers. **Slips:** 100, guest docking available, overnight $15 up.

Allegheny River Boat Club *314 Arch, Verona. 7 days 24 hrs.* **828-7775.** Power, showers, picnic facilities. Restaurant/bar, public launch $10. **Slips:** 90, 6 free for restaurant patrons, overnight $10 up.

Aspinwall Marina *285 River Ave, Aspinwall. 7 days 8am-10pm.* **781-2340.** Accessible dock, fuel, service, supplies, public ramp $8. **Slips:** 200, 15-20 for guests, overnight $20.

Bell Harbour Marina *1 River Road, Blawnox. 7 days 10-9.* **828-3477.** Fuel, service, supplies, facilities, showers, snacks. Ramp $10. **Slips:** 55, 5 guest $8-$15, overnight $10-$15.

Dave's Marina *Grantham/River Ave, North Shore 7 days 9:30-9:30, fuel 8-8.* **231-9860.** Fuel, facilities, ramp $7, snack bar. **Slips:** 95, guest/overnight available.

Downtown Yacht Club/Strip—Down by Riverside *between Veterans & 16th St bridges.* **471-2226.** Restaurants/disco/patio bar. **Slips:** 60 at Yacht Club, 50 guest slips around Boardwalk free to patrons.

Dock of the Bay *River Rd, Sharpsburg. 7 days 8-8.* **782-4176.** Last marina before Lock #2. Fuel, supplies. **Slips:** 250, guest slips vary, overnight $15.

Fox Chapel Yacht Club *1366 Old Freeport Rd, Fox Chapel.* **963-8881.** Private club, full-service. **Slips:** 110 members. Free docking restaurant patrons.

Hunt's Marina *10 Washington Ave, Oakmont, next to Bootlegger's. 7 days 8-8.* **828-1260.** Full service, fuel, power, showers. **Slips:** 140, 10 guest, overnight $10.

Washington's Landing

Washington's Landing *(former Herr's Island) 2 miles upriver from Golden Triangle. 7 days 8-8.* **741-1077.** Fuel, service, ship's store, laundry facilities, deli, members' club/lounge. Public park with river overlook, tennis complex, Three Rivers Rowing Assn facilities. (Future plans for the $4.4 million, 42-acre project include jogging/biking trails, nautical store, Town Center shops—open in '92.) **Slips:** 160 dry stack/150 wet slips; guest docking, overnight, $25.

North Shore Marina *River Ave/Mendota. 7 days 10-8.* **231-2333.** Full service, fuel, supplies, snacks. **Slips:** 100, 4 guest. Stadium docking $7, overnight $15—water/elec $20 extra.

Outboard Haven *228 Arch Street, Verona. 7 days 9-9.* **828-4944.** Very accessible dock. Fuel, supplies, facilities, shower, snacks. **Slips:** 250, guest slips vary. Overnight $20-$25.

MONONGAHELA

Beach Club Marina *124 S Union St, New Eagle, off Rt 88. 7 days 8-8.* **258-2088.** Fuel, power, facilities, showers, picnic facilities, volleyball, horseshoes. Public launch $5. **Slips:** 170, 10 guest, overnight 50¢ per ft.

Boat World *119 River Road, Speers, near Belle Vernon Bridge. Weekdays 10-7, Sat 10-4, Sun 12-4.* **483-3337.** Fuel, service, parts, supplies, facilities, picnic area. **Slips:** 180, 8 for guests, docking fees/overnight vary.

Green Cove Yacht Club *Rt 88 at Ten Mile Crk, Millsboro. 7 days 8-5.* **377-0184.** Longest pool (lock to lock) on Mon, blue-green water. Fuel, service, supplies, snacks, restaurant, camping; launching weekdays only, $10. **Slips:** 325, unlimited guest, overnight 50¢ ft, water/elec extra.

Marinas/River Fun

Engel's Holiday Harbour *Rt 88 at Ten Mile Creek, Millsboro. 7 days 9-7.* **377-0151.**
Fuel, service, facilities, showers, supplies, snacks. **Slips:** 65-70, 4-5 slips overnight only, 35¢ ft.

South Side Public Launch *South Side Riverfront Park, foot of Birmingham Bridge, entrance at 18th St. 7 days 6am-midnite.* **255-2390.**
Public launch ramp, picnic area.

Sandcastle on the Mon *Between Homestead/Glenwood bridges.* **462-6666.**
Docking for patrons with admission fee $2-$12. Food, DJ dancing eves.

OHIO

B & L Marina *4621 Royal Avenue, Coraopolis. 7 days 24 hrs.* **269-9569.**
On back channel. Service, facilities, restaurant, launching $10. **Slips:** 25, guest if space.

C & E Marina *200 Dawson, Sewickley under Glenfield Bridge. 7 days 9-5.* **741-6810.**
Fuel, service, supplies, facilities, shower. Dry-stacking, park/launch. **Slips:** 25, 2 guest—overnght only, $15.

Groveton Boat Club *Royal Ave, Neville Island. Back Channel. 7 days 8-11.* **264-6776.**
Fuel, supplies, snacks, 8 acres picnic grounds, launching $5. Courtesy Marine Exam (CME) for safety Coast Guard sticker. DJ Sat/holidays. **Slips:** Guest slips always available, no overnight.

Gr Pgh Aquatic Club *Pine Street, Neville Island. Back Channel.* **264-9978.**
Fuel, elec/water, docking. Members only.

Vic's Boat Park *1 River Road, McKees Rocks. Back Channel. 7 days 10-10.* **771-DOCK.**
Fuel, service, towing, facilities, supplies, ce/snacks, launching $10. **Slips:** 120, ew guest, overnight $25.

River City

Pittsburgh is truly a river town, beautifully situated at the Point of three rivers—where the Allegheny and Monongahela merge to form the Ohio. The largest inland port in the U.S., Pittsburgh's waterways carry more commercial tonnage (33.4 million in 1989) than any other inland port in the country, far ahead of St Louis, second with 26 million. And Pittsburgh ranks a surprising 17th of all U.S. ports including deep water coastal and Great Lakes ports. Allegheny County also has one of the largest number of registered pleasure boats in the U.S.—28,700 in 1990—second only to Miami's Dade County. And as new riverfront projects reclaim city waters for recreation and entertainment, Pittsburgh's River Renaissance is here!

8

RIVER CELEBRATIONS

Pgh Three Rivers Regatta
Point State Park. First weekend in August. Celebration on all three rivers opening with downtown Regatta Parade, fireworks, food booths, entertainment, sternwheeler races, "Anything That Floats" contest, hot air balloon races, air show, International Formula I Grand Prix speedboat races. **261-7055.**

Oakmont Yacht Club Regatta
Oakmont. Last weekend in July. Food, fun, fireworks, boat races on the Allegheny River. **828-9047.**

Maritime Day Celebration
Station Square. Mid-May. Sponsored by the Propeller Club, Port of Pittsburgh. Two days of fun events with emphasis on the working river, Natl Line Throwing Contest, rope tying, monkey line, marine diving demos, 40 exhibits. **751-9445.**

BOATERS/OUTDOOR EATERIES

River Fun

RIVERWALKS

South Side Riverfront Park 3/4 mile, Walking, jogging, biking.

Strip—Down by Riverside 1/2 mile, Walking, jogging, biking.

Sandcastle Water Park Scenic walk along the Mon length of park.

Station Square Plaza/Riverwalk Plaza/park next to Gateway Clipper, plus mile-long path with industrial artifacts, length of Station Sq from Panhandle Bridge to Ft Pitt Bridge. ('92-'93)

Washington's Landing One and a half miles walking, jogging, biking trails circling the island. (Open '92)

Pgh Technology Center Park 2nd Ave, Hazelwood. Proposed public park on the Mon; picnic, riverwalk promenade entire length of complex. ('92-'93)

Three Rivers Heritage Trail
Pittsburghers may one day be able to walk 12 miles on Pittsburgh's riverfronts along a proposed Three Rivers Heritage Trail. The continuous walkway would begin at Washington's Landing crossing the Allegheny on a picturesque old railroad bridge. It would join the riverside walkway in Roberto Clemente Park passing the Sculpture Court in Allegheny Landing, continue along the Mon passing through Station Square and Pgh History/Landmarks Foundation's planned river plaza and mile-long riverwalk featuring Pittsburgh industrial artifacts. Above the 10th St Bridge the trail becomes a wooded pathway joining South Side Riverfront Park at the Birmingham Bridge. And, hopefully, on to Sandcastle.

Head of Ohio Crew Regatta
September. Crews from all over vie in annual Mercy Hospital/Three Rivers Rowing Assn contest drawing national and international oarsmen. **232-7506.**

Mississippi/Delta Queen Riverboats
Cruise boats dock at the Mon Wharf, Downtown in Jul/Aug and Oct creating riverfront excitement. **800-543-1949.**

Mon-Yough AquaFest
Riverfront Park, McKeesport. 3rd Sun July. Part of Mon-Yough celebration on the Mon & Youghiogheny **678-1727.**

Albert Gallatin Regatta
Point Marion, 3rd wknd May. **725-9190.**

Armstrong County Regatta
Kittanning. Aug. **548-3226.**

Beaver Co River Regatta
3rd wknd Aug. **728-0212.**

White Water Rafting
Ohiopyle State Pk. Apr-Oct. **329-8591.**

"Yough Slalom" White Water
Boat Races Ohiopyle State Park. 1st Sat Sept. **329-8591.**

Yough River Days
Connellsville. 2nd wknd Jun. **628-5500.**

Clipper Cruises
Best way to see Pittsburgh and appreciate its unique geography is by water. **Gateway Clipper** cruises from one to three hours run every day from the Station Square dock. You can sail on everything from the Good Ship Lollipop to the 365-ft Majestic. **355-7965.**

Three Rivers Rowing
The Three Rivers Rowing Association, with home-base and 120-ft dock on the back channel at Washington's Landing, has 300 area members who row year round—indoors in winter on machines. For information call **231-8772.**

8

Allegheny Brewery & Pub

Troy Hill Road, North Side. Across 16th St Bridge. Tues-Sat 11-12am. AE,MC,V. **237-9402.**
In summer the cobblestone courtyard is transformed into a German biergarten with beer taps, long tables for fun in sun & shade. View of the city from deck above. Great German wursts, sauerkraut, spaetzle and beer fresh from brewery. Live bands Wed-Sat. Lunch/Dinner $5-$10.

Artery

5847 Ellsworth, Shadyside. Tues-Sat 5-11, Sun til 10. AE,DC,MC,V. **361-9473.**
Umbrellaed brick patio at this restaurant/art gallery/showcase. Light appetizers to popular mesquite chicken & fish on the outdoor grill, $7-$10.

Bentley's

5608 Wilkins Avenue, Squirrel Hill. Mon-Thur 11:30-10, Fri-Sat til 11. Sun 5-9. AE,MC,V. **421-4880.**
Neighborhood favorite with awninged sidewalk patio, full menu. Lunch/Dinner $4-$13. All-you-can-eat Ribs Thur, $13.

A Little Bit of Heaven In Heart of Town

Garden Cafe

Heinz Hall Plaza, 6th/Penn, Downtown. Mon-Fri 11:30-3. AE,MC,V. **392-4887.**
This little outdoor cafe is an oasis for lunch in the busy city...complete with murmuring waterfall and greenery. Light fare at tables with fresh flowers, a variety of soups, salads, desserts, hot entrees, coolers/cocktails from the bar. $3-$8. Pittsburgh at its best.

Brady St Bridge Cafe

2228 E Carson Street, South Side. Mon-Thur 11:30-10, Fri til 11:30, Sat 5-11:30. AE,D,DC,MC. **488-1818.**
Charming enclosed patio in intriguing Victorian restoration with pieces of Pittsburgh's past. Light nouvelle Calif cuisine. Lunch $3-$7, Dinner $10-$18.

Sidewalk Cafes, Patios

Bunznudders

305 S Craig Street, Oakland. Sun-Thur 8-10, Fri-Sat til 12. **683-9993.**
The white tables on the steps at Craig Square Shops are for happy eaters from this neon-lit ice creamery/bakery with homemade ice cream, yogurt, delicious cinnamon buns, meat/cheese croissants, espresso, lemonade. Inexp.

Cafe Azure

317 S Craig Street, Oakland. Mon-Thur 11:30-9:30, Fri-Sat til 10:30. AE,DC, MC,V. **681-3533.**
Classic dining on sleek outdoor terrace, the sophisticated French cuisine tempered by breezy museum/university atmosphere. Dinner music Wed-Sat. Gourmet Lunch $6-$10, Dinner $13-$20.

Cafe 401

401 Shady Ave, Shadyside. Mon-Sat 11:30-2am. Sun 11-2. AE,MC,V. **361-1900.**
There's a continental feel to this spacious patio (on site of old Red Bull Inn) seating 80 amid greenery 'neath blue/white umbrellas. Inside is a big bar, stylish restaurant with Italian cuisine. Very pleasant summer place. Lunch $5-$8, Dinner $7-$16.

Cafe Sam

5242 Baum Blvd, Oakland. Lunch Mon-Fri 11:30-4, Dinner Sun-Tues 5-10, Wed-Thur til 11, Sat-12. AE,MC,V. **621-2000.**
A rooftop patio with blue awnings and umbrellas complements this charming restaurant with innovative cuisine at good prices. Full dinner menu, late snacks, $4-$13.

PPG "Lemonade Stand"

Bring your lunch to the tree-shaded outdoor tables at PPG Place between Bldgs #2 and #3 off Market Square with a view of the shimmering glass bldgs. The "PPG Pushcart" provides the lemonade.

Cheese Cellar

Shops at Station Square. 7 days 11:30-2am. AE,DC,MC,V. **471-3355.**
A front row seat to watch the Station Sq crowds and horse & buggies go by at charming sidewalk cafe, romantic under lighted trees at night. Entrees, fondues, salads, desserts, $6.50-$13.

Dingbat's City Tavern

Oxford Centre, Downtown. Mon-Thur 11:30-12, Fri-Sat til 2. Bar til 2 daily. AE,MC,V. **392-0350.**
This 'sunken' patio at the foot of Oxford Centre has a Rockefeller Plaza atmosphere, lovely outdoor dining at pastel umbrellaed tables by the terraced waterfall. Great day/night menu— entrees, light fare, salads from $3-$13.

Doc's Grille

5442 Walnut Street, Shadyside. Mon-Fri 5-2am, Sat 4-2am. AE,DC,MC,V. **681-3713.**
Roof patio atop Doc's Place with inside/outside dining, entrees, appetizers, grills, sandwiches. Moderate.

Elbow Room

5744 Ellsworth, Shadyside. Mon-Sat 11-2am. Sun 11-11. AE,MC,V. **441-5222**
Tree-shaded bricked courtyard behind popular restaurant/bar, a favorite haunt of Shadysiders. Friendly, informal with good prices on soup, burgers, salads, sandwiches from $1.50-$8.

Foster's/Holiday Inn

100 Lytton Street, Oakland. 7 days Breakfast/Lunch 6:30am-2, Dinner 5-10. Sun Brunch 10-2. AE,D,MC,V. **682-6200.**
Pleasant outside patio enlivens hotel diningroom; Jazz Fri-Sun. Breakfast/Lunch $4.25-$9.50. Dinner $10-$19.

Froggy's

100 Market Street, Downtown. Wed-Thu 4:30-10, Fri til 2, Sat 7pm-1am. AE,DC, MC,V. **471-3764.**
Small 3rd-fl patio amid the rooftops of downtown, with bright Cinzano umbrellas; a wonderful sundown hideaway, popular after-five spot. No food, just good times, big 4-oz drinks $4 up.

Sidewalk Cafes, Patios

Harris Grill
5747 Ellsworth Avenue, Shadyside. 7 days 11-2am. AE,MC,V. **363-0833.**
An easy mix of people at the tables in front of this popular Shadyside hangout—and the owner is interested in them all. Good cafe food from burgers to moussaka $3-$9. Great place for lunch, dinner or 'night break.' Inside the restaurant, a three-story house, are simple rooms in the Greek manner.

Kane's Courtyard
303 S Craig Street, Oakland. Mon-Fri 7am-6pm, Sat 10:30-6. **683-9988.**
Charming eatery with little white tables in the courtyard of the Gallery Shops & in an indoor skylit patio. Gourmet pastries & coffee—try the chocolate croissant—and some of city's best sandwiches—egg/chicken salad, ham, capicolla on great bread; soup, pasta, seafood salads. Take-out too. $2-$5.

Le Petit Cafe
809 Bellefonte, Shadyside. Tues-Thur 11:30-9:30, Fri-Sat til 10:30. Sun Brunch 11:30-2:30. AE,MC,V. **621-9000.**
Tables from this charming little French bistro spill out onto the sidewalk for romantic trysts and a wonderful look at Shadyside street life. Full gourmet menu. Lunch $5.75-$12, Dinner $7.50-$18.

Paradise on Craig
420 South Craig St, Oakland. Mon-Sat 11:30-9:30. AE,MC,V. **681-9199.**
A few outdoor tables grace this trendy vegetarian eatery, a great place for a quick cappuccino, a piquant Red Zinger iced tea, unique sandwiches and sweets from a bakery case as you watch the Craig St world go by. $1-$5.

Piccolo, Piccolo
1 Wood Street, Downtown. Mon-Sat 11:30-3, 5-10. AE,DC,MC,V. **261-7234.**
Five sidewalk tables front this popular downtown spot. Full lunch on famous Italian & before/after dinner drinks & appetizers. Continental... you can have your cappuccino outside. Lunch $5-$7.50.

First Outdoor Dining On The Mount

Grandview Saloon
1212 Grandview Ave, next to Duquesne Incline, Mt Washington. Sun-Thur 11-12am, Fri-Sat til 1. Bar til 2. AE,DC,MC,V. **431-1400.**
There are two decks overlooking the city in this smashing new restaurant with five levels cantilevered over the hillside and a fantastic view of the Point. The Mount's first outdoor eatery, it's young, casual with a busy bar on 1st level. Sandwiches, salads, burgers, light dinners from $5, mostly under $10.

Pietro's
Hyatt Regency Pittsburgh, Downtown. Patio Lunch Mon-Fri 11-2. Sun Brunch 11-2. AE,DC,MC,V. **288-9326.**
Outdoor cafe overlooking city adds a charming touch to lunch in this sleek, contemporary dining room. Fine dining on N Italian specialties $6-$12.

Promenade Cafe
Pittsburgh Hilton, Gateway Center, Downtown. 7 days 6:30-8pm. AE,DC,MC,V. **391-4600.**
This 'cafe on the park' has a lovely vista of Gateway greenery; luminous light under bright awnings, formally set tables give a garden party feel to one of city's best open air settings. Elegant lunch—light fare, sandwiches, salads $5-$8,—tall, cool drinks add to outdoor delight. Restful al fresco.

Suzie's
130 6th St, Downtown. Mon-Thur 11-9, Fri-Sat til 11. No credit cards. **261-6443.**
Busy little awninged cafe off bustling sidewalk in true Greek tradition. Everything's special—homemade pasta, breads, authentic Greek cuisine. Lunch/Dinner $4-$13. Real favorite!

8

Sidewalk Cafes, Patios

Tramps
212 Blvd of Allies, Downtown. Mon-Thur 11:30-10:30, Fri-Sat til 11:30. Bar til 2. AE,DC,MC,V. **261-1990.**
New addition to this downtown charmer is white-latticed patio off "Dolly's Boudoir," a 2nd-fl party room. Full menu soups, salads, sandwiches, entrees $2-$14.

SUBURBS

Cain's
3239 W Liberty, Dormont. Mon-Thur 4-12am, Fri-Sun 4-1am. AE,D,MC,V. **561-7444.**
A large, relaxing 2nd-fl roof deck at neighborhood favorite specializing in ribs, chicken & pizza, $7-$16.

Chiodo's Tavern
107 W 8th Ave, Homestead. Mon-Sat 10-2am. No credit cards. **461-9307.**
This famous Homestead bar has an outdoor beer garden in true Italian fashion (nestled behind a billboard) for your more outgoing summer nights. Try a 'mystery sandwich'—meats & peppers on a submarine ($2.25 half, $4.25 whole)—and one of 125 beers. Good fun, and host Joe Chiodo himself making sure everyone has a wonderful time. You won't feel lonely.

Hideaway Restaurant
Venango Golf Course, Rt 19, Cranberry Twp. Mon-Sat Lunch 11:30-2:30. Dinner 5-10. Sun 2-7. AE,MC,V. **776-4400.**
Pastoral scene for lunch/dinner with lovely patio overlooking golf course, pavilion for parties. Amer-Continental cuisine. Lunch $5-$7, Dinner $11-$16.

Houlihan's
300 Mall Blvd, Monroeville Mall. Mon-Thur 11-11, Fri-Sat til 12:30. Sun 10-10. AE,DC,MC.V. **373-8520.**
Outdoor patio at colorful, lively restaurant. Sandwiches, light dinners $6-$14 plus weekday Happy Hour specials.

IKEA
2001 Park Manor Blvd, Robinson Twp. Mon-Fri 11-8:30, Sat 10-8:30, Sun til 4:30. D,MC,V. **747-0747.**
Big, wooden patio with a relaxing view of the countryside on the roof of famous furniture store. Hot/cold Swedish delicacies—meatballs, salmon, herring, great desserts. $3-$6.

J J Rose's
One Altoona Place, Mt Lebanon. Mon-Sat Lunch 11-2, Dinner 5-10. AE,D,DC,MC,V. Reser sugg. **344-4604.**
Outdoor deck at this charmer, a 'townhouse' with posh decor/cuisine—crab cakes, beef, fresh seafood. Lunch $7-$15, Dinner $17-$27.

Mad Anthony's Bier Stube
13th & Merchant, Ambridge. Tues-Sat 11-2am. AE,MC,V. **266-3450.**
Outdoor courtyard, rustic atmosphere with German food, thick sandwiches, lite entrees. Live bands Fri-Sat. $3-$12.

Papa J's
200 E Main Street, Carnegie. Mon-Thur 11-10, Fri-Sat til 11. Sun 12-9. AE,DC, MC,V. **429-7272.**
Enjoy veal, pasta, other Italian dishes a small sidewalk cafe, famous for white pizza. $4-$13.

The Pour House
215 E Main Street, Carnegie. Mon-Thur Lunch 11-2. Dinner Mon-Thur 6-1. Fri-Sa 11-1am. D,DC,MC,V. **279-0770.**
Small, fenced-in patio behind little eatery; stews/sausage, lite fare. $4-$5.

TGI Fridays
240 Mall Blvd, Monroeville. 7 days 11:30-2am. AE,D,DC,MC,V. **372-6630.**
Sunny outdoor deck at trendy restaurant with menu of 300 items—everything from quiche to sirloin—$5.65-$12.50. Check out the myriad paraphernalia inside.

9

Sunday Brunch, a popular Pittsburgh pastime, is an economical way to enjoy the city's best cuisine.   Most brunches are buffets with limitless servings and savings on gratuities. Many of the larger brunches require reservations.   Bars open Sunday at 1 pm. Remember, Early Birds get the best brunch!

Aussie's Downunder Pub

4617 Liberty Ave, Bloomfield.
AE,DC,MC,V. **681-2290.**
Hours: 10-2.
Cost: Menu $4-$8.
Complimentary champagne at lively brunch in Australian theme pub. Pancakes, NY strip, "Australian Omelet" with pineapple & BBQ sauce.

Blarney Stone

30 Grant Avenue, Etna at Rt 8 & 28.
AE,DC,MC,V. **781-1666.**
Hours: 11-3:30.
Cost: Menu $7.95; under 12, $4.95; under 2 free.
Hearty home cooking with a Gaelic flavour. Juice, salad bowl, delicious Irish date bread, hearty bean soup plus choice of seven entrees i.e. ham & eggs, chicken a la king, roast lamb, poached salmon, stuffed peppers. Good family fare.

Cheese Cellar

Station Sq. AE,DC,MC,V. **471-3355.**
Hours: 10:30-2:30.
Cost: Buffet $9.95; under 12, 25¢ a yr.
Delightful brunch in rathskeller atmosphere, outdoors in summer; made to order waffles & omelettes, cheese/chocolate fondues, salad/dessert bars. Free champagne mimosa, Bloody Mary or screwdriver. Good and lively.

Duranti's

Park Plaza, 128 N Craig, Oakland.
AE,DC,MC,V. **682-1155.**
Hours: 11-2.
Cost: Menu $5.50.
Attempting array of appetizing breakfast/lunch items—pancakes, French toast, sausage; sandwiches, salads. Good after-church stop.

Foster's

Holiday Inn, 100 Lytton Ave, Oakland.
AE,D,DC,MC,V. **682-6200.**
Hours: 10-2.
Cost: Buffet $10; 6-12, $7; under 6 free.
Bright diningroom, patio in summer. Breakfast items plus beef, ham, seafood, salad, desserts . . . and jazz sound track.

Jazz Brunch
Shadyside Balcony

Theatre Mall, 5520 Walnut, Shadyside. AE,DC,MC,V. **687-0110.**
Hours: 11-3.
Cost: Menu $8-$12 plus $1 buffet.
The popular Balcony Brunch is back with jazz piano/soloist and a wonderful array of food. . .10 entrees—French toast, eggs Benedict, vegetable frittata, big combo breakfast. Plus cold buffet with muffins, vegetables, sweet breads.

Grand Concourse

Station Square. AE,DC,MC,V. **261-1717.**
Hours: 10-2:30.
Cost: $13.95; under 12, $5.95.
Beautiful buffet in elegant setting, live music, gourmet items—smoked/poached salmon, English trifle, fresh juice, hot breads. Take your plate to River Room for wonderful view. Free coffee/hot doughnuts in Gandy Dancer while you wait. A city favorite.

Great Scot

413 S Craig Street, Oakland. Reser.
AE,DC,MC,V. **683-1450.**
Hours: 10-3:30.
Cost: Menu $4.95-$7.95.
Lovely victuals—Amaretto French toast, Belgian waffles, fresh baked breads, eggs Benedict—all served with Scottish potatoes & bacon/ham/sausage. Luscious lunches with Maryland crab cakes, Cajun chicken, sausage/buttermilk biscuits. Oakland favorite.

Houlihan's

Shops at Station Square. Reser.
AE,D,DC,MC,V. **232-0302.**
Hours: 10:30-2:30.
Cost: Semi-buffet $6-$8.
Fashionable crowd in cheery Art Nouveau decor, great Sunday place. Start with mimosa or "Houlihan's Cappuccino"—steamed milk, 6 kinds of booze, chocolate shavings, $3.50. Menu to match—brioche French toast with bacon, strawberries, eggs Benedict, breads, desserts from buffet table.

Le Petit Cafe

Bellefonte/Walnut Sts, Shadyside. Reser 5 or more. AE,MC,V. **621-9000.**
Hours: 11:30-2:30.
Cost: Menu $3.50-$9.
Eggs Benedict, gourmet omelettes join luncheon menu for a delightful brunch in atmospheric cafe. Melon with prosciutto, pates, chicken crepes, Caesar & nicoise salads, shrimp angel hair, crab cakes, wonderful breads, sweet butter, house wine. Sunny way to start the day.

Museum Cafe

Scaife Gallery, The Carnegie. Forbes & Craig. AE,MC,V. **621-3217.**
Hours: 12-2.
Cost: Buffet $7.50 inc bev.
Very pretty buffet with glass-walled view of fountain, marble tables, pink napkins. Eggs, bacon, blueberry pancakes, mini-croissants plus pasta, meat, vegetable dishes. And for dessert pastries, fruit. . . and the museum!

Orchard Cafe

Pittsburgh Vista, Liberty Center, Reser. AE,DC,MC.V. **281-8162.**
Hours: 11-2:30.
Cost: $20.50, 12 & under $8.95; under 5, $3 per foot. Bountiful repast in bright garden setting with pianist/Dixieland band. Gourmet items—smoked fish, pates, seafood, prime meats, unique salads, health foods plus Belgian waffles, fresh fruit, fabulous desserts. . . and glass of champagne. Costly, but city's biggest, best.

Pietro's

Hyatt Regency Pgh, Chatham Ctr. Reser sugg. AE,DC,MC,V. **288-9326.**
Hours: 11-2.
Cost: Buffet $15, 12 and under $7.95; under 5 free.
Hearty North Italian festa beginning with appetizer pizzas, antipasto. Eggs to order, fancy waffles, crepes with walnut sauce, ham, chicken, salmon, orange roughy champagne sauce; great desserts —sundaes, tiramisu, cream puffs. Festive!

Dim-Sum Oriental Brunch
(Light Chinese Appetizers)

Liang's Hunan

Liberty Center, 1001 Liberty Ave, Downtown. Free parking at Pgh Vista. AE,DC,MC,V. **471-1688.**
Hours: 11:30-3:30.
Cost: $2-$12.
A Dim-Sum cart brings delightful variety of appetizers in stunning decor. 40-50 dishes inc pork, beef, dumplings, noodle crepes, fish & chicken in varied sauces.

Oriental Balcony

5846 Forbes Avenue, Squirrel Hill. AE,DC,MC,V. **521-0728.**
Hours: 11-3.
Cost: $2-$10.
Oriental specialties & desserts— fluffy shrimp & meat dumplings, fried wonton, shrimp toast, fried chicken wings, egg rolls, soup & oodles of noodles in relaxing atmosphere.

Peking Royal Kitchen

2018 Murray Avenue, Squirrel Hill. No credit cards. **421-1920.**
Hours: 11:30-2 (also Sat).
Cost: $2-$10.
Choose from 36 Chinese delicacies at this weekend brunch—baby pork buns, hot sesame noodles, rice dumplings, baby spare ribs, steaming pots of tea.

And A Thai Buffet. . .

Thai Place

775 Freeport Road, Harmarville. AE,MC,V. **274-9222.**
Hours: 11-2.
Cost: Buffet $7.95; under 12 $3.95.
Delightfully different Thai specialties—soup, noodles, veggies, curry appetizers, cashew/sweet & sour chicken, pork, curry, Thai omelet—a thin crepe with pork/vegetables—and Thai Toast with chicken/shrimp batter.

9

BRUNCH/SUNDAY

Suburbs

Sunday Brunch At Heinz Hall

A music lover's special is Brunch in the **Mozart Room** two hours before Sunday afternoon performances only (around 12 or 12:30.) There's a breakfast buffet plus meats, vegetables, fish, salads, fruit and dessert . . . and you won't have to rush to the performance. All credit cards accepted, $13.95. Reservations a must. **392-4887.**

Reflections

Sheraton Hotel, Station Sq, AE,DC, MC,V. **261-2000.**
Hours: 10-3.
Cost: Buffet $14.95 inc bev, 6-12 half price, under 6 free.
Sunny brunch with spectacular riverfront view; made-to-order omelettes, beef, fish, chicken, pasta, big salad bar, sundaes. Nice Sunday afternoon.

Southern Platter

6947 Kelly Street, Homewood. No credit cards. **441-7217.**
Hours: 1-6.
Cost: Dinner Buffet $7.95 inc bev, 10 & under 1/2 price.
Sunday "soul" buffet—roast beef, Southern fried/smothered chicken, Virginia ham, fish, greens, black-eyed peas, yams, soup/salad bar. Summer barbecue under tent. Homewood tradition.

The Terrace Room

Westin William Penn, Mellon Sq. Reser 5 or more. AE,DC,MC,V. **553-5065.**
Hours: 10-2 (also holidays).
Cost: Buffet $17.95, 12 & under $12.95, 4 & under free.
Glass of champagne/white zinfandel starts off brunch in this splendid room off the grand lobby with fresh flowers, piano music and an array of 30 gourmet dishes. Eggs Benedict, pates, fresh fruit, smoked fish, roast beef and famous William Penn Cheesecake. Elegant.

SUBURBS

Chestnut Ridge Inn

Rt 22, Blairsville. Reser sugg. AE,D,DC,MC,V. **459-7191.**
Hours: 11-2.
Cost: Menu $8.95, 12 & under $4.95.
Belgian waffles with 20 toppings, omelettes made to order, chef's French bread, cakes & pies, salads, vegetables bacon, sausage, fish/meat specialties in beautiful country club setting.

Cross Keys

599 Dorseyville Road, Fox Chapel. Reser sugg. MC,V. **963-8717.**
Hours: 11-2.
Cost: Semi-buffet $7.95; under 10, $4.95.
Beautiful, woodland drive on a sunny day whets your appetite for charming brunch in quaint, restored 1800's inn. Salad & dessert bar, omelettes, eggs Benedict, seafood, soup, fruit, cheese, delicious salads, coffee cakes. Lovely bargain.

Dingbat's

Fox Chapel: Waterworks Shopping Center. **781-7727.** Robinson Twp; Towne Centre. **787-7010.** AE,D,DC,MC,V.
Hours: 10-2.
Cost: Buffet $9.95, under 12 free.
Lavish spread—including made-to-order omelettes, eggs Benedict, crabmeat, shrimp, smoked sable, mackerel, lox, pepper steak & rice, Napoleons, cheese cake, trifle. A winner!

Elephant Restaurant & Bar

5242 Clairton Blvd, Rt 51, Pleasant Hills. Reser sugg. AE,MC,V. **885-0151.**
Hours: 10-2:30.
Cost: Buffet $9.95, under 12 free with adult.
Complete buffet in trendy favorite—omelettes, waffles, French toast, eggs Benedict, salad, fajitas, ham, beef, chicken specialties plus bottomless glass of champagne—$2.95.

Fox Chapel Yacht Club
1366 Old Freeport Road, Fox Chapel.
Reser sugg. AE,MC,V. **963-8881.**
Hours: 10-2.
Cost: Buffet $11.95; under 10, $5.95.
Dining with a pleasant river view. Vast array of breakfast/lunch dishes—10 hot including carved beef/ham, 30 salads, fresh veggies, fruit cheese, 25 desserts. Good Sunday experience.

Greenery
Holiday Inn, Greentree. AE,CB,D,DC, MC,V. **922-8100.**
Hours: 10-2.
Cost: Buffet $10.95, under 12 free, Sr Citizens $9.95.
Lovely pink and green decor for hearty chicken, carved beef, ham plus eggs to order, salads, juice, dessert bar.

L & N Seafood Grill
Galleria, Mt Lebanon. Reser. AE,DC, MC,V. **343-6855.**
Hours: 11-2.
Cost: Buffet $8.95. Children's menu $1.95.
Unique brunch with a seafood flair. First choose your egg dish or omelette to order, then to the buffet for smoked salmon, spiced shrimp, soup, seafood, chicken/fruit salad, six warm dishes and wonderful biscuits, desserts.

Max & Erma's
1910 Cochran Road, Greentree. AE,D, DC,MC,V. **344-4449.**
Hours: 10-2:30
Buffet: $9.95; 8 to 12, $5.95; under 8, 50¢ per year.
Casual, homey. Ham, chicken, beef, smoked salmon, peel & eat shrimp, oysters Rockefeller, salads, mousse, fruit.

Bach, Beethoven & Brunch
Watch for **Pittsburgh Center for Arts** classical Sunday brunches 10-12 thru July on the lawn of Mellon Park. You can bring your own basket or purchase from gourmet booth there $1-$5. **361-0873.**

Holiday Inn Buffets
Servico Holiday Inns
Airport: Beers School Rd. **262-3600.**
Greentree: 402 Holiday Dr **922-8100.**
N Hills: McKnight Road **366-5200.**
Meadowlands, Washington **222-6200.** *Braddock Hills: Brinton* **247-2700.** *AE,DC,MC,V.*
Hours: 10-2.
Cost: $9.95-$12.95, special rates for child, Sr Citizen.
Sunday brunch a specialty at these Holiday Inns. Tables laden with breakfast/lunch dishes, pleasant surroundings.

Oxford Dining Room
Radisson Hotel, Monroeville Mall. AE,DC,MC,V. **373-7300.**
Hours: 9:30-2.
Cost: Buffet $13.25; ages 6-12, $6.25; under 5, $4.25.
Popular family brunch in warm Colonial room with four hot entrees, breakfast goodies, omelettes, plus steamship round of beef, chicken, seafood, fabulous desserts—mousse, trifle.

Pastel's
Royce Hotel, Thorn Run Rd, Coraopolis, near Airport. **262-2400.**
Hours: 10-2.
Cost: $10.95; 5-12, $5.95; Sr Cit $9.95. Omelettes, waffles, breakfast items plus dinner inc roast beef, ham in lovely mauve/pink decor.

Prime House
Greentree Marriott, Greentree. AE,D,DC,MC,V. **922-8400.**
Hours: 8-2.
Cost: Buffet $9.95, 12 & under $4.95, under 5 free.
Appetizing breakfast buffet in plush room with fruit, biscuits, omelettes made to order, eggs Benedict, blintzes, bread pudding, pies, mousse.

9

BRUNCH/SUNDAY

Suburbs

River Room
Sewickley Country Inn, 801 Ohio River Blvd. AE,D,DC,MC,V. **741-4300.**
Hours: 10-2
Cost: Buffet $10.95, Sr Cit & ages 6-12, under 6 free.
Charming atmosphere for roast beef, fish, ham, pasta plus Belgian waffles, omelettes, sundae bar.

Shajor
422 McMurray Road, Bethel Park. AE,MC,V. Reser sugg. **833-4800.**
Hours: 10-2.
Cost: Menu $6-$15.
Creative menu in elegant gray-mauve contemporary restaurant. Seafood, steak & eggs, "Eggs Blackstone," French toast with apples/apricots.

Tremont Cafe
Cranberry Sheraton Inn, Mars. AE,D,DC, MC,V. **776-6900.**
Hours: 10-2.
Cost: Buffet $11.95, 6-12 $6.95; under 5 free, Sr Citizens $8.50.
Pleasant surroundings for big buffet— ham, beef, spare ribs, seafood newburg, omelettes, Belgian waffles, salads, fruits & ice cream bar.

One of Best in US!
Horn of Plenty
Rt 8, 20 mi from Pgh. MC,V. **898-3030.**
Hours: Sun 11:30-8:30 (Tues-Sat 4:30-8:30).
Cost: Sat-Sun Buffet $10.50; 5-10, $4.50, under 5 free. (Tues-Fri $7.95; under 10, $4.50.)
Rated one of the three top buffets in the US & Canada by Mobil Travel Guide, **Horn of Plenty's** bountiful table features 55-75 items in pleasant diningroom away from city bustle. Roast beef, baked chicken/stuffing, ham & fish, delicious French fried mushrooms, homemade soup, mousse, bread pudding, cake. A family feast worth the ride out of town!

Brunch All Week At Le Peep
Le Peep
Wilkins: 3498 Wm Penn Hwy. **825-0725.** *S Hills: 2101 Greentree Rd.* **276-3525.** *7 days 7-2:30pm. AE,DC,D,MC,V.*
You can brunch all day everyday at these charming eateries...on pampered eggs, strawberry whipped-cream pancakes, frittatas, French toast...plus lunch. Breakfast lover's dream. $2-$6.50.

TGI Friday's
Monroeville: 240 Mall Blvd **372-6630.** *Bethel Park: 2800 Oxford Dr* **854-5610.** *McCandless: 5300 Corporate Dr.* **367-1101.** *AE,DC,MC,V.*
Hours: 11:30-3.
Cost: Menu $4.25-$6.75, Child $2.
Lively brunch in colorful Art Nouveau; croissants, 3-layer omelettes, Belgian waffles, pecan French toast, Mexican, 'filet mignon Benedict' & cocktails.

Valentine's
Howard Johnson, Wm Penn Highway, Monroeville. AE,D,MC,V. **372-1022.**
Hours: 10-2.
Cost: $8.95, 6-12 $4.95; Sr Citizens $6.95.
Breakfast items plus hot dishes, pastries, desserts, beautiful surroundings.

Vernon's
South Hills Village, Ft Couch Rd, Bethel Park. Reser 6 or more. AE,DC,MC,V. **531-3688.**
Hours: 10-3.
Cost: Buffet $9.95; under 12, 35¢ yr.
Free Champagne/Bloody Mary/Screwdriver at big brunch long on breakfast items—eggs, homemade waffles—plus meats, seafood, salad/sundae bar.

BUDGET BRUNCHES

Amarraca
Supermarket adjacent to Northway Mall.
AE,MC,V. **366-9700.**
Hours: 10-3:30.
Cost: $5.89, 2-10 yrs half price, Sr Citizens 10% disc.
Fresh from larder of this super-modern market—fruit, salads, chicken, beef, seafood, breakfast. Stay on to shop.

Bagel Nosh
5885 Forbes, Squirrel Hill. MC,V.
521-5834.
Hours: 8-9 pm.
Cost: Menu $2-$8.
Brunch on your own from the menu at this popular deli. 10 kinds of bagels with eggs, cheese, as French toast, noshes, with pastrami, corn beef. Full deli menu.

Eat'n Park
53 city, suburban sites. Some take credit cards. **923-1000.**
Hours: 11-2.
Cost: Buffet $5.95, 10 & under half price.
Breakfast items plus hot entrees—scrambled eggs, chicken, ham, biscuits. Go early.

Elbow Room
5744 Ellsworth Ave, Shadyside.
AE,MC,V. **441-5222.**
Hours: 11-3.
Cost: Menu $1.50-$6.
Informal Shadyside brunch—omelettes, soups, burgers, salads—summer patio.

Harley Hotel
Off Rodi Road, Penn Hills.
AE,D,DC,MC,V. **244-1600.**
Hours: 9-12.
Cost: Buffet $5.50, 10 & under $2.95.
A big breakfast buffet in Rivers Three diningroom with pleasant windowfront view. Fresh fruit, cream cheese/bagels, eggs, hash browns, bacon, sausage, pastries. For the breakfast lover.

IKEA
Robinson Twp: Robinson Town Centre.
AE,D,DC,MC,V. **747-0747.**
Hours: 11-2.
Cost: Buffet $4.50; under 10, $1.99.
Brunch with a Swedish touch in popular furniture store's gourmet deli. Bacon, sausage, omelettes, Swedish meatballs, desserts, delicious pastries.

King's Family Restaurants
Various suburban sites. Some take credit cards.
Hours: Open 24 hours.
Cost: $4-$7.
Good family brunch in cheerful surroundings. Famous for all-day breakfast— waffles, hot cakes, eggs plus dinners. Special—bacon, eggs, hot cakes $1.89.

Max & Erma's
5533 Walnut St, Shadyside. AE,CB, D,DC,MC,V. **681-5775.**
Hours: 11:30-2:30.
Cost: $4-$6.95.
Popular, brassy 2nd floor. Omelettes, quiche, eggs Benedict, menu lunch items, make-your-own-sundae & pasta bars.

Pamela's
Squirrel Hill: 5813 Forbes. **422-9457.**
Oakland: 3703 Forbes. **683-4066.**
Shadyside: 5527 Walnut. **683-1003.**
No credit cards.
Hours: 7 days 6:30am-7pm, Walnut 8-7pm.
Cost: Menu $2.95-$6.95.
Long lines for breakfast specials at these favorite eateries—sausage, bacon at low prices, best pancakes in town; sandwiches.

What's Cookin' at Casey's
608 Allegheny River Blvd, Oakmont. MC,V. **826-1400.**
Hours: 8-2.
Cost: Menu $3-$5.
Cozy, country breakfast til 2. Hot cakes, eggs, French toast, omelettes with 3 fillings, corned beef & hash plus lunch menu.

9

Sunday Guide

These listings include only restaurants in major city areas. For suburban restaurants
check the Best of the Suburbs Section.
Code: B-Brunch, L-Lunch, D-Dinner, LS-Late Supper.
Price Index: Inex-$10 & under, Mod-$10-$20, Exp-$20 & over.

Name	Address	Phone	Cuisine	Price	B	L	D	LS	Hours
DOWNTOWN/STRIP									
Brandy's	Penn & 24th	566-1000	Amer	Mod-Exp			D	LS	3-11
Chinatown Inn	522 Third	261-1292	Chin	Inex-Mod			D	LS	2-11
Common Plea	308 Ross	281-5140	Amer	Mod-Exp			D		5-10:30
Orchard Cafe	Vista Intl	281-8162	Eur-Am	Mod	B		D		7-10:30
Jakes Above Sq	430 Market	338-0900	Cont	Mod-Exp			D		4-10
Mick McGuire's	Market Sq	752-7526	Irish	Inex-Mod	B	L	D		8-7
Pietro's	Hyatt Pgh	288-9326	Ital	Mod-Exp	B	L	D	LS	6-30-11
Primanti's	46 18th St	263-2142	Amer	Inexp	B	L	D	LS	24 hr
Promenade Cafe	Hilton Hotel	391-4600	Amer	Mod	B	L	D		6:30-8
Ruddy Duck	Bigelow Apts	281-3825	Amer	Mod		L	D		11-10
Ruth's Chris	PPG #6	391-4800	Amer	Mod-Exp			D		5-9
Spaghetti Whse	2601 Smallman	261-6511	Ital	Inex-Mod		L	D		12-10
Sterling's	Hilton Hotel	391-4600	Cont	Mod-Exp			D		5:30-11
Terrace Room	Westin Wm Penn	553-5235	Cont	Mod-Exp	B	L	D	LS	6:30-11
Top of Triangle	USX Bldg	471-4100	Amer	Mod-Exp			D		4-9
STATION SQUARE									
Bobby Rubino's	Commerce Court	642-7427	Amer	Inex-Mod		L	D		11-9
Cheese Cellar	Freight House	471-3355	Amer	Inex-Mod	B		D	LS	10:30-11
Gandy Dancer	Landmark Bldg	261-1717	Amer	Inex		L	D	LS	2:30-10
Grand Concourse	Landmark Bldg	261-1717	Amer	Mod-Exp	B		D		10:00-8:30
Houlihan's	Freight House	232-0302	Amer	Mod	B	L	D	LS	10:30-11
Kiku's	Commerce Court	765-3200	Jap	Mod		L	D		12-10
Reflections	Sheraton Hotel	261-2000	Amer	Mod-Exp	B				10-3
River Cafe	Freight House	765-2795	Amer	Mod		L	D		11:30-10
Sesame Inn	Freight House	281-8282	Chin	Mod		L	D		12-9
Tequila Junct	Freight House	261-3265	Mex-Am	Inex-Mod		L	D		12-10
Waterfall Terr	Sheraton Hotel	261-2000	Amer	Mod	B	L	D	LS	6am-12
MT WASHINGTON									
City Deli	1216 Grandview	481-8585	Amer	Inex		L			10-6
Georgetowne Inn	1230 Grandview	481-4424	Amer	Mod			D		4-10
Grandview Saloon	1212 Grandview	431-1400	Amer	Inex		L	D	LS	11-12
LeMont	1114 Grandview	431-3100	Cont	Exp			D		4-9:30
SOUTH SIDE/DORMONT									
Bankok House	3233 W Liberty	341-8888	Thai	Mod			D		5-10
Beehive	14th/Carson	488-4483	Coffee	Inex		(24 hr til 1 am)			
Cafe Allegro	51 S 12th	481-7788	Fr/Ital	Mod			D		4:30-9:30
Cain's	3239 W Liberty	561-7444	Amer	Inex-Mod			D	LS	4-1
Chinese-Carson	1506 E Carson	431-1717	Chin	Mod			D		4-10
Hunan Gourmet	1209 E Carson	488-8100	Chin	Inex-Mod			D		3-9:30
J J's	21st & Carson	481-2900	Amer	Mod			D		4:30-8:30
Mario's Saloon	1514 E Carson	381-5610	Ital	Inex-Mod		L	D		1-10
Moriarity's	1832 E Carson	431-9387	Amer	Inex-Mod			D		2-8
Muffy's	2024 Sarah St	431-2040	Amer	Inex-Mod		L	D		12-10
Pgh Steak Co	1924 E Carson	381-5505	Amer	Mod			D	LS	4-11
Rumors	1828 E Carson	431-4500	Amer	Mod			D		4-10
Sarah's	52 S 10th St	431-9307	Slavic	Mod-Exp			D		4-8

Sunday Guide

Name	Address	Phone	Cuisine	Price	B	L	D	LS	Hours
NORTH SIDE									
Billy's Bistro	1720 Lowrie	231-9277	Amer	Inex		L	D	LS	11:30-10
Maggie Mae's	110 Federal	231-8181	Amer	Inex			D		3-9:30
Max's Tavern	Middle & Suismon	231-1899	German	Inex		L	D		11-8
Mr Lee's Garden	415 E Ohio St	321-4888	Chin	Inex	B		D		11-10
Park House	403 E Ohio St	231-0551	Amer	Inex			D	LS	5:30-2am
OAKLAND									
Ali Baba	404 S Craig	682-2829	Mid-East	Inex			D		4-10
Cafe Sam	5242 Baum Blvd	621-2000	Cont-Amer	Mod			D		5-10
Darbar	4619 Centre	687-0515	Indian	Inex-Mod			D		5-10
Duranti's	128 N Craig	682-1155	Ame	Mod	B		D		11-8
Foster's	100 Lytton	682-6200	Amer	Mod-Exp	B	L	D	LS	7:30-11
Great Scot	413 S Craig	683-1450	Amer	Mod	B		D		10-10
Jacqueline's	4415 5th Ave	683-4525	French	Exp			D		5-9
Khalils	4757 Baum	683-4757	Mid-East	Inex			D		4-10
More	214 N Craig	621-2700	Cont	Mod-Exp			D		5-9
Museum Cafe	4400 Forbes	622-3225	Amer	Inex	B				12-2
Samreny's	4808 Baum	682-1212	Mid-East	Inex-Mod			D		4:30-10:30
SHADYSIDE									
Artery	5847 Ellsworth	361-9473	Amer	Inex-Mod			D		5-10
Cafe 401	401 Shady Ave	361-1900	Amer	Mod		L	D	LS	11:30-11
Cafe Giovanni	Walnut/Aiken	621-8881	Amer	Mod-Exp			D		4:30-9
Cappy's	5431 Walnut	621-1188	Amer	Inex		L	D	LS	12-2am
China Palace	5440 Walnut	687-7423	Chin	Mod			D		2-9:30
Elbow Room	5744 Ellsworth	441-5222	Amer	Inex	B	L	D	LS	11-11
Hotlicks	5520 Walnut	683-2583	Amer/Ribs	Inex-Mod			D		4:30-9
Harris Grill	5747 Ellsworth	363-0833	Gr/Amer	Inex-Mod			D	LS	11-2am
Jimmy Tsang's	5700 Centre	661-4226	Chin	Inex-Mod			D		3:30-9
Le Petit Cafe	809 Bellefonte	621-9000	French	Mod	B		D		11:30-8:30*
Max & Erma's	5533 Walnut	681-5775	Amer	Inex	B	L	D		11:30-10
Minutello's	226 Shady	361-9311	Ital	Inex-Mod		L	D		1-9
Pamela's	5527 Walnut	683-1003	Amer	Inex	B	L			9-2
Pasta Piatto	736 Bellefonte	621-5547	Ital	Mod			D		4:30-9
Shdyse Balcony	5520 Walnut	687-0110	Amer	Inex-Mod	B				11-3
Szechuan Gourm	709 Bellefonte	683-1763	Chin	Inex-Mod			D		4:30-10
SQUIRREL HILL									
Bagel Nosh	5885 Forbes	521-5834	Deli	Inex	B	L	D		8-8
Bentley's	5608 Wilkins	421-4880	Amer	Mod			D		5-9
Gullifty's	1922 Murray	521-8222	Amer	Inex-Mod	B	L	D	L	10-12
Oriental Balc	5846 Forbes	521-0728	Chin	Inex-Mod	B	L	D		11-10
Pamela's	5813 Forbes	422-9457	Amer	Inexp	B	L			9-2
Peking Kitchen	2018 Murray	421-1920	Chin	Inex-Mod	B	L	D		11-10
Poli's	2607 Murray	521-6400	Amer	Mod-Exp			D		1-9:30
Rhoda's	2201 Murray	521-4555	Deli	Inex	B	L	D	L	7-11
Suzie's	1704 Shady	422-8066	Greek	Inex-Mod			D		4-9
Sweet Basil	5882 Forbes	421-9958	Amer	Inex-Mod			D		4-9

*closed 2:30-5:30

9

Early Birds

You can savour some of the city's best cuisine at these 'Early Bird' dinners with special prices on complete meals— usually at earlier hours. A great way to eat the best for less!

Gandy Dancer
Landmarks Bldg, Station Square. AE,DC,MC,V. **261-1717.**
Hours: Mon-Thur 11:30-11pm, Fri til 1. Fabulous seafood bargains half price weekdays. Check for bargains on tub of mussels, blue crab, shrimp, oysters, clams, fish sandwich, $3 up. And fun besides. (See Review)

Grand Concourse
Landmarks Bldg, Station Square. AE,DC,MC,V. Reser. **261-1717.**
Hours: Mon-Sat 4:30-6, Sun 4:30-9.
Cost: $9.95-$15.
Elegant dinner with appetizer/salad/ soup, dessert & beverage at one of city's top restaurants with choice of four fish, 11 other entrees plus sunset view of the river. (See Review)

Klein's
330 4th Ave, Downtown. AE,DC,MC,V. **232-3311.**
Hours: Mon-Fri 3-6, Sat 4:30-6.
Cost: $7.95-$12.95.
Complete dinner with appetizer, vegetable/potato, salad, dessert, beverage. Here's your chance to eat at Pgh's famous seafood house at half the cost...salmon, scrod, lemon sole, 1-lb lobster, petite steak, fried clams, lobster tail, crab cakes, shrimp, casseroles. Wonderful buy.

Poli's
2607 Murray Ave, Squirrel Hill. AE,DC,MC,V. **521-6400.**
Hours: Tues-Sat 3-6.
Cost: $6-$8.50.
Seafood lovers crowd these early birds. Choice five entrees with seafood items like lemon sole, lobster newburg, scallops, shrimp plus chicken cordon bleu, salmon croquettes, Swiss steak—with soup, salad, vegetable. Good value.

Economy—First Class

Accolades to **Duranti's,** 128 Craig St, for better-than-average cuisine at super prices for the Oakland 'apartment set.' Good lunches $3.95-$6, dinners $7.95-$11 and a $6.95 Early Bird 7 days from 5-9 make for economical eating here. Satisfying traditional dishes plus old favorites i.e. Turkey Devonshire, Hot Roast Beef/Turkey Sandwich, homemade soups. Delivery immediate area 2-5 pm—order before 4. **682-1155.**

SUBURBS

Eastwood Inn
4268 Verona Road, East Hills. MC,V. **241-4700.**
Hours: Mon-Fri 4-6.
Cost: $4.95-$6.50.
Wide variety of pastas, fish, chicken, eggplant Parmesan with salad & bev.

Fairchild's
Jonnet Bldg, Monroeville. AE,D,DC, MC,V. **372-1511.**
Hours: Mon-Sat 5-6:30.
Cost: $9.95-$12.95.
Nightly special at this rooftop room— crab cake imperial, scrod citrus, chicken cordon bleu, including salad, vegetable and potato.

Mama Lena's
Library Rd, Rt 88, Castle Shannon. AE,DC,MC,V. **884-8484.**
Hours: Tues-Sun 4-6:30.
Cost: $7.80.
Twelve daily specials—Mama's famous spaghetti, scrod, chicken marsala, chopped sirloin—with salad, vegetable & potato/pasta. Good buy.

Oxford at Radisson
Radisson Hotel, Monroeville Mall, AE,DC,MC,V. **373-7300**
Hours: Sun-Thur 5-7.
Cost: $11.95.
Four choices—prime rib, chicken, orange roughy, scrod/shrimp—with salad, veg, potato, ice cream/sherbet.

BUDGET EATS - CITY

Apollo Cafe
429 Forbes Ave, Downtown. Mon-Fri 7am-3pm. No credit cards. **471-3033.**
Unique gourmet fast food—quiche, homemade soup, great shish-kabob, sandwiches, desserts $5-$7. Breakfast $2 up.

Dave's Lunch
237 Third Ave, Downtown. Mon-Fri 6:30am-5:30pm. No credit cards. **391-2409.**
Favorite downtown lunchroom, $1.35 breakfast, good soup, chili, burgers with onions & hot peppers. $1.65-$4.

Federal Building Cafeteria
2nd fl, Grant/Liberty, Downtown. Mon-Fri 6:30am-4pm. No credit cards. **261-3660.**
Breakfast, lunch with lots of choices — soup, sandwiches, salad bar, entrees with soup/salad, potato, veggie $3-$4.

First Presbyterian Church
316 6th Ave, Downtown. Mon-Fri 11am-1:30pm. **471-3436.**
Popular daily business lunch— homemade soups, salads, sandwiches, cakes, pies 75¢-$2. Daily entree i.e. stuffed pork chops, Swiss steak, chicken breast with potato & veg. $2-$2.50. Great buy!

Gateway Cafeteria
Gateway #2, lower level, Downtown. Breakfast 7-10, Lunch 11-2. **261-9671.**
Underground favorite with downtown workers, shoppers. Delicious breakfast/lunch, hot & cold entrees, sandwiches, salads, homemade desserts, $1-$4.

Poor Man's Dream
Super buffet at **Amarraca**, a plus modern market at Northway Mall, features 80 items—meats, cheeses, casseroles, desserts Mon-Sat, Lunch 11-3:30, $4.89 & Dinner 4-7:30, $6.89. AE,MC,V. **366-9700.**

McCrory's
318 5th Ave, Downtown. Mon-Sat 9:30-6, Mon-Thur til 7. D,MC,V. **281-1969.**
Old-fashioned coffee shop, booths or counter. Breakfast thru dinner—soup & sandwich, burgers, great salads, nourishing entrees i.e. meatloaf/turkey. $2-$5.

Nicky's
Grant Bldg Lobby. Mon-Fri 7-4. No credit cards. **391-3900.**
A Grant Street institution. Busy breakfast from continental to Belgian Waffles, $3. Lunch $2-$5 for sandwiches/ omelettes.

Original Oyster House
20 Market Sq, Downtown, Mon-Sat 9am-11, Sit down 10-6 **566-7925.** *Also: 801 Liberty, Mon-Fri 10:30-7, Sat 10:30-5* **566-9630.** *3710 Forbes, Oakland, Mon-Sat 8-9, Sun 10-8* **687-9043.** *No credit cards.*
Historic old saloon with city's best fish sandwich $2.40; Seafood Platter with fish/shrimp/crab, fries & slaw—a-meal-in-itself for $4.40; oysters, clams, buttermilk, beer. Old Pgh at its best. You can eat outside in Market Sq.

10

Palmer's
Gulf Bldg, Seventh, 7-3:30 **471-0511**; *Gateway #4, 7-6:30* **471-5366**; *Porter Bldg, Grant, 6-3* **391-3483**; *437 Smithfield, 6-8* **471-0514**; *Alcoa Bldg, 6-3:30* **471-0553.** *No credit cards.*
A Pgh institution for good quick breakfast/lunch $1-$5.50. Sandwiches, salads, daily hot specials i.e. stuffed pork chops, sauerkraut & wieners, chicken pot pie $2.50-$5.50. Good buy, fast service.

Park House
403 East Ohio St, North Side. Mon-Fri 11:30-2, Sat-Sun 5:30-2. AE,DC,MC,V. **231-0551.**
Old-time barroom atmosphere, good food—the highest at $5.95. Shrimp, nachos, appetizers, salads, soups, sandwiches hot & cold; good selection of imported beer, coffees.

BUDGET EATS

Primanti Brothers

Strip: 46 18th St. Mon-Sat 24 hrs. Sun 8am-11pm. **263-2142.** *Oakland: 3803 Forbes. Mon-Thur 10am-3am, Fri-Sat til 4am, Sun noon-3am,* **621-4444.**
Famous hearty food including meal-in-one sandwiches with kolbassi, pastrami and fries and slaw in the sandwich. Good antipasto, chili $2.75-$6.

Richest Restaurant

140 6th, Downtown. Mon-Sat 9-9, later Heinz Hall events. AE,DC,MC,V. **471-7799.**
Favorite downtown deli. Blintzes, hot pastrami, Reubens, great corned beef, 'matzo ball' soup, $3-$6. Platters $5.25 & Early Bird dinners from 4-8, $6.75.

Tic-Toc

First floor, Kaufmann's Dept Store. Store charge only. **232-2680.**
Some of the best coffee shop food in town. 99¢ breakfast, great ham salad, chopped olive/cheese, delicious ice cream, unique coffee soda. $1-$5.

Trinity Episcopal Church

325 Oliver. Mon-Fri 11-2. **355-0461.**
Open since 1914, this church lunchroom offers daily home cooking i.e. veal Parmesan, salisbury steak, meatloaf with vegetables $2.70. Soups, sandwiches, homemade desserts, 55¢-$1.60.

EAST END

Eat 'n Park

44 locations, most open 24 hrs. No credit cards. **923-1000.**
'Fast' family eatery cut above the rest. Breakfast anytime, burgers, salads, entrees in $4-$5 range. Big buffet $5.95. Sat-Sun Brunch 11-2:30, $4.45.

Howard Johnson

3401 Blvd of Allies, Oakland. MC,V. **681-6300.**
Dependable for locals, travelers. Great blueberry pancakes, hot dogs on toasted buns, famous ice cream, $3-$9.

Italian Oven

5859 Ellsworth, Shadyside. Sun-Thur 11-10, Fri & Sat til 11. MC,V. **361-6836.**
Popular new "up" cafe with crisp pizzas from wood-fired brick oven, 23 pastas $4.25-$8.50. Kids love it.

Pamela's

Oakland: 3703 Forbes. 7 days 6:30am-7 **683-4066.** *Shadyside: 5527 Walnut. 7 days 8-4.* **683-1003.** *Squirrel Hill: 5813 Forbes. 7 days 8-4.* **422-9457.**
Casual East End breakfast/lunch favorite. Good low prices for best hot cakes in town; sandwiches, light fare. $2-$5.

Paski's

2533 Penn, Strip. AE,DC,MC,V. **566-2782.**
Friday night Fish Fry 5:30-10 is a big draw, all-you-can-eat broiled or fried fish with potatoes, slaw for $6.95.

Rhoda's

2201 Murray, Squirrel Hill. Sun-Thur 7-11, Fri-Sat til 12. **521-4555.**
Real deli food, homemade soup, potato pancakes, Reuben platter, stuffed kishke, chicken, meatloaf dinners under $5. Kids Menu $2 & under.

Ritter's Diner

5221 Baum Blvd, Oakland. 7 days 24 hours. No credit cards. **682-4852.**
A Pgh tradition for good solid food around the clock. Breakfast bargains—buckwheat cakes, real maple syrup, sandwiches under $2, entrees $3-$5.

11

Where do Pittsburgh executives/professionals dine in their on-the-job hours? At a handful of traditional restaurants, generally with comfortable, club-like atmosphere conducive to a working meal or a relaxing end to a business meeting. Or they lunch in executive dining rooms and the city's private membership clubs. Many of these restaurants assume a more festive air at night-- ideal for introducing visiting executives to an extraordinary side of the city.

Brandy's

2323 Penn Avenue, Strip District. AE,DC,MC,V. **566-1000.**

A unique decor, brick & hanging greenery and an out-of-city feel make this a business favorite for dining & relaxing. There's a bar with real Pittsburgh flavour, and private 'board rooms' for larger meetings in a warm, informal atmosphere. An added plus to the veal/seafood menu are delicious Brandyburgers and liqueur ice-cream desserts. A good place to further business friendships. (The Brandy Van picks up groups from downtown by reservation.)
Lunch: Mon-Sat 11-4 ($4-$8).
Dinner: Mon-Sat til 2. Sun til 12 ($10-$15).

The Carlton

One Mellon Bank Center, Downtown. AE,MC,V. Reser. **391-4099.**

This is a handsome, burnished room with lots of private space, a quiet, unruffled atmosphere for confidential conversations. At night it takes on a more festive air. . .with free limo service to and from Heinz Hall and Benedum Center by reservation. The menu is traditional—grilled meats, chops, seafood, with business luncheon specials. Free dinner parking in One Mellon Bank Center.
Lunch: Mon-Fri 11:30-3 ($8-$16).
Dinner: Mon-Thur 5-10, Fri & Sat til 11 ($16-$24).

Christopher's

1411 Grandview Avenue, Mt Washington. Reser. AE,D,DC,MC,V. **381-4500.**

The right site for decision-making at the highest level with the lighted city for background and inspiration. Superb views from glass walls on three sides, an entire wall made of coal, a Sports Hall of Fame and a mini-museum of Pittsburgh memorabilia provide a showcase for Pittsburgh products. Visitors leave with a wonderful impression. Valet parking.
Dinner: Mon-Thur 5-11, Fri & Sat til 12am ($18-$35).

City Club

119 6th St, Downtown. AE,MC,V. **391-3300.**

This downtown athletic club's Cafe Restaurant, open to the public for lunch, provides a private setting for a quick repast for many businessmen/women. For members it's a convenient stop after a noon-day workout. The serene two-level room has a unique glass-wall view of the club pool and courts. There's an inexpensive salad bar, soup, sandwiches. . .and 25 imported beers. You can continue your talk at the bar (open til 10:30 in the evening).
Lunch: Mon-Fri 11:30-4, Light Menu 4-8 ($3-$7).

The Colony

Greentree & Cochran Roads, Mt Lebanon. Reser. AE,DC,MC,V. **561-2060.**

The best steak in town—and an atmosphere for relaxing—or business talk—by the open grills of this informal room. It's mellow, comfortable, an ideal site for beginning or finishing up business, then relaxing with nightly entertainment in the Lounge. A weary executive will appreciate your thought.
Dinner: Monday-Sat 5-11:30, Sun 4-9 ($20-$27).

Common Plea

308 Ross Street, Downtown. Lunch reser suggested. AE,DC,MC,V. **281-5140.**

An interesting second floor room with a Renaissance atmosphere—heavy wood tables, high backed chairs, a rococo decor—and lots of comfort for leisurely dining, a favorite haunt of Pittsburgh's legal profession. The cuisine—especially the seafood and veal—is top-flight.
Lunch: Mon-Fri 11:30-2:30 ($7-$10).
Dinner: Mon-Sat 5-10:30, Sun (except summer) 4-9 ($16-$25).

D'Imperio's

3412 William Penn Highway, Wilkins Township. AE,DC,MC,V. Reser. **823-4800.**
A businessman's favorite, this restaurant's fine cuisine and calm ambience draws executives from all over. Famous six-course dinners—trout, sole, veal, steak impeccably served in gracious surroundings with special attention to business needs and international dishes for corporate guests. Good place to take a serious gourmet.
Dinner: Tues-Sun 5-11 ($16-$25).

Grand Concourse

Station Square. AE,DC,MC,V. Reser. **261-1717.**
Still the grandest location to impress visiting executives with the big changes in Pittsburgh. This magnificently restored P&LE Station, with its soaring stained glass ceiling, is a fitting place for a luncheon or dinner feast. While you're there take the opportunity to look around Station Square.
Lunch: Mon-Fri 11:30-2:30 ($6.50-$12).
Dinner: Mon-Thur 4:30-10, Fri & Sat til 11 ($11-$20).

Harvest Room

Pittsburgh Vista, Liberty Center, Downtown. Reser sugg. AE,D,DC,MC,V. **281-8160.**
Warm elegance—glass, brass, a genial comfortable bar—greet you in this intimate room, sure to be a favorite of your international visitors. While the decor's Edwardian the menu's Amer/Continental, the finest quality ingredients in the best of regional favorites—Maine lobster, Louisiana redfish, wild game, chicken, American desserts and a "55 minute lunch" Mon-Fri for busy executives. Matchless service by a European-trained staff. Your visitors from near and far will be delighted!
Lunch: Mon-Fri 11:30-2:30 ($12-$20).
Dinner: Mon-Sat: 5:30-10:30 ($18-$26).

Jacqie's/Jacqueline's

Webster Hall, 5514 Fifth Avenue. Reser. AE,DC,MC,V. **683-4344/683-4525.**
The casual elegance of Jacqie's lends itself to an informal business lunch/dinner for handsomely presented 'modern Italian' and fine wines. It's a favorite of Oakland's university/high-tech professionals. Adjoining Jacqueline's is a perfect 'manor house' setting for classical French cuisine—for your connoisseur guests.
Lunch: Jacqie's—Mon-Sat 11:30-3 ($5-$13).
Dinner: Jacqie's/Jacqueline's. Mon-Thur 5:30-10, Fri & Sat til 11. Sun Jacqueline's only—5-9. Jacqie's ($15-$26) Jacqueline's ($23-$27).

Jake's Above the Square

430 Market Street, 2nd level. Reser sugg. AE,DC,MC,V. **338-0900.**
Jake's offers diners a sweeping view of Market Square in stylish surroundings. A great spot for important business lunches, it specializes in North Italian and regional American cuisine—grilled seafood and homemade pasta and pastries. Nightly piano adds to dining pleasure.
Lunch: Mon-Fri 11:30-5 ($8-$16).
Dinner: Mon-Thur 5-11, Fri & Sat til 12, Sun 4-10 ($20-$33).

Klein's

330 Third Avenue, Downtown. AE,DC,D,MC,V. **232-3311.**
A fast break from your deliberations for an in-city lunch/dinner at one of the area's busiest seafood houses, famous for its lobster, bouillabaisse, garlic rolls & salt sticks. A favorite lunching spot for businessmen/lawyers, this is a great place to take a visiting seafood lover. Parking lot across the street.
Lunch/Dinner: Mon-Thur 11-9:30, Fri til 10, Sat 4:30-10 ($4.50-$16).

11

Le Mont

1114 Grandview Avenue, Mt Washington. AE,DC,MC,V. 431-3100.
An impressive place to take visitors for continental cuisine and a spectacular view of the city from banquette seating facing a sheer glass wall. The decor is plush and dramatic—for those who like to do business with a flair. Valet parking.
Dinner: Mon-Fri 5-10:30, Sat til 11:30, Sun 4-9:30 ($17-$30).

Le Pommier

2104 E Carson Street, South Side. Reser. AE,DC,MC,V. 431-1901.
This fine little Country French restaurant is a disarming choice for a special guest. Connoisseur diners, women executives will appreciate its simple charm and outstanding cuisine. Perfect setting for a private business tete a tete.
Lunch: Mon-Fri 11:30-2:30 ($4.50-$8.95).
Dinner: Mon-Thur 5:30-9, Fri & Sat til 10 ($15-$23).

More

214 N Craig Street, Oakland. AE,DC,MC,V. 621-2700.
Famous for its food, this Oakland standby is always a reliable executive choice. The fine cuisine—seafood, veal, fish, salads, pasta—won't disappoint and the surroundings are comfortable and relaxing and the drinks are superb.
Lunch: Mon-Fri 11:30-2:30, Sun 5-9 ($4.50-$7.50).
Dinner: Mon-Fri 5-10, Sat til 11, Sun 5-9 ($9.50-$20).

Per Favore

Royal York Apartments, 3955 Bigelow Blvd, Oakland. Reser sugg. AE,DC,MC,V. 681-9147.
Here's a bright, hospitable room for business talk and N Italian specialties—veal, chuck roast braised in barolo wine, pastas, intriguing pizzas. Your visitor will feel at home. Dinner piano. Thur-Sat. Valet parking.
Lunch: Mon-Fri 11-4 ($3.95-$21.95).
Dinner: Mon-Thur 4-10, Fri & Sat til 11 ($9.95-$21.95).

Piccolo Mondo

Foster Plaza, Greentree. 15 min from Airport. Reser. AE,MC,V. 922-0920.
Rico Lorenzini of North Hills Rico's fame has taken over this beautiful restaurant atop the hills of Greentree, the perfect site for a relaxing repast out of the city. Renowned for its French & N Italian cuisine and special service to business clients, it serves some of the city's best fish, veal, rack of lamb in a lavish decor. Nearby hotel limousines offer service to the door. An impressive experience.
Lunch: Mon-Fri 11-2:30 ($5-$10.50).
Dinner: Mon-Fri 5-10, Sat til 11 ($12-$25).

Pietro's

Hyatt Pittsburgh at Chatham. AE,DC,MC,V. 288-9326.
Spacious, two-level room with modern decor, glass walls and patio looking out over the city. Good Uptown meeting place for fine N Italian dining, fabulous Sunday Brunch "Festa." Good place for power breakfast.
Breakfast: Mon-Fri 6:30-11, Sat & Sun til 11:45 ($3.95-$15).
Lunch: Mon-Fri 11-5, Sat/Sun 11:45-5 ($6-$13).
Dinner: 7 days 5-11 ($11-$20).

Ruddy Duck

Ramada Hotel, Bigelow Square, Downtown. Reser sugg. AE,DC,D,MC,V. 281-3825.
This warm club-like room centered around a big brass bar is a gracious setting for an early breakfast or executive lunch in comfortable surroundings. There's traditional grilled fish & meat plus creative variations on duck—hence its name. Handy to city businessmen. A real favorite. (Parking in Ramada garage.)
Breakfast: Mon-Fri 6:30-11 ($1.50-$5)
Lunch: 7 days 11-4 ($5.50-$8).
Dinner: 7 days 4-10 ($9-$11).

Private Membership Clubs

Ruth's Chris Steak House
6 PPG Place, Downtown. DC,MC,V. Reser sugg. **4391-4800.**
The latest "in" downtown restaurant, a sophisticated but comfortable room in which to wine and dine your clients—a must for steak lovers. Also delicious lobster, chicken and chops. Good lunch bargain. Free evening parking in PPG garage from Third or Fourth Ave.
Lunch: Mon-Fri 11:30-3 ($5.95-$15).
Dinner: Mon-Sat 5-11, Sun 4-8 ($15 & up).

Tambellini's
860 Saw Mill Run Blvd (Rt 51), near the Liberty Tunnels. AE,DC,MC,V. **481-1118.**
A famous Pittsburgh name in seafood. They come all over to this big, spacious restaurant for stellar lobster, seafood Louis, fish, veal, chicken and pasta. A repast here can turn a business meeting into a convivial gathering.
Lunch: Mon-Fri 11:30-3:30 ($6-$8.25).
Dinner: Mon-Sat 4-11 ($9.75-$25).

Terrace Room
The Westin William Penn, Mellon Square, Downtown. AE,DC,MC,V. **553-5235.**
An elegant room, newly restored to its 1916 splendour, this Pittsburgh landmark is a traditional favorite for executive breakfast, lunch or dinner. Its ornate ceiling, chandeliers and fine service make an impressive setting for seafood, steak, best prime rib in town. A must for hearty beef lovers.
Breakfast: 6:30-11:30 ($4-$9).
Lunch: 11:30-5 ($11-$17).
Dinner: 5-11 ($13-$24).

Top of the Triangle
USX Tower, 600 Grant. AE,DC,MC,V. **471-4100.**
A spectacular view of downtown Pittsburgh from the 62nd floor makes this an impressive choice for visiting VIPs. With traditional offerings, fine service and relaxing music in the Lounge, it's a good place to unwind when business is done. Beautiful day/night city views.
Lunch: Mon-Fri 11:30-3, Sat 12-3 ($4.75-$9).
Dinner: Mon-Fri 5:30-10, Sat til 12, Sun 4-9 ($13-$20). Lounge Mon-Sat til 2.

Sterling's
Pittsburgh Hilton, Gateway Center. Reser sugg. AE,DC,D,MC,V. **391-4600.**
A handsome hotel grill with an exclusive feel and lots of privacy for discussion. Seafood, steaks and Continental dishes...a good executive/traveler's retreat. Valet parking.
Dinner: 7 days 5:30-11 ($10-26).

PRIVATE MEMBERSHIP CLUBS

The Allegheny Club
Three Rivers Stadium, Fourth Level. **323-0830.**
Membership: Open. 1400 members. Established 1970.
Dinner for major events and following daylight football games. The glass-walled diningroom overlooks the Point and has a marvelous terrace view of Pirate/Steeler games. Private facilities for member-sponsored functions.
Hours: Lunch Mon-Fri 11:30-4, Sat & Sun 11-2. Late Bites Mon-Fri 5:30-8:30.

The City Club
119 6th Street, Downtown. **391-3300.**
Membership: Open. Established 1981.
Modern health club with restaurant/cafe, conference room; full health club facilities—racquetball, squash, nautilus/free weights, jogging track, whirlpool, swimming pool, aerobic studio, pro shop.
Hours: Mon-Fri 6am-10pm, Sat & Sun 9-7. Breakfast/Health Food Bar Mon-Fri 7-9:30, Lunch Mon-Fri 11:30-4, Light Menu 4-8.

The Duquesne Club
325 Sixth Avenue, Downtown. **391-1500.**
Membership: By sponsor. 2600 members. Established 1881.
The brass lions outside this familiar, awninged brownstone guard Pittsburgh's oldest and most exclusive club. Prestigious leaders meet to eat, work and relax in its 56 meeting/dining rooms; health club, barber shop, corporate suites, overnight guest rooms.
Hours: 7 days, 24 hours. Breakfast/Lunch/Dinner: Mon-Sat 7am-10pm.

11

Private Membership Clubs

Engineer's Society W Pa
337 Fourth Avenue, Downtown.
261-0710.
Membership: Professional sponsorship. 1200 members. Established 1880.
A social and business meeting place for engineers and engineering-related professionals and students. Comfortable private dining rooms, bar and lounge, members' seminars and club functions.
Hours: Mon-Fri 8:30-5. Dinner by arrangement.

The Gateway Center Club
Three Gateway Center, 24th fl.
566-1300.
Membership: Open—with references. 900 members. Established 1973.
A luncheon club with a sweeping view of the Point, favorite of Gateway Center executives and Greater Pgh Chamber of Commerce members. Dining facilities and meeting rooms for private parties.
Hours: Mon-Fri 11:30-7. Lunch 11:30-2:30.

Harvard-Yale-Princeton Club
619 William Penn Place, Downtown.
281-5858.
Membership: Sponsorship by members, limited to graduates or those listed in Harvard, Yale or Princeton alumni books; associate membership to other university graduates. 600 members. Established 1930.
Pittsburgh's oldest downtown residential buildings, these charming red brick "houses" off a tiny courtyard are headquarters for the city's Ivy League alumni. Dining rooms and three private meeting rooms are available for members/non-members.
Hours: Mon-Fri Lunch 12-2, Dinner 6-7:30. Cocktail Lounge til 8.

Igloo Club
Civic Arena, Uptown. **642-1890.**
Membership: Pgh Penguins full-season ticket holders. 800 members. Established 1967. This modern/neon two-level club offers hockey fan members a la carte entrees at Icing's restaurant on the first level and a Bar/Buffet on the second floor for pre & post-game revels.

The facility is also available to members and the public for private parties.
Hours: Two hours before game time.

Pittsburgh Athletic Association
4215 Fifth Avenue, Oakland. **621-2400.**
Membership: Sponsorship by member. 2500 members. Established 1909, opened 1911.
This beautiful five-story Venetian Renaissance building with its ornate frieze is a second home to Pittsburgh's top business and professional leaders. It houses one of the city's most complete athletic facilities for men and women—a marble/terra-cotta swimming pool and bowling alleys—an elegant, rococo first floor diningroom and smaller private rooms. It also houses guests—some of them permanent.
Hours: Mon-Fri 6:30-9, Sat & Sun 9-6. Breakfast/Lunch/Dinner: Mon-Fri 7-11:30, Sat 8-11:30, Sun 8-8.

The Rivers Club
One Oxford Centre, Downtown.
391-5227.
Membership: Sponsorship by member. 1000 members. Established 1983.
This sleek health club on the fourth floor of Oxford Centre has a main dining area, four private dining rooms and first-class athletic facilities—pool, track, nautilus, weights, racquetball, squash, sauna, steam room, whirlpool.
Hours: Mon-Fri 6am-9, Sat 9-5. Lunch Mon-Fri 11:30-2, Dinner Wed-Sat 6-10.

The University Club
123 University Place, Oakland.
621-1890.
Membership: College graduates. Sponsorship by member. 2000 members. Established 1890.
Facilities include private dining rooms, health club—squash, sauna, whirlpool, bowling alleys; largest private library in the city, parties, summer dances and outdoor dining on handsome roof garden overlooking Oakland. Also guest rooms for members. Member luncheon privileges at the Downtown Club of Pittsburgh, 62nd floor, USX Bldg.
Hours: 7 days. Breakfast 7-11, Lunch 11:30-2:30, Dinner 5:30-9, wknds til 10.

Whether it's a brown bag for office workers...a festive box for picnickers... or a sumptuous gourmet basket for special events....Pittsburghers are increasingly eating as Europeans do - from movable feasts of bread, cheese fruit and take-out dinners to eat in city parks, plazas, by the riverside or by your own hearth. And you can now have meals delivered to your home!

GOURMET TO GO

Benkovitz Seafoods
23rd & Smallman, Mon-Fri 8:30-5:30, Sat 8-5. **263-3016.**
People come from miles around for stellar seafood, famous fish sandwich, delicious shrimp bisque, clams, seafood platter, potato pancakes, fish hoagie. $2-$6.

Busy Day Gourmet
3845 Old Wm Penn Hwy, Murrysville. Mon-Fri 9-8, Sat til 6. D,MC,V. **327-1260.**
Three local women conspire to turn out gourmet treats for eating on premises or take-out. Quiche, gourmet sandwiches, chicken salad, tuna/pecan salad, homemade soup, baked goods/pies. $2 up.

Catz 'n Kids
2114 Murray Ave, Squirrel Hill. 7 days 7-9. No credit cards. **421-9500.**
If you're yearning for kosher food this is the genuine thing. Meats, deli sandwiches, soup, potato pancakes, sides, platters $1.50-$7. Feed a family on Big Jack Sandwich—corned beef, pastrami, salami, swiss on a whole loaf of rye—with fries & slaw, $14.50! Wry waitresses make this a real eat-in experience!

Faxing...
A New Food Fad

Several deli's and restaurants are encouraging businesses and private patrons to fax in their orders. Many offices save worktime by faxing in multiple lunch orders from a "Fax Menu" before 10:30am or by 5 the night before for pick-up or delivery next day. Taking fax food orders downtown are: **Liang's Hunan,** Liberty Center **Fax 471-1557. Rosenbaum's Deli,** 614 Smithfield **Fax 391-4944. Subway** 401 Wood St **Fax 471-7279. Brown Bag Deli's** Fax 288-1354. **Also Ghengis Cones,** 5349 Penn, Bloomfield **Fax: 363-4113.**

Dinner For Two

How about a McGinnis Sisters' dinner right on your own hearth. You can pick up the makings for a Surf 'n Turf dinner for two—including fresh lobster tail, filet mignon, Idaho potatoes, broccoli, 1/2 lb fresh mushrooms, rolls and butter to cook in your own home. $50-$60 for 2 to 4-oz tails, $65-$75 for 6 to 8-oz tails. Give them 3-4 days notice. Pick up at 3825 Saw Mill Run Blvd **882-6400,** Penn Ctr, Monrv. **824-6330. MC,V.**

Genghis Cones
5349 Penn Ave, Bloomfield. Mon-Thur 11-10, Fri til 11, Sat til 12. Sun 4-10. AE,MC,V. **363-3248.**
Very interesting Oriental take-out—unique Korean short-ribs, Peking duck, pork, chicken, shrimp sandwiches, BBQue, cold sesame noodles, $3.50-$10.50. Whole Duck with mushu pancakes, plum sauce & onions, $15. Free delivery $10 & over.

H & M Gourmet Food
Bourse Shops, Greentree Rd. Mon-Fri 9-8, Sat til 7, Sun til 5. Galleria, Mt Lebanon . Mon-Sat 10-9:30. Sun 10-5. No credit cards. **276-2899.**
Great gourmet breads—herb, sausage, cheese. Appetizers, soups, salads, croissant sandwiches, salads & desserts plus daily specials from stuffed chicken to saffron rice. $1 up. Also Gourmet Feasts for 4, $35-$130 on 48-hrs notice.

HoneyBaked Spiral Ham
South Hills: 1600 Washington Rd **835-2400.** North Hills: 4780 McKnight Rd **364-1800.** No credit cards. Mon-Sat 10-6.
Your guests will rave about this ham, so tender it falls off the bone, uniquely sliced in a spiral, with a delicious crunchy glaze. 6-16 lbs, $27-$70. Also BBQ ribs, turkey, cheeses, salads, cheesecakes, mustards of all kinds.

Hot Licks Express

Shadyside: Theatre Mall, 5520 Walnut St
683-2583. Mt Lebanon: Galleria.
341-7427. Mon-Thur 11:30-10, Fri-Sat til
12. Sun Shadyside 4:30-9, S Hills
12-10. AE,DC,MC,V.
Ribs, wings, great sandwiches—mesquite & Cajun chicken, smoked turkey
to go—$4.50-$10. **Pig-Out Party**—Ribs,
Chicken or Combo with baked beans,
homemade chips, slaw/potato salad—for
4 to 100. $12 person up.

Kiku Express

229 S Highland Ave, Shadyside.
Mon-Sat 11-10. Sun 12-9. No credit
cards. **661-5458.**
A-1 Japanese 'fast food.' Indoor/patio
eating plus take-out of teriyaki, sukiyaki,
other delicacies, economical $2-$3.
Sushi of all kinds—shrimp, vegetable,
fish, California roll $2-$5. Deliciously
different.

La Charcuterie

Ellsworth Plaza, Ellsworth & College.
Tues-Fri 10-8, Sat til 6, Sun til 4. MC,V.
661-2262.
Take out extraordinaire from famed
Laforet chefs Michael and Candy
Uricchio... with a few stand-up tables.
Almond/grape chicken salad, curried
shrimp, foie gras, truffles, osso buco,
huge selection of rare mushrooms you
can't get elsewhere...and some of the
restaurant's marvelous pastries. From
$1.85 for a slice of cake to decidedly
upscale—but deliciously worth it!

A Pittsburgh Welcome

Welcome a newcomer to Pittsburgh or just say thanks with a
unique basket of the city's finest
gourmet products—plus copies of
the **Rich/Poor Man's Guide to
Pittsburgh** and the **Pgh Walking
Map & Guide.** They'll love you for
giving them a head start in discovering the city. $16 & up. A
unique gift from **Basketique,** 1032
MacArthur Drive, Russelton.
MC,V. **265-4553.**

Roast Pig
In Your Own Back Yard

Kelson's

1721 5th Avenue, Uptown.
261-2740.
Here's something different for that
business or private bash. How
about a Pig Party...they'll set up
the charcoal grill and big rotisserie and roast a pig in your own
back yard...with all the trimmins'...a unique idea for business, private parties. ($22 per
person up.) Or grill strip steaks,
ox rounds, BBQ chicken, ham,
spare-ribs—prices vary. Also party
trays from $5 up.

McGinnis Sisters

South Hills: 3825 Saw Mill Run Blvd.
Mon-Sat 9-7. Sun 9-5. **882-6400.** Monroeville: Penn Center. Mon-Sat 9-7, Sun
11-5. **824-6330.** MC,V.
Three sisters, Bonnie, Sharon and Noreen—gourmet cooks all—are a local
legend for their succulent hams, Amish
chicken, Black Angus beef, Foley's Boston seafood, and 50 more items—
salads, goodies from the bake shop,
cheeses/meats from the deli, $3 up.
Free delivery on a "working lunch."

Robert E & Lee Food Co

728 Copeland Street, Shadyside. Mon-Sat 9-6. Sun 9-2. **687-4300.**
Some of the best food in town from a
repertoire of 100 gourmet items—
tarragon/pesto chicken salad, shrimp
salad, smoked turkey breast, delicious
breads, soups, hot entrees, i.e. chicken
cordon bleu, shrimp & scallops Barsac,
Italian subs. $4 & up.

Shadyside Market

Mineo Bldg, 5414 Walnut St, Shadyside.
Mon-Fri 9-6, Sat 9-5. **682-5470.**
Menu varies daily, wonderful gourmet
versions of chicken, veal, beef, stuffed
shells, soups. $2-$10.

12

GOURMET TO GO

Meal Delivery To Your Door

Wheel Deliver

East End, Fox Chapel. Call in Mon-Fri 10:30-10, Sat & Sun 4-10. **421-9346.**

An idea whose time has come, this restaurant home delivery service is a boon to busy careerists and the homebound. Customers in the East End and Fox Chapel areas place lunch/dinner orders from a Wheel Deliver menu brochure and meals from nearly 20 participating restaurants are delivered by a tuxedoed driver usually within 45 minutes. You can order anything from sandwiches to gourmet feasts with a minimum of $10 and a 15% delivery charge for the luxury of eating in your own home. Lunch is delivered in the East End from 11:30-2:30 Mon thru Fri and dinners in both East End and Fox Chapel 7 days a week from 7 to 10. Participating restaurants include: **East End:** Shadyside Balcony, Hotlicks, Great Scot, Paradise on Craig, Suzie's, Star of India, Darbar, Mai Thai, Wok Inn, Peking Gourmet, Oriental Balcony, Alexander's Pasta Express, Minutello's, Stephen's La Piccola Casa and Simply French. **Fox Chapel:** Abate's, Dingbat's, Thai Pei, Simply French. **Laundry Pick-Up:** Wheel Deliver also provides a 48-hr. pick-up laundry/dry cleaning service.

Rhoda's

2201 Murray Avenue, Squirrel Hill. Sun-Thur 7-11, Fri-Sat til 12. No credit cards. **521-4555.**

Restaurant/deli items to go. Delicious noodle kugel, potato salad, short ribs, chopped liver, smoked salmon, pickled herring, matzo ball, latke (potato pancakes) chicken soup, dark rye, sandwiches made to order, and of course corned beef. $3-$10.

Simply Delicious

1200 Old Freeport Road, Fox Chapel. Tues-Sat 8:30-9, Sun & Mon til 4. AE,MC,V. **963-0636.**

You can now eat in a peach & white parlor behind the deli counter at this creative gourmet house...or take out all of their wonderful goodies. Gourmet sandwiches, hot/cold soups, salads, hot casseroles, filet Bearnaise, other specialties changing daily. Also desserts—how about Peach Schnapps Ice Cream? From $1.50 to "sky's the limit" depending on your imaginative appetite!

Tokyo Japanese Food

Ellsworth Plaza, Ellsworth/College, Shadyside. Mon-Sat 10-8, Sun 10-7. No credit cards. **661-3777.**

City's biggest selection of Oriental foods; best sushi in Pgh $2.75-$4, great Japanese vegetables, soups, cookies. Sushi feasts for 3—California Roll, Vegetable Roll Oinari-san $16; Fish Sushi or Sashimi Feast—tuna, octopus, shiromi, salmon, squid, both $30. Also feasts for 6—$120 or for 10—$270 on beautiful Japanese ceramic plates... two hours notice, please.

USA Gourmet

2031 Penn Avenue, Strip. Mon-Sat 7-4:30. No credit cards. **471-6333.**

Stand up or take out fantastic-looking, great-tasting food—chicken/ham salad, quiche, fruit salads...all exceptional. Feast for the eyes. Also wonderful desserts—raspberry/vanilla/chocolate cheesecake, tarts, brownies, you name it...you'll love it. $1-$7.

Wholey's

1711 Penn Avenue, Mon-Thur 8-5:30, Fri 8-6pm, Sat til 5. **391-3737.**

Really fresh seafood—jumbo fish sandwich, shrimp in basket, deviled crab, soups, complete deli ($1.99-$3.50). Seating on 'Captain's Deck' upstairs, Chinese fast food on the first level.

PICNIC BOXES, BASKETS

Applebee's
Downtown: 214 5th Ave **566-2441.**
Forbes/Wood **391-2296.** 411 Smithfield
261-2277. Mon-Fri 7-5:30.
Box Lunches: to eat in downtown
parks or by the riverside. Sandwiches,
salads, desserts, croissants, brownies &
fine cheesecake. $5-$6.

Blarney Stone
*30 Grant Ave, Etna. Tues-Thur 11-9, Fri-
Sat til 11. Sun 10:30-9. AE,MC,V.*
781-1666.
Baskets: Fried chicken with a biscuit or
roast beef/corn beef croissant, plus cole
slaw, Italian macaroni salad, cheese,
fresh fruit, brownie. Basket with table-
cloth & utensils! $8 person. We're
impressed! Handy for Hartwood picnics.

Brown Bag Deli
Downtown: Triangle Bldg **566-1795.**
Kossman Bldg **355-0270.** 701 Penn
471-2360. Market Sq **765-1561.** 411
Wood **391-0806.** 220 Grant **261-9697.**
Chatham Ctr **471-3354.** 625 Stanwix
281-3403. Union Trust Bldg **263-2120.**
Liberty Center **261-5111.** Mon-Fri 7-5.
Bag Lunch: Changes daily—sand-
wiches, salads, soups, snacks, fruit,
ice cream. $1.99-$3.59.

'Pittsburgh Gourmet' Half-Time Special

Give a Pittsburgh flavour to your
party with the Halftime Special at
Clara's **Pittsburgh Pirogies**, 2717
Library Road, Castle Shannon (Rt
88 off Rt 51). For $37 you get 8
Kielbasa sandwiches, 50 perogi,
onion and butter sauce, plates,
knives, forks, napkins, salt. Order
ahead. You can pick up at drive-
thru window. No credit cards.
882-3555.

Busy Day Gourmet
*3825 Wm Penn Hwy, Murrysville. Mon-
Fri 9-8, Sat til 6. D,MC,V.* **327-1260.**
Box Lunches: A very special lunch in a
white box, green tissue paper. Your
gift—a croissant sandwich, salad, homemade cookies, fruit from this gourmet
house. Flatware, condiments included.
$8.50 up.

Fluted Mushroom
*109 S 12th St, South Side. Mon-Fri 9-5.
No credit cards.* **381-1899.**
Picnic Boxes: Posh picnics, elegant
goodies in little white boxes tied with a
green ribbon. Min of 10, delivered to
home/office. Gourmet salads, sandwiches i.e. mustard chicken salad, Italian veal meatloaf, shrimp with red
peppers, Black Forest ham/brie sandwich. $8-$13 person.
Exec Box: Maryland crab cakes, cole
slaw, fruit cup, roll, chocolate brownie,
Chinese walnuts, $8.50. **Special Box::**
Oven baked chicken, fruit cup, potato
salad, roll, chocolate chip cookies &
Chinese walnuts, $8.50.

Food Gallery
Shadyside: 5550 Centre Ave **681-1500.**
Fox Chapel Plaza: Freeport Rd
781-4424. Mt Lebanon: 1082 Bower Hill
Rd **279-8645.** Valley Brook: Rt 19 4 mi
s of S Hills Village **942-0600.** Mon-Sat
8-10, Sun 9-6.
Instant Picnic: —9-piece bucket of
chicken, quart of cole slaw, half doz
rolls for 4-6. Mem Day-Labor Day. No
advance notice. $9.99.
Picnic Trays—meats, cheeses, veggies,
dip, fruit, salads, rolls. $2.25-$5.95 person, 48-hr notice.
Two for the Road Special (Valley
Brook only Apr-Sept) 2 grilled
burgers/cheeseburgers/hot dogs, chips.
$1.99-$2.49.

12

Picnic Boxes, Baskets

H & M Gourmet Food

Greentree: Bourse. Mon-Fri 9-8, Sat til 7, Sun til 5. Mt Lebanon: Galleria. Mon-Sat 10-9:30, Sun 10-5. No credit cards. **276-2899.**
Baskets/Tins: Picnic for 4 in basket or tins—BBQ baby pork back ribs, BBQ chicken, homemade cole slaw, Dijon potato salad, pecan bars and a baguette of bread. Plastic utensils, condiments provided. $39 for 4. Beautiful!

Kane's Courtyard

303 S Craig Street, Oakland. Mon-Fri 7-6. Sat 10:30-6. **683-9988.**
Box Lunches: Some of the city's best sandwiches—choice of meat, cheese, bread—plus potato salad/cole slaw, cookie, beverage for $5.75. Good bargain. Free delivery to East End.

McGinnis Sisters

South Hills: 3825 Saw Mill Run. Mon-Sat 9-7, Sun 9-5. **882-6400.** *Monroeville: Penn Center. Mon-Sat 9-7, Sun 11-5.* **824-6330.** *MC,V.*
Box Lunches: Croissant sandwich— choice of baked ham, lean roast beef, NY style corned beef, gourmet turkey breast. Choices of cheese, salad and brownie, carrot or apple cake. Utensils, napkins, condiments. $4.50.

Robert E & Lee Food Co

728 Copeland Street, Shadyside. Mon-Sat 9-6. Sun 9-2. **687-4300.**
Party Boxes: Tissue-papered party boxes—soup & quiche, chicken salad, quiche & veggies, chili & potato salad, $6.50-$8.50.
Baskets: Beautiful baskets with gourmet items ($50 deposit) china, crystal, choice of items, about $20 person.

Susan Bakes & Cooks

2316 Penn Ave, Strip. No credit cards. **471-3777.**
Picnic Boxes: A very fancy picnic, unique boxes with tomato tarts, vegetables provencale, Susan's famous French roll, sweet butter, brownie & lemon squares. Plastic flatware. $13.90 a person. Call ahead.

Simply Delicious

1200 Old Freeport Rd, Fox Chapel. Tues-Sat 8:30am-9pm, Sun-Mon til 4. AE,MC,V. **963-0636.**
Bag Lunches: Made to order. Choice of chicken salad/tuna/roast beef/turkey/ ham sandwich $4, on croissant $4.75. Fruit, cole slaw, potato quiche 75¢-$2.25.
Picnics. Bring in your picnic hamper/ box at least a day ahead and they'll fill it with your favorite goodies.

USA Gourmet

2031 Penn Ave, Strip. Mon-Sat 7-4:30. No credit cards. **471-6333.**
Box Lunch: Choice of roast beef/cheddar, Virginia ham/American cheese or smoked turkey breast/Swiss with potato salad, cole slaw or pasta primavera and cookie. Condiments, paperware. $6.25 person.

Picnic Boxes Under the Stars

You can enjoy food with your music at Star Lake, the exciting new outdoor amphitheatre on Rt 18 open May-Sept. Call ahead for Gourmet Picnic baskets *available only to box seat ticket holders.* Deluxe Barbecue Basket for 6— Southern Style Chicken BBQ, Ribs, Peel 'n Eat Shrimp, red-skin potato salad, sourdough bread, sweet butter, cheddar cheese & crackers, fresh strawberries, beer nuts plus dessert tray with homemade brownies, cookies & an 8" Granny Smith apple pie, ($75-$90). You can also have Shrimp by the Dozen, Fruit & Pepperoni for 6, Antipasto & Hoagy picnic baskets. 48 hours notice. Or you can eat on the lawn from food booths at the theatre. Call **947-7415.**

ORIENTAL/ASIAN

One of the fastest growing, most popular cuisines in the city is exotic Asian/Oriental. Here are fifty of the city's favorite Chinese...Japanese ...Indian...Thai...Vietnamese...and even a Filipino restaurant with exciting new tastes, many with smashing decors.

13

159

Chinese

Cathay Inn
*1000 Greentree Rd, Greentree.
Lunch Tues-Sat 11:30-2, Dinner Tues-Sun 4-9:30. MC,V.* **921-9770.**
Small, family, out-of-way find. Good prices for Cantonese, sweet/sour dishes, good beef oyster sauce. Inexp.

China Palace
Shadyside: 5440 Walnut St. Mon-Thur 11:30-10:30, Fri-Sat til 11:30. Sun 2-9:30. **687-7423.** *Monrv: Jonnett Plaza, 4059 Wm Penn Hwy. Mon-Thur 11:30-9:30, Fri & Sat til 10:30. Sun 3-9.* **373-7423.** *Sewickley: 409 Broad St. AE,MC,V.*
Above-average Szechwan, Hunan, Mandarin in tasteful surroundings. Great sampler Pu Pu Platter—grill your own & saute in spicy sauce. Excellent "Happy Family"—beef, pork, broccoli. Mod-Exp.

Chop Stix
1034 Freeport Rd, Fox Chapel. 7 days 11:30-10, Fri-Sat til 11. AE,MC,V. **782-3010.**
On site of former Anna Kao's; Szechwan, Hunan, Peking dishes, 20-30 min duck, special pork in bean sauce. Buffet Sun-Tues 5:30-8:30 ($8.99). Mod-Exp.

Chinatown Inn
520 Third Ave, Downtown. Mon-Thur 11-11:30, Fri-Sat 12-11:30, Sun 2-10. AE,DC,MC,V. **281-6708.**
Favorite downtown lunching spot, one of the last vestiges of Pittsburgh's old Chinatown. All the regulars & excellent Kung Pao Chicken and Fung Mei Har—shrimp in bacon in sweet sour sauce, Mod.

Chinese on Carson
1506 E Carson Street, South Side. Mon-Thur 11-10, Fri-Sat til 11. Sun 4-10. AE,DC,MC,V. **431-1717.**
A rarity in Chinese restaurants, a modern room in lavender, black & neon, one of the city's handsomest. Great Szechwan, Cantonese, Burmese; chicken curry, unique Lobster Egg Rolls, braised duck with seafood. Mod-Exp.

Elegant Oriental
Liang's Hunan
Liberty Center, Downtown. Sun-Thur 11:30-10, Fri-Sat til 11. AE,DC, MC,V. **471-1688.**
Downtown's newest, elegant Oriental with smashing decor; gourmet Hunan, Szechwan — Asparagus Prawns, smoked duck, pheasant, venison, rabbit, frog's legs; delicious crispy whole fish $19.50. Dim Sum Sat/Sun 11:30-3. Mod-Exp. Worth it!

Dynasty Express
633 Smithfield, Downtown. Mon-Fri 10:30-8pm. No credit cards. **281-9818.**
Small eat-in/take-out place, favorite of office workers; Hunan Mongolian beef/chicken; Szechwan chicken, seafood. Lunch specials. $4-$8. Inexp.

Empress
Waterworks, Fox Chapel. Mon-Fri 11:30-9:30, Sat 12-10:30. Sun 12-9. AE,D,MC,V. **781-3727.**
Big good-looking room with authentic Szechwan cuisine, chicken, beef; Potato Basket with shrimp, lobster, scallops & vegetables. Inexp-Mod.

Golden Palace
206 Shiloh, Mt Washington. Mon-Thur 11-10, Fri-Sat til 11, Sun 4-10. AE,MC,V. **481-8500.**
First Chinese on Mt Washington. Casual, modern with good vegetarian dishes, great eggplant with garlic sauce, bean curd. Inexp.

Great Wall
Pines Plaza, 1130 Perry Hwy, Ross. Mon-Thur 11:30-10, Fri-Sat til 11. Sun 3-9. AE,DC,MC,V. **369-5858.**
Full Mandarin menu, Szechwan, Peking, Kwonton in modern decor. Seafood special—crabmeat, shrimp, scallops; also seafood with lobster sauce, sizzling rice & chicken. $6-$13. Mod.

ORIENTAL/ASIAN

Chinese

Jimmy Tsang's
Kennilworth Apts, 5700 Centre, Shady-
ide. Mon-Thur 11:30-10, Fri-Sat til 11.
Sun 3:30-9. AE,DC,MC,V. 661-4226.
Big, busy restaurant with fancy-to-
asual dining, city's favorite for wide
variety of Chinese/Korean—"over 100
best-loved Peking, Szechwan, Shang-
hai, Cantonese dishes." Detailed menu
xplains cuisine, helps you order.
Mod-Exp.

King Wu
04 Plaza on Mall, Monrv. Sun-Thur
1:30-10, Fri-Sat til 11. AE,MC,V.
73-5464.
Chinese modern for Szechwan, Man-
arin, Hunan. Good wonton chips, Gen
so's chicken. $5 lunch specials.
nexp-Mod.

Mark Pi China Gate
Galleria, 1500 Washington Rd, Mt Leba-
on. Mon-Thur 11:30-10, Fri-Sat til 11.
un noon-9. 341-9582.
xquisite decor, contemporary atmos-
here. Expensive but worth it for Szech-
an, Mandarin, Hunan specialties.
esame Beef, Hunan Shrimp, Dragon &
hoenix—prawns, scallops, chicken,
bster, scallop rumaki. Good date
ace, excellent service. Mod-Exp.

Kosher Chinese

King David
2020 Murray Avenue, Squirrel Hill.
Mon-Thur 11-10, closed Fri-Sat in
summer, open Sat in winter an
hour after sundown til midnite. Sun
2-10. AE,D,DC,MC,V. 422-3370.
How about Kosher Chinese, a
most unusual mix...and some
Amer food too! Soup & Egg roll,
hot Chinese vegetable platter,
sesame chicken. $1.50-$14. Also
take-out. Phone greets you with
"Shalom."

Four Gourmet Stars

Mandarin Gourmet
YWCA Bldg, 305 Wood Street,
Downtown. Mon-Sat 11-9.
AE,D,DC,MC,V. 261-6151.
One of Harold & Mrs Jou's four fab-
ulous "gourmet" houses with excel-
lent Mandarin, Hunan, Cantonese.
All-day Dim Sum. Try Dragon
Phoenix—half chicken, half lobster
with veggies...mmm! Inexp-Mod.

Hunan Gourmet
1209 E Carson St, South Side.
Mon-Thur 11:30-10, Fri-Sat
11:30-11. Sun 3-9:30.
AE,D,DC,MC,V. 488-8100.
One of city's newest, best; a
serene room with Dim Sum all
day, outstanding shrimp/scallops
in garlic sauce, best Gen Tso's
Chicken in town. Mod.

Cathay Gourmet
4812 McKnight Road, N Hills. Mon-
Thur 11:30-10, Fri-Sat til 11, Sun
3-9:30. AE,D,DC,MC,V. 366-9111.
One of city's best, renowned cuisine,
delicious beef, pork, lobster, great
Dragon-Phoenix Soup, Pu Pu Platter $9 for 2. Mon Buffet $8.50.
Lunch/Dinner $4.50-$9. Mod.

Szechwan Gourmet
709 Bellefonte St, Shadyside. Mon-
Thur 11-10, Fri-Sat til 11. Sun 4:30-10.
AE,D,DC,MC,V. 683-1763.
Longtime favorite, same great
"Gourmet" dishes, special Szech-
wan Chicken. Mod.

Liu Garden
10500 Perry Hwy, Wexford. Mon-Thur
11:30-10, Sat til 11. AE,MC,V. 935-1880.
Pgh's first Mongolian barbecue—you
select your own food for all-you-can-eat
stir fry on giant grill, $12 weekdays, $13
Fri-Sat. Lunch $4.50. Sun Brunch 12-3,
$8.95. Mod.

13

ORIENTAL/ASIAN

Chinese

Special Places

Sesame Inns
Shops at Station Sq: Upper Level
281-8282. Mt Lebanon: 715
Washington Rd **341-2555.** Mon-Thur
11:30-10, Fri-Sat til 11. Sun 12-9 (Mt
Leb 4-10). AE,DC,MC,V.
Terrific Szechwan, Hunan cuisine in
lovely atmosphere. Try the fried
dumplings, cold noodles with sesame
paste, Orange Beef, Seafood
Supreme, Gen Tso's Chicken, Ses-
ame/Walnut Shrimp. $8-$15.

Sichuan Houses
*Squirrel Hill: 1900 Murray Ave. Sun-
Thur 4-10, Fri-Sat til 11.* **422-2700.**
Mt Lebanon: Va Manor Shops, 1717
Cochran Road. Same hours. MC,V.
563-5252. Fox Chapel: 1335
Freeport Rd. Mon-Sat Lunch 11:30-3,
Dinner 4:30-10, Fri-Sat til 11. Sun
4:30-10. AE,MC,V. **967-0789.**
Some of city's best, creative Chi-
nese, mild to spicy. Good portions at
moderate prices. Specialties Gen
Tso's Chicken, Sea Delight, great
Peking Duck for 2 $24.95. Inexp-Mod.

Oriental Balcony
*5846 Forbes, Squirrel Hill. Sun-Thur
11-10, Fri-Sat til 11. AE,D,MC,V.*
521-0728.
Very pleasant 2nd-fl room, famous for
Burmese curries, shrimp, Lobster Kai
Kew, Ginger Chicken, hot beef and
"Strange Taste" chicken with ginger,
garlic & chili. Dim Sum Sun 11-3. Mod.

Peking Gourmet Kitchen
*2018 Murray Ave, Sq Hill. Lunch Mon-Fri
11:30-2. Dinner Sun-Thur 2:30-9:30, Fri-
Sat til 10:30. Sat-Sun Dim Sum 11-2:30.
No credit cards.* **421-1920.**
Favorite for Peking Duck from $16.90
for eight-course feast to Duck with Chinese Pancakes, $28 for 4. Also Manda-
rin, Szechwan & Hunan dishes.
Inexp-Mod.

Tantalizing Take-Out

Genghis Cones
*5349 Penn Avenue, Garfield. Mon-
Thur 10-10, Fri til 12, Sat 11-11.
Sun 3-9. AE,MC,V.* **363-4248.**
Unique take-out of spicy N Chinese & 200 other items under $9.
Korean beef short ribs; pork ribs
cooked in wooden hot box—14 rib
rack $13.75, half rack $7.25, with
hot/sweet mustard. Lunch Box
specials $4.50. Free Delivery $10
& over. Inexp-Mod.

Cafeteria, Chinese Style

Yum Wok
*Oakland: 400 S Craig St. Mon-Sat
11-10.* **687-7777.** Downtown: 124
Sixth St, Downtown. Mon-Sat
11-9. **765-2222.** No credit cards.
A unique idea, a Chinese cafeteria! Off Craig Street in a very
tasteful setting—tile tables, high-
backed chairs, great food (mostly
Cantonese), wonderful prices. You
can snack cheap on 50-cent rice
& noodles and $3.25 dinner spe-
cials i.e. Cashew Chicken/Crab
Rangoon, Honey Pineapple
Chicken, Moo Goo Gai Pan. You'll
see lots of Asian patrons. (Also
Downtown) $2-$6. Inexp.

Sichuan Palace
*Penn Hills Shopping Ctr, Penn Hills.
Mon-Thur 11:30-9:30, Fri-Sat til 10:30.
Sun 12-9:30. MC,V.* **241-7110.**
Small, graceful room with Szechwan,
Hunan; Mongolian beef, lobster and stea
cubes, seafood. $7-$12. Inexp-Mod.

Tai Pei
Fox Chapel: 124 Freeport Rd **781-4131**
Greentree: The Bourse **279-8811.** Mon-Thu
11:30-10, Fri-Sat til 11. AE,D,DC,MC,V.
Light, airy, comfortable room with
Hunan lamb, Gen Tso's chicken, sea-
food, Peking Duck. Mod.

JAPANESE
WHERE TO GET SUSHI

Kabuki
635 Brown Ave, Turtle Creek. Lunch Mon-Fri 11:30-2, Dinner Mon-Sat 5-10. AE,DC,MC,V. **823-0750.**
Authentic Japanese cuisine in spare, serene setting; first sushi in Pgh. Seating at tables or floor cushions in tatami room. Mod.

Kiku of Japan
Shops at Station Square. Lunch Mon-Sat 11:30-2:30, Dinner Mon-Fri 5-10:30, Fri-Sat til 11. Sun 12-10. AE,DC,MC,V. **765-3200.**
Sushi bar or table service. Full Japanese menu, fabulous swordfish teriyaki, great broiled Hijiki seaweed. Mod-Exp.

Oakside Inn
256 N Craig Street, Oakland. Lunch Mon-Fri 11:30-2:30, Dinner Mon-Sat 5-9. No credit cards. Reser sugg. **681-9883.**
Small sushi bar, table service...and Johnnie from old Anna's Place, Downtown. Sushi's good, order ahead for quick service. Inexp.

Samurai Japanese Steak House
2100 Greentree Rd, Greentree. Mon-Thur 11:30-10, Fri/Sat til 11. Sun 4:30-9. AE,DC,MC,V. **276-2100.**
Dramatic dining at habachi tables with performing chefs; great decor, steaks, seafood, tropical drinks. Mod-Exp.

Shogun
3 Tech Dr, near Monrv Mall. Mon-Fri 11:30-2, 5:30-9:30, Fri-Sat til 10:30. AE,DC,MC,V. **372-0700.**
Japanese chefs perform at your table in this handsome restaurant; tempura, sushi & sashimi. Lunch $4-$8, Dinner $8-$24.

Tokyo Japanese Food Store
Ellsworth Plaza, Ellsworth/College, Shadyside. Mon-Sat 10-8, Sun 12-8. No credit cards. **661-3777.**
Food store with city's best sushi/sashimi, big selection of exotic fish, vegetable rolls. Call ahead for take-out. Delivery.

Sushi To Go

Kiku Express
229 S Highland, Shadyside. Mon-Sat 11-10pm, Sun 12-9. No credit cards. **661-KIKU.**
Main dishes and sushi and maki to go at this bright new Japanese take-out...all at wonderful prices. Tuna sushi, California roll plus shrimp, teriyaki, noodle soup and oyako—soy marinated chicken/veggies...under $5.

Young Bin Kwan
4305 Main St, Bloomfield. Mon-Fri 11-10:30, Sat-Sun 1-10:30. AE,DC,MC,V. **687-2222.**
Sushi/Japanese/Korean/Chinese. Standards plus exotic Asian dishes, tableside cooking. Atmospheric private Japanese tatami rooms, wishing bridge. Mod-Exp.

INDIAN

Darbar
4519 Centre Ave, Oakland. Lunch Mon-Sat 11:30-2:30, Dinner 5-10, Fri-Sat til 10:30. Sun 5-10. AE,MC,V. **687-0515.**
Pleasant neighborhood room with excellent mostly N Indian Punjab cuisine. Excellent paneers, tandoori, curries & biryanis. Inex-Mod. (See Review)

Star of India
412 S Craig St, Oakland. Lunch 11:30-2:30, Dinner Sun-Thur 5-10, Fri-Sat til 10:30. AE,MC,V. **681-5700.**
Excellent cuisine in pleasing room, vegetarian thali, mixed grill tandoori, paneer & bhartha—herb spiced eggplant; good Indian breads, desserts. Mod. (See Review)

Taste of India
4320 Penn Ave, Bloomfield. Lunch Mon-Sat 11-2:30. Dinner Sun-Thur 5-10, Fri-Sat til 11. AE,DC,V. **681-7700.**
New little eatery specializing in North Indian dishes—tandoori, chicken jal frezi, shrimp kabob, Mod-Exp.

13

Thai/Vietnamese

Tropical Delight

Teody's La Filipiniana
5321 Butler St, Lawrenceville, Wed-Sat 5-10. No credit cards. **781-8724.**
Surprise of the year is this charming little tropical oasis in Lawrenceville with a soothing decor and four-star Philippine cuisine, a delightful blend of Thai, Indian and Spanish. Unusual marinated Adobo chicken, delicate curries, trout steamed in banana leaves with traces of ginger, unique appetizers, unusual desserts. Don't miss the Oriental salad. Five-course special $9.95. Dinner $7.50-$13. BYO wine.

THAI

Bangkok House
3233 W Liberty, Dormont. Sun-Thur 5-10, Fri-Sat til 10:30. AE,MC,V. **341-8888.**
Rare Thai gourmet in lovely room. Curries, Phad noodles, chicken, shrimp, boxer chicken, specials for 2. Mod-Exp. (See Review)

Bangkok Taste
428 Forbes, Downtown. Mon-Fri 11-9, Sat noon-8. AE,MC,V. **338-9111.**
Wonderful noonday stop for business buffet—spring rolls, soup, curries, vegetable dishes, dessert for $6.95. Excellent dinner under $10. Inexp.

House of Siam
7905 McKnight Rd, N Hills. Lunch Tues-Fri 11:30-3, Dinner Mon-Fri 4:30-9:30. Fri-Sat til 10:30. Sun Dinner 11:30-9. AE,DC,MC,V. **367-9888.**
Exotic specials—try stir-fry noodles, green curry chicken, scallops, BBQ skewered satay chicken, fish cakes. Bring your own liquor. Dinner $7.50-$10. Inexp-Mod.

Mai Thai
328 Atwood St, Oakland. Mon-Fri Lunch 11:30-2:30, Dinner Mon-Sat 4:30-9:30. AE,D,DC,MC,V. **683-7066.**
City's first Thai house; popular favorites—try #31 Chicken in Basil, Pad Thai noodles or any green curry. Average meal $8. Inexp-Mod.

Thai Place
775 Freeport Road, Harmarville. Tues-Fri Lunch 11-2:30, Dinner Tues-Thur 5-10, Fri til 10:30. Sat noon-10:30. Sun Brunch 11-2, Dinner til 9:30. **274-9222.**
One of city's best. Owner Surin (Serene), a macrobiologist, does the cooking. Try crispy Angel Wings stuffed with ground shrimp & chicken, soft, fluffy jasmine rice & Seafood Platter—clams, orange roughy, shrimp, scallops, squid, crab legs, all stir-fried in Thai curry paste topped with a shrimp/potato bird...mmmmm! After dinner you can go downstairs to Orchid Club for DJ & live entertainment.

VIETNAMESE

Kim's Coffee Shop
5447 Penn Avenue, Garfield. Tues-Thur & Sun 11:30-9:30, Fri-Sat til 10:30. No credit cards. **362-7019.**
Upstairs/downstairs Vietnamese & Mandarin; try the crispy chicken wings stuffed with shrimp & crab. You can get really spicy here! Bring your own wine, beer. Inexp.

Me Lyng
213 W 8th Ave, Homestead nr High Level Bridge. Mon-Thur 11-9:30, Fri-Sat til 10. Sun 3-9. AE,MC,V. **464-1477.**
A sister restaurant to Kim's. Vietnamese/Chinese. We suggest Sour Soup with homemade eggrolls, crispy beef with orange peel, Me Lyng shrimp. Friendly casual, under $10. Inexp.

Unique Indian, Chinese, Vietnamese

Wok Inn
370 Atwood St, Oakland. Lunch Mon-Fri 11:30-2:30, Dinner 7 days 4:30-9:30. AE,D,DC,MC,V. **621-6400.**
Great Indian, Chinese, Vietnamese cuisine. Tandoori, Indian bread, Basmati rice, curries, chicken and chick pea masala. Try beef or chicken lemon grass, shrimp in brown bean sauce if you like Vietnamese. Inex-Mod.

14

Whether it's a boat, train, or a magnificent museum....beautiful and unique places for private/business parties abound. Here are some of the city's best with exciting atmosphere and that element of surprise that transforms a gathering into a celebration and makes *you* a successful partygiver. Enjoy!

PARTY ROOMS

The Benedum

Hold a business/social meeting at the resplendent Benedum Center for the Arts—home of the city's opera, ballet, dance and Broadway shows. The restored grand lobby is a glamorous setting for a wedding or reception and the promenade and mezzanine, rehearsal studios and downstairs galleries are all available for parties. Combine business with pleasure and arrange a free 45-minute tour before a luncheon.
Capacity: 20-400.
Cost: Varies, smaller rooms $2.75 person; with hors d'oeuvres $3.75 up. Also sitdown meals.
Contact: Adm Office—**456-2600.**

Brandy's Restaurant

Penn Ave & 24th St, Strip.
A favorite scene for business meetings, Christmas parties and football gatherings are two private rooms with the stained-glass and oak-wood atmosphere of the restaurant. There's a first floor 'Board Room'—ideal for business groups—and a larger upstairs room with a private bar, fireplace and dance floor for informal office revels and rehearsal dinners. The Board Room can also accommodate early seatings 'of parties.
Capacity: 25-50.
Cost: Buffet $12-14, Dinner $12-$22.
Contact: Janet Holzer—**566-1000.**

The Castle

Wilmerding.
This turreted, turn-of-the-century stone castle broods over the landscape, dominating the town. It's a perfect setting for a 'murder mystery party' and an unusual backdrop for business meetings, weddings, showers. There are six to eight available rooms, some with fireplaces big enough for two men to fit inside, and the furniture's still the original. Built by George Westinghouse as a clubhouse for his employees, the building's now a non-profit training center. Catering is from Wilmerding's famous Station Brake Cafe. Atmospheric.
Capacity: 20-150 per room.
Cost: $100-$275 per room. Catering from $4 to $20 a person.
Contact: Tom Setz—**823-1600.**

Party On Your Own Houseboat

A dream of a party. . . rent your own 56-ft houseboat, the luxurious Sunseeker of **Three Rivers Cruises, Inc.** The boat is equipped with a hot tub for 15, water slide, stereo, wet bar and full galley with a microwave to heat up your own or catered eats. A relaxing milieu and a real change of scene for your next sales meeting, corporate party, wedding, or just a 'friendly' celebration.
Capacity: 1-60.
Cost: $400-$700 base rate for 4 to 6 hr cruises (off-season Oct-Dec $350-$450) plus charge for captain/fuel.
Contact: Three Rivers Cruises Inc—**831-1188.**

The Carnegie

4400 Forbes Avenue, Oakland.
Some of the city's most magnificent interiors are available for private celebrations at the Carnegie museums. Imagine your guests in the Music Hall's ornate gilt and marble foyer, dancing or banqueting beneath the gold baroque ceiling. . . a spectacular site for a sumptuous private party. Or in the white marble Hall of Architecture, the huge architectural casts an imposing background for a special event. Or—imagination soars—your gathering in the Museum of Art's graceful Scaife foyer overlooking the beautiful Sculpture Court and fountain. . . a lovely space by day. . . enchanting on a summer's night as guests wander outside amid the Court's illuminated trees and statues. . . the golden lights reflected in the Gallery's sheer glass walls. If you have it—what a better way to spend!
Capacity: Music Hall—2000 reception, 500 for banqueting; Hall of Architecture—400 reception, 250 banquet; Museum of Art foyer, 500 reception.
Cost: Music Hall, $1950 base rental for three hours; Hall of Architecture $960 base rental; Museum of Art foyer $1885 base rental. Museum catering available
Contact: Eileen Dewalt—**622-3360.**

Fountainview Room

2nd Level, Sheraton at Station Square.
This romantic room, redecorated in teal, salmon and dusty rose, has a splendid view of the city skyline. It's plush decor fits the scenery—a superb place for a wedding or cocktail party.
Capacity: 100.
Cost: Room charge varies. Cocktails $8 person up, Lunch $8.95 up, Dinner $15.50 up.
Contact: Sales Dept—**261-2000.**

Grand Concourse

Station Square.
The 'grand hotel' atmosphere of this famous restaurant can't be beat for an elegant wedding breakfast or anniversary party. Tables are separated in the main dining room but marvelous atmosphere and gracious service prevail for first-class partying.
Capacity: 20-200.
Cost: No room charge. Hors d'oeuvres $3.75 up, Lunch $7-$11, Dinner $14-$21.
Contact: Sherry Ackerman—**391-3474.**

A Floating Party On Pittsburgh's Rivers

The Gateway Clipper's six vessels are unique sites for weddings, receptions, private parties, business and social events. You can tie the knot with the Point Fountain in the background and a salute from the Captain's horn. Or celebrate by releasing many-coloured balloons over the waters. The vessels can be chartered for up to three hours—the Liberty Belle or River Belle accommodate up to 240 ($1750); the Party Liner, up to 600 ($2400); or the elegant 265-foot Majestic which can accommodate up to 1000 for $4000. Gateway will cater anything from a $4 picnic box lunch to a $35 per person sit-down dinner and arrange for music, magician and vocalists. Landlubbers can settle for a party in the dockside Riverboat Lounge for $50 an hour. Contact **355-7965.**

Carnegie Science Center

Another new party facility with a river view is Carnegie Science Center with multiple areas—including the outdoor dining terrace—available for party rental. You can also tie in with special exhibitions for a unique event. Call **237-3400.**

Fox Chapel Yacht Club

1366 Old Freeport Road, Fox Chapel.
An unconventional conference center with a relaxing view of river greenery and the club marina, full audio-visual facilities and famous cuisine to keep your attendees happy. It's an out-of-city favorite for corporate affairs, seminars, retirement dinners, small or large parties. And the big, pale gray ballroom has an outside deck overlooking the river—great for weddings, business, social events.
Capacity: 10-1500.
Cost: Room cost varies. Catering from $5-$24.50 a person.
Contact: Susan Cohen—**963-8881.**

Hyeholde Cabaret

190 Hyeholde Drive, Coraopolis. 5 min from Airport.
Here comes the bride . . . down the beautiful curved stairway, a dramatic entrance into this elegant silver, white and gray Art Deco room at one of Pittsburgh's most celebrated restaurants. Connected to Hyeholde's Tudor mansion by an art gallery/loggia, the Cabaret has a two-story glass wall overlooking six acres of pine trees. In summer, parties can spill out onto the lawn, a romantic setting for a wedding, reception, cocktail or business party. And guests can revel in Hyeholde's four-star cuisine.
Capacity: 10-100, using lawn 125.
Cost: No rental cost for room (except Sun). Catering from restaurant menu $12.50-$20 per person, less for hors d'oeuvres.
Contact: Diane Robinson—**264-3116.**

14

Hartwood

Saxonburg Blvd, Rt 8, Allison.
A garden party on the beautiful lawn at Hartwood... under spacious yellow & white striped tents...a rare experience. Your guests can also tour the impressive Tudor mansion and grounds. Daytime only til 7:30 pm. Bring your own caterer.
Capacity: 75 people.
Cost: $150.
Contact: Del Cook—**767-9200.**

Heinz Hall

Sixth Avenue & Penn, Downtown.
The possibilities here are endless. Imagine a reception or wedding in the grand marble lobby with its gold, white and red plush decor...or a summer cocktail party under the stars in the outdoor plaza—available on non-performance nights. There are also the Grand Tier and Overlook bars, the Mozart Room and downstairs Regency Room ... for everything from large corporate parties to very small receptions.
Capacity: 25-350.
Cost: Varies from budget to lavish depending on group size and catering.
Contact: Terry Neugebauer/Jean Ross—**392-4887.**

Pittsburgh Party

Chiodo's Tavern

104 W 8th Avenue, Homestead.
How about a real Pittsburgh party in the backroom of this famous neighborhood tavern...or in the wooden-benched Italian beer garden outside in summer. One hundred beers will flow, Joe will serve his famous 'mystery sandwiches' and regale your guests with tales of the city's most famous bar. Here's to good friends. They'll wonder why *they* never thought of it!
Capacity: 50-75.
Cost: Reasonable.
Contact: Call Sam—**461-9307.**

Lawrence Convention/Expo Center

1001 Penn Avenue, Downtown.
Pittsburghers often forget the 24 rooms on the third level of the Convention Center, ideal for everything from business meetings to wedding receptions. Some of them have gorgeous views of the Allegheny. There are also two full-service lounges with outdoor terraces ...ideal for cook-outs on a summer's night. In-house catering.
Capacity: 12 to 6000.
Cost: Varied rentals, waived for events.
Contact: Tracy Brailey—**564-6014.**

L C Simpson's

3220 W Liberty Ave, Dormont.
South Hills has a beautiful new party facility in the elegant, chandeliered party rooms of this Dormont restaurant. Soft shades of peach and seafoam green make a pleasing background.
Capacity: 10-150.
Cost: No rental fee. Catering $6-$20 person.
Contact: Debbie—**531-0666.**

Max's Allegheny Tavern

Middle & Suismon Streets, North Side.
A unique Pittsburgh meeting place, this historic tavern has all of the atmosphere of a German gastehaus. Four connecting second floor rooms with fireplaces, Victorian wallpaper and lace curtains are just right for an informal party, business meeting, rehearsal dinner. And the food's unique too.
Capacity: 10-80.
Cost: $50 rental for catering under $400.
Contact: Peggy Quillan—**231-1899.**

Metropol Coffee House

2600 Smallman, Strip District.
Perfect get-together space for local civic, arts, cultural organizations—from small meetings to big events. 6500 sq-ft of industrial space, state-of-the-art audio-visuals for multi-media events. Coffee, specialty teas, desserts plus bar. Hors d'oeuvres are available.
Capacity: 50-600.
Cost: Flexible, depending on event.
Contact: **261-2221.**

The Pennsylvanian
1100 Liberty Ave, Downtown.
One of the city's best kept secrets is this beautiful party space in the magnificent Concourse of the restored Pennsylvania RR Station—now a fashionable downtown address. Your guests make a grand entrance from beneath the lofty outdoor rotunda into the Concourse's breathtaking space...the skylight ceiling, marble floors, restored wall paintings a beautiful setting for everything from private weddings to huge corporate parties and fund-raising balls.
Capacity: 150-1700.
Cost: Rental $1000-$6000.
Contact: Carol Gamble—**391-6730.**

The Priory
614 Pressley Street, North Side.
This Victorian in-city inn, a charmingly restored abbey, is a delightful choice for secluded meetings and parties. The diningroom and courtyard are romantic background for a wedding/reception and the Inn's quiet rooms are perfect backdrops for business and private parties. Large groups can extend into the hall, sitting room, elegant library and, in good weather, to the charming courtyard.
Capacity: 45 for dinner, 60-75 for cocktails.
Cost: Rooms $250. Receptions $375.
Contact: Barbara Beisel—**231-3338.**

Brew "On Tap" For Charities

The Ober Brau Haus, a taproom attached to the historic Pittsburgh Brewing Company at 3340 Liberty Avenue, Lawrenceville, is available for use by non-profit community groups & charities. Bring your own food, Iron City & IC Light beer is on tap. Seats 80 comfortably. Call Patricia Sheets **682-7400.**

Party—by the Riverside

A brand new party facility is the **Riverwatch** banquet hall out on the floating Boardwalk of exciting new Strip—Down by the Riverside. On the second level, it has space for 250-300, an outer deck and a great river view. Call **257-1500.**

Sandcastle on the Mon
West Homestead.
Your guests will never forget their beautiful summer evening along the riverfront at Pittsburgh's fantastic water park. Sunday thru Tuesday (after the park closes) they can be transported to a Hawaiian Luau, an Island Buffet or a Beach Party, enjoying the park's giant hot tubs, volleyball courts, music, dancing, fun.
Capacity: Minimum of 100 to 2000.
Cost: $9.95-$28 per person.
Contact: Bob Henninger/Andy Quinn—**464-9931.**

Shiloh Inn
123 Shiloh Street, Mt Washington.
A well-kept secret...high above the city in this mellow restaurant with a Civil War flavour are two small drawing rooms with an atmosphere perfect for small parties.
Capacity: 10-75.
Cost: No room charge. Food costs vary.
Contact: John Edgos—**431-4000.**

Tramps
212 Blvd of the Allies, Downtown.
261-1990. What better spot for a party than Dolly's Boudoir or Madame's Room on the second floor of this charming downtown restaurant—the site of one of Pittsburgh's first bordellos. Four upstairs rooms—small, intimate, with quaint touches, two full bars and outside patio. Ideal for business meetings, cocktail parties or a unique bachelor party.
Capacity: 70.
Cost: No charge for room. Hors d'oeuvres $6-$11, sit-down $8-$15.
Contact: Debbie Bradley—**261-1990.**

14

Children's Parties

Children's Parties

The Carnegie

Make your child's next birthday a unique adventure with a Carnegie museum party. Choose a Dinosaurs or Polar World theme for ages 8-12, Sat & Sun only from 1:30-3:30. Invitations, favors, ice cream, cake, beverage are included.
Cost: Members $10 child, $11 nonmembers. Reserve far in advance, there's a long waiting list.
Contact: Beverly Dickson —622-3289.

Good Ship Lollipop

Gateway Clipper Fleet, Station Sq.
Take your party aboard the colorful Good Ship Lollipop for a one-hour Birthday Cruise on Pittsburgh rivers. Included are hot dogs, cupcakes, balloons and entertainment with Lolly the Clown! A kiddie favorite. Or you can rent the whole boat for $450 an hour for a private party.
Capacity: up to 100.
Cost: $9.95 person.
Contact: Maria Kehlbeck— 355-7965.

The Factory

7501 Penn at Braddock, East End. Kiddies love this mall full of games.
Grand Slam: You can have a party on your own here with a sports entertainment ticket for indoor miniature golf, batting cages, baseball, video... and eat at East End Co-op Cafe. Individual 25¢-$2. Entertainment Ticket $5. **731-7526.**
ShadySkates PartyLine: Or have a supervised party at ShadySkates for

4 and older—roller skating, miniature golf, gymnastics, sports, beauty parlor—and for eats... pizza. $165 for 15 children 4 & up. **731-4937.**
Playful Parenting: Supervised parties for tots 4 and younger with miniature trampolines, tree house, trapeze, swings. $75 for 15 tots 1-3. **247-4100.**

Hartwood Hayride/Sleighride

Saxonburg Blvd, Rt 8, Allison Park.
What better site for a party than a good old-fashioned **Hayride** on a summer's eve or a **Sleighride** through North Hills beautiful winter scenery. Guaranteed fun!
Cost: A one-hour ride for 20 children (or 16 adults) is $50.
Contact: 767-9200.

Kennywood Park

West Mifflin.
A novel idea—for both kiddies and adults—is a birthday party at Kennywood Amusement Park. For 25 people or more you can get discounts off the ride-all-day admission price. Bring your own picnic or have the park cater hot dogs, hamburgers & watermelon or charbroiled steak & potatoes served in an outdoor pavilion. It's a trip down memory lane for adults who remember their wonder years at Kennywood.
Capacity: 25 to 1000 or more.
Cost: Admission $9.50-$13.50. Catering $5.10-$6.95 person.
Contact: Bob Henninger/Andy Quinn—461-0500.

Citiparks has everything from a small shelter in Frick for up to 40 ($60) to a large shelter at Riverview for 300 ($150). Permits are necessary for formal events. $25 permit for alcohol. **255-2370.**

County Parks has picnic shelters in the $5-$10 range but also offers various packages with or without catering; range of attractive shelters and renovated barns & buildings for $90-$250. Call **392-8474.**

TRAVELING PARTIES

In a Super Coach...

Travel in style and party at the same time...in a deluxe $325,000 motor coach (not a bus!) from Executive Transportation Company. The carpeted custom-built coach is equipped with everything from sofas to a shower, galley, bar, TV and a stereo system for a little travelin' music. It rents for $2.50 a mile or $800 a day (whichever is greater), a bargain when the cost is shared by groups of 20-25. You can hire a hostess or bartender and really 'lay back' and enjoy the fun all the way to your destination. Make arrangements at least one month in advance with Jim or Patricia West—**242-6267.**

In A Railroad Car

You can host daylight parties for up to 15 guests in a refurbished 1926 Pullman-Standard antique railroad car, stationary at the Conrail yard office in Sharpsburg. The car, which has hosted movie stars and government officials, is complete with lounge, four staterooms (sleeping eight), ceramic tile showers, all electric kitchen, formal diningroom and an observation platform at the rear to watch the scenery. For traveling parties of eight it's a wonderful way to see the U.S.A...anywhere that Amtrak goes. Arrangements can be made for larger parties with additional cars. What a wonderful way to go!
Capacity: 8-15.
Cost: Stationary, $400 a day. Travel rates vary.
Contact: John R Owen—**531-3652.**

Or By Balloon

How's this for a thrilling party...transport your guests to the skies for a fantastic hot air balloon ride with **Ragge & Willow Enterprises,** Rt 30, East Greensburg. The 45-60 minute flights, at sunrise and a few hours before sunset, include a complimentary breakfast

UNIQUE WEDDING SCENES

Pittsburgh Aviary

The lush foliage of the Tropical American Marsh Room is a unique background for wedding ceremonies with exotic, multi-coloured birds swooping nearby.
Cost: $100 fee, limit 50 guests.
323-7235

Heinz Chapel

A jewel of a wedding site, this exquisite Gothic chapel on the Pitt campus is open only to students, alumni, relatives and employees. Capacity 450. Available Thur, Fri & Sat.
Cost: $395. **624-4157.**

Phipps Conservatory

The perfect wedding scene...you choose the room—the flower arrangements are magnificent. Limit 35 guests, daily from 9-3 during non-show times.
Cost: $100. **622-6915.**

Pittsburgh Parks

Outdoor weddings in the greenery of Pittsburgh's city/county parks are becoming more popular. Favorite sites are Schenley, Hartwood, North & South Parks. Consider a back-up shelter in case of rain and be sure to get a permit.
Cost: City Shelters $60-$150.
255-2370. County $50-$250.
392-8455.

(on morning flights) and the traditional Champagne Party on landing. Six balloons can accommodate up to 25 guests. Year round, Sat/Sun only.
Capacity: 25 guests.
Cost: $150 person.
Contact: 836-4777. Reser three weeks in advance.

14

RIBS TO GO

Pittsburgh ribs are second to none! You can check them all out at the annual Allegheny Co Rib Cook-Off at South Park Fairgrounds, Labor Day weekend when rib-makers from all over compete with local chefs. For info -- 392-8455.

Stand Up...Sit Down...Take Out

Blue Lou's
1510 E Carson, South Side. Tues-Sat 11-1:30. AE,DC,MC,V. **381-7675.**
Tangy pork ribs in fun eatery. Slab $13, half $10; mild to hot. Chicken, platters. Sit down. Take out.

Bobby Rubino's
Shops at Station Sq. Mon-Thur 11-10:30, Fri-Sat til 12:30. Sun 1-9. **642-RIBS.**
Mellow rib dinners in posh decor. Steel City—2 slabs $17.95, slab $15 with baked potato/fries; great onion ring loaf $2-3.50. Sit down/take out.

Damon's
Waterworks, Freeport Rd, Fox Chapel. Mon-Thur 11-11, Fri & Sat til 1 am, Sun til 10. AE,DC,MC,V. **782-3750.**
Pleasant restaurant with meaty, pungent ribs. Slab $13.95, half $10.95 with salad & baked potato; Rib Lunch $5.95 with sides. Full menu. Sit down/take out.

Genghis Cones
5349 Penn, Garfield. Mon-Thur 10-10, Fri 11-12, Sat 11-11, Sun 3-9. AE,MC,V. **363-4248.**
Tender pork ribs uniquely cooked in wooden hot box, rack $13.75, 1/2 $7.25 with hot Alabama mustard or mild sweet sauce. Tantalizing Korean beef short ribs marinated in sesame oil, ginger $8. Take out only. Free delivery $10 & over.

Hot Licks
Theatre Mall, 5520 Walnut, Shadyside. **683-2583.** *S Hills, Galleria.* **341-7427.** *Mon-Thur 11:30-10, Fri & Sat til 12. Sun 4:30-9, S Hills 12-10. AE,DC,MC,V.*
Big favorites $14 rack; $7.95 1/2 with cole slaw. Sweet & mild, smoky medium or Zeb's Screamin' Killer-Willer! Eat in/take out.

House of Sauce
4707 Centre, Oakland. Mon-Thur til 2:30am, Fri/Sat til 3:30. Sun 1-11:30. **682-9888.**
Great tastin' hot & spicy, slab $19, 1/2 $10, sandwich $7; also BBQ chicken, potato salad and sweet potato pie. Sides 50¢-65¢. Real thing. Stand-up/take out.

Mr P & P Ribs
1501 Fifth/Pride, Uptown. Mon-Thur 11-12, Fri-Sat 11am-2:30am. Sun 12-6. No credit cards. **566-2773.**
Open-pit grilled, rack of 12—$17, 1/2 rack $8.80. Chicken, Texas toast, great baked beans, cakes & pies, $2.65 up. Eat in, take out, delivery.

Original Hot Dog Shop
3901 Forbes, Oakland. 7 days 10am-4am. No credit cards. **621-0435.**
The Big "O" is into zesty ribs, slab $8.80 with cole slaw & potato; mild to hot. Stand up, sit down, take out.

Piero's Pit
2117 Penn Avenue, Strip. Mon-Sat 11-9. AE, DC. **471-6911.**
Whole $14.95, half $8.50 with 2 sides, mild to fiery. Sit down, take out.

Red River Bar-B-Que
E Liberty: 5945 Penn. **363-7427.** *Edgewood Towne Ctr.* **241-0300.** *Castle Shannon Sq.,* **882-9500.** *Monroeville* **372-2500.** *Wexford* **935-9200.** *Mon-Thur 11-10. Sun 4-9 (E Lib 12-7). AE,DC,MC,V.*
Alleg Co Rib Cook-Off winner; hickory-smoked, Slab $12-$13, half $6-$7, sides 89¢-$1.59. Mild, hot, daredevil. Sit down, take out.

Ribb House
2125 Murray Ave, Squirrel Hill. Tues-Thur 4-10:45, Fri 3-10:45, Sat 1:30-10:45, Sun 1:30-8:30. **521-8827.**
Pungent, mellow, mild to extra hot. Rack $14, half $7.49; smoked potatoes, sides 59¢ up. Famous Buffalo wings, dinners $4-$8. Sit down, take out.

Wilson's Bar-B-Q
700 N Taylor & Buena Vista, N Side **322-7427.** *3404 Penn, E Liberty.* **683-1616.** *Mon-Wed 12-12, Thur-Sat 12-2. Sun N Side 12-8.* Pungent, hot & tangy, some say city's best. Slab $15, plate $8; sides, 85¢. Stand up/take out.

Woodside
7610 Frankstown, Homewood. Mon-Wed 11am-12, Thur-Sat til 1:30. **371-1949.**
Secret open pit recipe—hot or mild. Slab $18.50, 1/2 $8.85. Take out only.

15

BEST OF SUBURBS

Exciting and unusual restaurants are continually opening around Pittsburgh beckoning both suburban and urban diners to discover new cuisine outside the city. Here are the best of the suburbs...North...South...East...West...many with restful country settings. Also included are popular family eateries with menus, entertainment and party atmosphere that children love.

SUBURBS NORTH

Abate's Seafood Co
Waterworks, Freeport Rd, Fox Chapel. 7 days 11:30-12. AE,CB,DC,MC,V. **781-9550.**
Bona fide Italian/seafood house, nautical theme; all kinds of fish, great hearth-baked pizzas, key lime pie. Lunch/Dinner $4-$18. Friendly, casual.

Blarney Stone
30 Grant Ave, Etna. Tues-Thur 11-9, Fri-Sat til 11. Sun 10:30-9. AE,MC,V. **781-1666.**
Irish/Amer cuisine, authentic Irish stew, corned beef/cabbage, pastries by Irish chef. Gaelic entertainment Fri-Sat, Sun Brunch. $4-$18.

Cathay Gourmet
4812 McKnight Road, N Hills. Mon-Thur 11:30-10, Fri-Sat til 11. Sun 3-9:30. AE,D,DC,MC,V. **366-9111.**
Renowned Chinese cuisine. Delicious beef, pork, lobster, great Dragon-Phoenix Soup, Pu Pu Platter for 2. Mon Buffet $8.50. Lunch/Dinner $4-$9.

Chili's Grill & Bar
7404 McKnight Rd, North Hills. Mon-Thur 11-11, Fri-Sat til 12. Sun 11-10. AE,DC,MC,V. **364-5678.**
Big, good looking; tasty Tex-Mex burgers, ribs, steak and, of course, chili. First-class fajitas, delicious baked onion. $4-$15. Close to the real thing!

Chop Stix
1034 Freeport Rd, O'Hara. 7 days 11:30-10, Fri-Sat til 11. AE,MC,V. **782-3010.**
Worthy successor to Anna Kao's. Szechuan, Hunan, Peking dishes, "20-30 Minute Duck," house special pork/bean sauce, $5.50-$24. Buffet Sun-Tues $8.99.

Cranberry Hall
Rt 19, Crider's Corners. Mon-Sat 4-8:30. Sun Dinner 12-8. MC,V. **776-9930.**
Good family fare, American home cooking—baked ham/raisin sauce, fried chicken, rainbow trout, great Strawberry Ice Cream Meringue. $13-$18.

Cross Keys
599 Dorseyville Rd, Fox Chapel. Tues-Fri 11:30-10, Sat 5-11. Sun 11-9. Reser weekends. MC,V. **963-8717.**
Charming little inn, an old stagecoach stop. Delicious steaks, veal, seafood. Lunch $4-$7, Dinner $13-$18.

Damon's
Waterworks, Freeport Rd, Fox Chapel. Mon-Thur 11-11, Fri-Sat til 1. Sun 11-10. AE,DC,MC,V. **782-3750.**
Great barbecue ribs, chicken, full dinners, sandwiches in pleasant decor; four big TV screens for sports fans. $4-$14.

DeFazio's
1026 Mt Nebo Road, Ohio Twp. Tues-Sun 4-10. AE,D,DC,MC,V. **364-9464.**
Old North Hills favorite with Italian veal, delicious prime rib, cassata cake, custard desserts. $5-$15.

Dingbat's
Waterworks, Fox Chapel. **781-7727;** *Ross Park Mall* **369-0440.** *Mon-Thur 11:30-12am, Fri-Sat til 1. Sun 10-12. AE,D,DC,MC,V.*
Bright, trendy with specialty drinks, fun foods, good portions; big variety of sandwiches, steaks, pasta. $7-$13.

Foxbriar
1044 Saxonburg Road, Glenshaw. Tues-Thur 5-10, Fri-Sat til 11. Sun 4-10. DC,MC,V. **486-6767.**
Elegant, candlelight dining. Beef, veal, chicken, seafood, many extras— sourdough bread, great desserts. $10-$17.

Fox Chapel Yacht Club
1366 Old Freeport Rd, Fox Chapel. Lunch Mon-Sat 11-3, Dinner Mon-Thur 5-9 (summer til 11), Fri-Sat til 11. Sun 10-9. Reser sugg. AE,MC,V. **963-8881.**
Fashionable room with riverfront view, piano Wed-Sat til 11, trio weekends. Veal, chicken, seafood, pasta. Lunch/Dinner $4.25-$19.

16

North

Franco's
Fox Chapel Plaza, Freeport Rd. Mon-Sat Lunch 11:30-2:30, Dinner 4-10, Fri-Sat til 11. AE,MC,V. Reser sugg. **782-5155.**
Chef Franco, originator of downtown's Bravo! Franco, is back in town in this polished room with delicious veal, seafood, pasta, tableside renditions. And his fans have found him! $6-$18.

Grant's Bar
114 Grant Ave, Millvale. Mon-Fri 11-11, Sat 4-11. Sun 3-8. CB,MC,V. **821-1541.**
Neighborhood landmark for sandwiches, dinners, jumbo butterfly shrimp. $6-$12.

Great Wall
Pines Plaza, 1130 Perry Hwy, Ross. Mon-Thur 11:30-10, Fri-Sat til 11. Sun 3-9. AE,DC,MC,V. **369-5858.**
Casual, modern with tasty, Mandarin, Szechwan, Peking. Good seafood, sizzling rice & chicken. $6-$13.

Gryphon at Stone Mansion
Stone Mansion Dr, Franklin Park. Lunch Tues-Fri 11-2, Dinner Tues-Thur 5-10, Fri & Sat til 11. AE,D,MC,V. **934-3000.**
Very good North & South American cuisine in rustic stone mansion, stained glass, warm wood. Fresh meat & seafood, light foods, 'no fried.' $9.50-$23.50.

Hamfeldt's
Freeport Rd, Aspinwall. Mon-Fri 11:30-2am, Sat 12-2am. Sun 4-12. AE,D,MC,V. **782-0444.**
Comfortable neighborhood tavern with great steak and lobster in dining room and sandwiches, ribs in the bar. $4 to $25 for steak/lobster.

Hampton Inn
Rt 8, Allison Park. Mon-Sat 11-1am. Sun 11-10. AE,D,DC,MC,V. **486-5133.**
Multi-paged menu, 100 sandwiches $2-$9. Design one & they'll name it for you. 18 dinners $6 up—seafood platter $16; best selection of imported beer. Fun!

Hideaway Restaurant
Venango Golf Course, Cranberry. Mon-Sat Lunch 11:30-2:30, Dinner 5-10. Sun 2-7. AE,MC,V. **776-4400.**
Great atmosphere, fireplaces, beautiful view; good steak, fish, veal, pasta. Patio. Lunch $5-$7, Dinner $11-$16.

Hotel Saxonburg
Main St, Saxonburg. Lunch Tues-Sat 11:30-4, Dinner Mon 5-9, Tues-Thur 4-10, Fri-Sat 4-11. Sun 4-9. AE,MC,V. **352-4200.**
Casual dining in charming 19th C inn, old stagecoach stop. Full menu $8-$25.

Iron Bridge Inn
Rt 19 N, 5 mi south of Mercer. Sun-Thur 11-10:30, Fri-Sat til 11:30. Sun Brunch 11-3. AE,DC,MC,V. **748-3626.**
A real experience—old lamp shades, moose heads, polar bears. Tangy Cajun seafood, tender prime rib. $2-$16.

Jergel's
3855 Babcock Blvd, Ross. Mon-Sat 11-2am, Sun 1-11. AE,D,MC,V. **364-9902.**
Casual, upbeat, good family homestyle. Sandwiches to Surf 'n Turf, Cajun, veal, seafood. Entertainment weekends. $3-$21.

Jimmy G's
225 Commercial Ave, Aspinwall. Mon-Thur 11:30-10, Fri-Sat til 11, Bar til 2. AE,D,DC,MC,V. **781-4884.**
Traditional American cuisine in paneled room; good steak, veal, & burgers too. Sat eve tableside entertainment $5-$22.

Juno Trattoria
Ross Park Mall, off McKnight Rd. Mon-Thur 11:30-10, Fri-Sat til 11. Sun 12-7. AE,D,DC,MC,V. **366-2737.**
Great Italian atmosphere, tile-topped tables, interesting art; homemade pasta in piccolo/uno servings, excellent sauces, wine. Lunch/Dinner $3-$13.

Kaufmann House
Main St, Zelienople. Mon-Thur 7am-9, Fri-Sat til 10. AE,DC,MC,V. **261-2024.**
Friendly room, outstanding kitchen; great broiled seafood platter, Alaskan King crab legs, & homemade desserts (try the peanut butter pie). $2.50-$17.

Kleiner-Deutschman
643 Pittsburgh St, Springdale. Tues-Sat 5-10. Sun 4-8. AE,MC,V. **274-5022.**
Adventures in German eating—wine, beer, music, great atmosphere; authentic pork, veal dishes. $8.50-$22.

Liu Garden
10500 Perry Hwy, Wexford. Mon-Fri 11:30-10, Sat til 11. Sun 12-10. AE,MC,V. **935-1880.**
You select your own food for unique all-you-can-eat stir fry on giant grill in first Mongolian BBQ house. $12, weekends $13. Lunch $4.50. Brunch Sun 12-3, $9.

Maggie Mae's Roadhouse
McKnight/Seibert Shp Ctr, 4885 McKnight Rd. Mon-Thur 11:30-11, Fri-Sat til 12. Sun 12-9. AE,DC,MC,V . **364-4300.**
Trendy restaurant, eclectic menu, 100 items—honey chicken, steaks, sandwiches; lively bar, $4-$12.

Montemurro
1822 Main St, Sharpsburg. Mon-Thur 11-11, Fri-Sat til 12. AE,D,DC,MC,V. **781-6800.**
Big Italian family menu, pleasant decor; seafood, pasta, veal, steaks. $8-$20.

Perrytowne Tavern
1002 Perry Hwy, Perrysville. Mon-Sat 11-12, Sun 2-12. DC,MC,V. **367-9610.**
Casual atmosphere for great beers, terrific hot chicken wings, beer-batter fish sandwich, pasta, seafood. $5-$12.

Pines Tavern
Old State Road, Gibsonia. Mon-Sat Lunch 11-3, Dinner 5-10. MC,V. **625-3252.**
Country inn tucked off highway, fireplace, antiques, atmosphere. Good seafood, turtle soup. Lunch/Dinner $4-$19.

Rico's Restaurant
Park Place, off Babcock Blvd, Ross. Lunch Mon-Sat 11:45-2:30. Dinner Mon-Thur 4-10:30, Fri-Sat til 11:30. AE,DC,MC,V. **931-1989.**
Fine dining in quaint old house on hill, get-away feel. Big reputation for fish, seafood, steak. Lunch $4-$8.50, Dinner $9-$23. (See Rich Man's Guide 3)

Simply Delicious
1200 Old Freeport Rd, Fox Chapel. Sun-Mon 8:30-4, Tues-Sat 8:30-9. AE,MC,V. **963-0636.**
Small delightful dining area at famed caterer's. Gourmet specialties—filet Bearnaise, french fried ice cream, great chicken salad, poppyseed/lemon/apple muffins. Breakfast to dinner $2-$13.

Tambellini North Park
Ingomar & Kummer Rds, Allison Pk. Mon 11:30-9, Tues-Thur til 10, Fri til 11. Sat 4-11. Sun 3-9. AE,MC,V. **935-6566.**
Another notable Tambellini's. Beautiful 'country estate,' fine service. Ital/Amer meat, seafood, pasta, $10-$26.

Tai Pei Chinese Restaurant
124 Freeport Rd, Fox Chapel. Mon-Thur 11:30-10, Fri-Sat til 11. AE,D,DC,MC,V. **781-4131.**
Light, airy with Hunan lamb, Gen Tso's Chicken, seafood, Peking Duck. Lunch $5.25-$6.50, Dinner $8-$12.

Thai Place
775 Freeport Rd, Harmarville. Tues-Thur 11-2:30, 5-10, Fri til 10:30. Sat 12-10:30. AE,D,DC,MC,V. **274-9222.**
Made-to-order Thai specialties i.e. Tropical Birdnest—shrimp, chicken, vegetables in roasted curry paste; whole yellow pike. $7-$12.50. Special Oriental Buffet $7.95.

Tremont House
Sheraton Pgh North, Warrendale Mon-Sat 4-11. Sun 3-10. AE,D,DC,MC,V. Reser weeknds. **776-6900.**
Stylish room noted for Fri Seafood Buffet with lobster tail, hot/cold entrees & Sat Prime Rib Buffet, both $17. Dinner $8-$25.

16

South

SUBURBS SOUTH

Amel's
435 McNeilly Rd, Baldwin. Mon-Sat 11:30-12am. Sun 4-10. AE,MC,V. **563-3466.**
Favorite Mid-East food; good mazza plate, Ital-Amer seafood $7-$18, homemade desserts $2.50.

Bado's
307 Beverly Road, Mt Lebanon. Mon-Thur 11-11, Fri til 12, Sat 8-12. Sun 8-10. No credit cards. **563-5300.**
Pizza parlor extraordinare; gourmet white/veg pizza—all-you-can-eat Mondays $4. Other great dishes. $2-$7.

Bachri's
3821 Willow Ave, Castle Shannon. Mon-Thur 11:30-10, Fri-Sat 11:30-11. No credit cards. **343-2213.**
Great Indonesian and Syrian specialties in small, cozy quarters. $5-$7.50.

Bangkok House
3233 W Liberty Ave, Dormont. Dinner Sun-Thur 5-10, Fri-Sat til 10:30. **341-8888.**
Extraordinary Thai cuisine in pleasant fountained room. Curries, Phad noodles, chicken, shrimp. $4-$13. (See Review)

Candle Keller
94 Center Church Rd, McMurray. Tues-Thur 5-10, Fri-Sat til 11. Sun 4-9. Reser weekends. AE,MC,V. **941-8424.**
Excellent Euro-American food in quaint rathskeller. Homemade schnitzel, wurst, great potato pancakes. $9-$14.

Cathay Inn
1000 Greentree Rd, Greentree. Lunch Tues-Sat 11:30-2, Dinner Tues-Sun 4-9:30. MC,V. **921-9770.**
Out of way find. Cantonese food at marvelous prices—Chicken Chop Suey/fried rice lunch, $3.30; dinners $5.25-$15. Try beef with oyster sauce, sweet/sour dishes.

Century Inn
Scenery Hill, Rt 40. Mon-Sat 12-3. Mon-Thur 4:30-7:30, Fri-Sat til 8:30. Sun 12-6:30. No credit cards. Reser. **945-6600.**
Charming trip to Colonial past in 1794 inn; traditional dishes—roast turkey, pork chops. Lunch $5-$9, Dinner $11-$25.

Colony
Greentree & Cochran Rds. Scott. Mon-Sat 5:30-11. AE,DC,MC,V. **561-2060.**
Warm, elegant atmosphere around open brick grill where suburbanites enjoy best in steak. Complete dinners $20-$26. Piano lounge. (See Rich Man's Guide 3)

Cousin's Restaurant & Bar
7 Parkway Ctr, Greentree. Mon-Sat 11:30-10. Sun 5-9. AE,DC,MC,V. **928-0700.**
Spacious room with happy atmosphere, oldtime baseball motif. Seafood, prime rib, chicken. Lunch $5 up, Dinner $7-$16. Night time fun. (See After Dark 4)

Elephant Bar
5242 Clairton Blvd, Pleasant Hills. Mon-Thur 11-10, Fri-Sat til 1-2. Sun 10-10. Bar til 1:30. AE,MC,V. **885-0151.**
Safari atmosphere, big Mexican, Ital, Creole menu with lots of fresh fish, pasta, fajita plus waffles & juice bars.

Fajita Grill
580 Old Clairton Rd, Pleasant Hills. Sun-Thur 11-9, Fri-Sat til 10. MC,V. **653-7230.**
Small eatery, authentic inc unique Mexican egg-rolls, Chili relleno, free margarita with meal. $4.50-$10.

Ferrieri's
2975 Washington Rd, McMurray. Mon-Thur 11-11, Fri-Sat til 12. Sun 4-11. AE,DC,MC,V. **941-3940.**
Casual, comfortable with nearly 100 entrees—fish, fowl, beef, veal, homemade ravioli, Ital specialties $7.50-$19. Pizza parlor annex.

The Forest—Redwood Inn
Banksville Rd/Potomac, Dormont. Mon-Fri 7am-2, Sat 8-12, Dinner 5:30-9:30. Sun 8-1, AE,D,DC,MC,V. **343-3000.**
Veal, beef, fresh seafood, 26 entrees $7-$20. Happy Hour Tues-Thur.

Fortunato's
2739 Library/McNeilly Rds, Rt 88 S, Castle Shannon. Tues-Fri 11-11, Sat 4-11. Sun 4-9. AE,MC,V. **881-4111.**
Down-to-earth cuisine, excellent veal, homemade pasta, fish, garlic toast. Lunch $2.50-$5, Dinner $6.75-$17.

Giovanni's
Bourse Shops, Greentree Road, Scott. Tues-Fri 4-11, Sat 5-11:30. Sun 4-10. AE,DC,MC,V. **279-1414.**
Warm, contemporary decor, pleasant view, one of city's best Italian—good seafood, veal, fowl, tantalizing desserts. Dinner $9-$16.50.

Houlihan's
Fort Couch & Washington Rds, Bethel Park. Mon-Thur 11-10:30, Fri-Sat til 12:30. Sun Brunch 10:30-3, Dinner til 10:30. AE,DC,MC,V. **831-9797.**
Casual dining in fun surroundings. great fajitas, chicken, beef, good onion soup. $9-$12. Sun Brunch $9.

J J Rose's
One Altoona Place, Mt Lebanon. Mon-Sat Lunch 11-3, Dinner 5-10. AE,D,DC, MC,V. **344-4604**
S Hills star, charming restored mini-mansion, elegant touches. Excellent veal, duck, salmon. Lunch $7-$15, Dinner $17-$27. Patio in summer.

Jose & Tony's
1573 McFarland Road, Mt Lebanon. Mon-Thur 11-12am, Fri-Sat til 12:30. Sun 4-10. No credit cards. **561-2025.**
Little take-out eatery that packs a Mexican wallop. Big Joe Dinner—taco, tamale, refried beans, Spanish rice, chili, cheese enchilada—all for $6.55! Bargain tacos, tamales, pizza.

Klay's Cafe
3105 Banksville Rd. Mon-Fri 11-11, Sat 4-12. Sun 3-9. AE,DC,MC,V. Reser. **341-3200.**
Newest S Hills favorite, excellent Greek/Italian food. Casual. Lunch $4-$6.50, Dinner $9-$15.

L&N Seafood Grill
Galleria, 1500 Washington Rd, Mt Lebanon. Mon-Thur 11:15-10, Fri-Sat til 12. Sun 11-9. AE,DC,MC,V. **343-6855.**
Stylish, informal, lots of favorites—mesquite-grilled fish, seafood lasagna, delectable biscuits. Sunday Brunch 9-11. Lunch $5-$9, Dinner $7-$22.

Le Peep
2101 Greentree Rd, Scott. 7 days Break/Lunch 7-3pm. AE,D,DC,MC,V. **276-3525.**
Breakfast lover's haven. Wonderful egg dishes—awesome omelettes, skillet 'pan-handled eggs,' pancakes, French toast plus sandwiches in perky decor. Definitely worth the stop. $3-$6.25.

Living Room
1778 N Highland Rd, Upper St Clair. Mon-Sat 5-11. AE,DC,MC,V. **835-9772.**
Sophisticated hideaway with good dinners, nightly piano bar. Italian specialties, exceptional cuisine $10-$20.

Maggie Mae's Roadhouse
1610 Cochran Road, Mt Lebanon. Mon-Thur 11:30-11, Fri-Sat til 12. Sun 12-9. AE,MC,V. **344-6200.**
Nice ambience, popular with young, old. A la carte snacks, Mexican, light cuisine, sandwiches, dinners. $2-$10.

Mama Lena's
Library Road, Rt 88, Castle Shannon. Tues-Fri 11:30-12am, Sat 4-12. Sun 4-9. AE,DC,MC,V. **884-8484.**
Good Ital with authentic touches—cannelloni, pasta, veal, seafood. Early Birds 4-6. $7-$12.

16

South

Mark Pi's China Gate
Galleria, 1500 Washington Rd.
Mon-Thur 11:30-10, Fri til 11. Sat 12-11,
Sun 12-9. AE,MC,V. **341-9582.**
Excellent Szechuan, Hunan, Mandarin
specialties; Three Moon combo—
sesame beef, moo goo gai pan, Hunan
shrimp. Lunch $3.75-$7, Dinner
$5-$12.50.

Naples
3600 Saw Mill Run Blvd, Brentwood.
Mon-Thur 11-11, Fri til 12. Sat 3-12. Sun
3-10. MC,V. **884-4899.**
Fans rave about the homemade cooking
here (from family of famed old Naples
downtown). Big portions of pasta, veal,
chicken, seafood in pleasant setting.
Lunch $3.75-$5.50, Dinner $5.50-$13.

Paule's Lookout
2627 Skyline Drive, West Mifflin. Tues-
Sat 11-9. Sun 12-7:30. AE,DC,MC,V.
466-4500.
Good family restaurant with great river
view. Seafood, lobster, prime rib.
$3-$11.

Piccolo Mondo
Foster Plaza—Bldg #7, Holiday Inn Dr,
Greentree. Lunch Mon-Fri 11-2:30, Din-
ner 5-10, Fri-Sat til 11. Reser sugg.
AE,MC,V. **922-0920.**
Beautiful room with sweeping view, ele-
gant cuisine, service. Noted for fish,
veal. Lunch $5-$16, Dinner $10-$22.
(See Rich Man's Guide 3)

Primo
15 DeWalt Ave, Whitehall. Mon-Thur
5-11, Fri-Sat til 12. Sun 4-9. AE,DC,
MC,V. **881-9493.**
Friendly Italian in comfortable surroundings. Rare fish specialties inc scogli—
shrimp, clams in tomato sauce—
pompano, grouper. $8-$13.

Prime House
Pgh Greentree Marriott. 7 days 7-11.
AE,D,DC,MC,V. **922-8400.**
Elegant room, first-class service, Amer
cuisine—inventive seafood, veal; daily
specials, tempting desserts. $13.50-$22.

Raffeale's
1215 State Hwy 885, Jefferson Boro.
Tues-Thur 11:30-10, Fri-Sat 4-11. Sun
3:30-8:30. AE,MC,V. **466-5910.**
Casual with some very special pasta,
salads, veal, beef. Good atmosphere,
service. Lunch $5-$8, Dinner $7-$18.

Shajor
922 McMurray Rd, Bethel Park. Dinner
Mon-Thur 5-10, Fri-Sat til 11. Sun 5-9,
Brunch 10-2. AE,MC,V. **833-4800.**
Upscale Amer/Continental, smoked
fresh seafood, veal, beef—from their
own smokehouse $13-$26. Cocktails in
lounge. $13-$26.

Sante Fe
25 McMurray Rd, Upper St Clair. 7 days
4-11. AE,DC,MC,V. **833-7075.**
Big, open room; heaping portions of
Tex-Mex dishes—grills, fajitas,
appetizers; great ribs. Dinner $8-$16

Samurai Japanese Steak House
2100 Greentree Road, Greentree. Mon-
Thur 11:30-10, Fri-Sat til 11. Sun 4:30-9.
AE,DC,MC,V. **276-2100.**
Dramatic dining at hibachi tables, performing chefs; steaks/seafood, tropical
drinks. Lunch $5-$7. Dinner $10-$18.

Sesame Inn
715 Washington Road, Mt Lebanon.
Mon-Thur 11:30-10, Fri-Sat til 11. Sun
4-10. AE,DC,MC,V. **341-2555.**
Authentic Chinese incl Gen Tso's
Chicken, orange beef, shrimp, sesame
shrimp. Lunch/Dinner $5-$15.

Sichuan House
1717 Cochran Rd, Mt. Lebanon. Sun-
Thur 4:30-9:30, Fri-Sat til 10:30. MC,V.
563-5252.
One of the city's best Chinese. Try the
Sea Delight, Chicken/Shrimp/Vegetables
& Gen Tso's Chicken. $7.50-$17.

Tai Pei Chinese Restaurant
Bourse Shops, Greentree Rd. Scott.
Mon-Thur 11:30-10, Fri-Sat til 11. Sun
11:30-9:30. AE,D,DC,MC,V. **279-8811.**
Comfortable room with Hunan lamb,
Gen Tso's Chicken, seafood, Peking
Duck. Lunch $5-$7, Dinner $9-$15.

SUBURBS EAST

Angie's
111 Middle Ave, Wilmerding. Wed-Thur & Sat 4-10, Fri 12-11. No credit cards. **829-7663.**
Secret find, a small place with great prices on delicious homemade pasta, gnocchi, spinach calzones, veal, fish, shrimp. $4.50-$11.50.

Birdie's
4733 William Penn Hwy, Monroeville. Dinner Mon-Thur 5-10, Fri-Sat til 11. Reser. AE,DC,MC,V. **372-9878.**
Intimate, elegant with good service. King-size cocktails, seafood, veal, steak, great garlic toast, $12-$26.

China Palace
Jonnet Plaza, 4059 Wm Penn Highway. Mon-Thur 11:30-9:30, Fri-Sat til 10:30. Sun 3-9. Reser 6 or more. AE,MC,V. **373-7423.**
Above average Szechwan, Hunan, Mandarin at great prices; good Pu Pu Platter $9.95 for 2. Gen Tso's Chicken, lobster, specialties $7.50-$12.95.

Dick's Diner
Rt 22, Murrysville. Sun-Thur 6:30am-10pm. Fri-Sat 24 hrs. No credit cards. **327-4566.**
A Pgh institution, big, modern, informal with wonderful family fare at great prices. Fabulous hot roast beef sandwiches, homemade pies. $2-$7.

D'Imperio's
3412 William Penn Hwy, Wilkins Twp. Dinner Tues-Sun 5-11. Reser. AE,MC,V. **823-4800.**
Gracious dining at city's finest; famous for seafood, lamb, fish from $16-$27. (See Review 1, Rich Man's Dining 3)

Eastwood Inn
7268 Verona Road, Penn Hills. Mon-Sat 4-11. MC,V. **241-4700**
Old favorite newly remodeled. Famous for soft shell crabs year around, good steak, veal, desserts, $8-$24.50. Early Bird 4-6 Mon-Fri $5-$6.50. Good bet!

Fairchild's
Jonnet Bldg, Monroeville. Lunch Mon-Fri 11-2:30. Dinner Mon-Thur 5-10, Fri-Sat til 11. AE,D,DC,MC,V. **372-1511.**
Inviting atmosphere, penthouse view, good service; beef, veal, fresh seafood, $11.75 to $32.50 for surf 'n turf, lamb chops & lobster combo.

Hoffstot's Cafe Monaco
533 Allegheny Ave, Oakmont. Mon-Thur 11:30-10, Fri-Sat til 11. Sun 3:30-9. Weekend reser. AE,DC,MC,V. **828-8555.**
Euro/Italian cafe with family flavour, sports bar, good prices. Great fish sandwiches, dark beer, fried ice cream, 50 dinner items. Deserves its accolades.

Hotel Benedict
400 2nd Street, Pitcairn. Mon-Thur 11:30-11, Sat 4-12. Sun 4-9:30. AE,MC,V. **372-9801.**
Comfortable, casual. Famed steak salad, lobster, prime rib weekends. Dinners $8-$24. Italian Buffet Wed $7.95.

Houlihan's
Monroeville Mall. Mon-Thur 11-11, Fri-Sat til 12. Sun Brunch 10-2, Dinner til 10. AE,DC,MC,V. **373-8520.**
You may see your favorite sports star at this lively place. Good eclectic menu, Mexican, grills, sandwiches, raw oyster bar. Lunch/Dinner $5-$14. Appetizers 1/2 price at Happy Hour; nightly disco.

Kabuki
635 Brown Ave, Turtle Creek. Lunch Mon-Fri 11:30-2, Dinner Mon-Sat 5-10. AE,DC,MC,V. **823-0750.**
The place for sushi, tempura, authentic Japanese cuisine at tables or on floor cushions in the tatami room. Moderate.

King Wu
304 Plaza on Mall Blvd, Monroeville. Sun-Thur 11:30-10, Fri-Sat til 11. AE,MC,V. **373-5464.**
Chinese modern setting for Szechuan, Mandarin, Hunan, good wonton chips, Gen Tso's chicken $3-$14. Lunch special—egg/spring roll, soup, rice, tea for $5.

16

BEST OF SUBURBS
East

Me Lyng Restaurant
213 W Eighth Ave, W Homestead. Mon-Fri 11:30-9:30, Sat 4-10. Sun 3-9. AE,MC,V. **464-1477.**
Beautiful Chinese/Vietnamese dishes—beef, shrimp, duck, fish, pork—110 in all. Lunch $3-$4.50, Dinner $6.25-$13. Take out too.

Nick Marie's
4000 Wm Penn Hwy, Monroeville. Mon-Sat 11-10:30. Sun 3-9. AE,D,DC,MC,V. **372-4414.**
Good Italian dishes—seafood, pasta, shrimp, veal. $4-$7 & up. Early Bird Mon-Sat 4-6:30.

Oxford Dining Room
Radisson Hotel Pgh, Monroeville Mall Blvd. Breakfast/Lunch Mon-Fri 6:30-2, Sat & Sun 7-2, Dinner 7 days 5-11. AE,DC,MC,V. **373-7300.**
Country atmosphere, romantic fireplaces, SW cuisine; Fri prime rib/pasta, Sat Ital buffet, both $15. Early Birds $6.95. Lunch $6-$13, Dinner $13-$20.

Penn Monroe Bar
3985 Wm Penn Hwy, Monroeville. 7 days 10-2am. Sun 11-1am. AE,MC,V. **373-1180.**
Casual dining, excellent homemade soups, sandwiches ($1.50-$4), authentic Ital—meatballs to steak, $5-$10. Mon Rigatoni $1.89. Sing-a-longs Sun/Tues.

Pizzeria Uno
Penn Center, Wilkins Twp. Sun-Thur 11-10, Fri-Sat til 12. AE,MC,V. **825-8667.**
Sassy new place for famous Chicago deep-dish pizza. Also winning wings, potato skins, salads, sandwiches, appetizers $2-$10. Five minute lunch $4.45.

Rivers Three
Harley Hotel, off Rodi Road, Wilkins Twp. Lunch 7 days 11-2, Dinner Sun-Thur 5:30-10, Fri-Sat til 11. AE,D,DC, MC,V. **244-1600.**
Quiet, elegant, hilltop view, dinner music, extra touches. Seafood, prime rib, steak. Sun Breakfast Buffet 8-12. Lunch/Dinner $4-$18.

Shogun Japanese Restaurant
Monroeville Blvd opp Racquet Club. Lunch Mon-Fri 11:30-2. Dinner Mon-Thur 5:30-9:30, Fri-Sat til 10:30. Reser sugg. AE,DC,MC,V. **372-0700.**
Delightful Japanese, hibachi-style steak, seafood, sushi prepared at table. Entrees with shrimp appetizer from $8-$24 for scallop/steak/lobster combo.

Spadaro's
Rt 22, Murrysville. Mon-Thur 11-10, Fri-Sat til 11. Reser wknds. AE,CB,DC, MC,V. **327-5955.**
Italian garden with gazebo, stained glass. Excellent seafood, super hot/cold salad bar $3-$7. Wed-Thur Prime Rib $10/Lobster $13. Lunch/Dinner $3.50-$23.

Station Brake Cafe
500 Station St, Wilmerding. Lunch Mon-Fri 11-3, Dinner Mon-Thur 5-10. Sun 4:30-9. AE,DC,MC,V. Reser wknds **823-1600.**
Gourmet cuisine in warm dining room, fireplace and lots of surprises. Fancy seafood, veal, lamb, beef. Lunch $5-$10, Dinner $14-$28. Lunchroom next door 10-4. (See Review)

TGI Friday's
240 Mall Blvd, Monroeville. 7 days 11:30-2am. Sun Brunch til 3. AE,D,DC, MC,V. **372-6630.**
Colorful Art Nouveau, brass, greenery and a long menu, a la carte to dinners $2-$13.50, outdoors in summer. Pleasant dining, nightlife at big brass bar.

Tigano's Inn
6202 Leechburg Rd, Penn Hills. Mon-Sat 5-11. Sun 4-9. AE,DC,MC,V. **795-5151.**
Small, busy, good Italian seafood, veal $5-$26. Tues Pasta Special $3.95.

Tivoli Restaurant
419 Rodi Road, Penn Hills. Lunch Mon-Fri 11-3. Dinner Mon-Sat 4-11. Sun 3-9. Reser weeknd. AE,D,DC,MC,V. **243-9630.**
Elegant dining in crystal/brass decor; veal, pasta, seafood, lobster, flambeed desserts $6.50-$18. Lunch $4.50-$7.

Veltri's
Rt 907 & Coxcomb Hill, Plum Boro. Dinner Mon-Thur 5-10, Fri-Sat til 11. Reser. AE,DC,MC,V. **335-4474.**
Romantic dining, beautiful river view. Ital-Amer, great veal Parmesan. $7-$21. DJ at Nikki's Lounge Wed-Sat.

What's Cookin' at Casey's
608 Allegheny River Blvd, Oakmont. Mon-Thur 7am-9, Fri-Sat til 10:30. Sun 8-9. MC,V. **826-1400.**
Country cozy, big variety sandwiches, casseroles, red/white pizza, strombolis. $4-$10. Worth the stop.

Winchester Room
1728 Lincoln Hwy, N Versailles. Mon-Thur Dinner 5-10, Fri-Sat til 11. Sun 4-8. Reser sugg. AE,CB,D,DC,MC,V. **823-9954.**
Famous for great steak, fresh fish, lobster in popular, busy rooms. $11-$20.

Wooden Nickel
4006 Berger Lane, Monroeville. Lunch Mon-Fri 11:30-2, Dinner 5-11, Sat til 12. Sun 4-10. AE,DC,MC,V. **372-9750.**
Quaint little restaurant, garden view. Pasta, veal, fresh seafood, barbecued shrimp. Wed-Sat Prime Rib. Lunch $3-$7, Dinner $7-$22. Good bet.

SUBURBS WEST

Beef & Burgundy
Holiday Inn Airport, 1406 Beers School Rd, Coraopolis. Mon-Sat 6am-2, 5-11. Sun Brunch 10-2, Dinner 5-10. AE,D,DC,MC,V. **262-3600.**
Comfortable, elegant room with fresh seafood, chef's specials. Lunch $5-$11, Dinner $11-$22. Dinner dancing.

Cathy's Windsor Tea Room
515 Locust Place, Sewickley. Mon 7am-4, Tues-Thur & Sun 7-7, Fri-Sat til 9. Reser sugg. **741-6677.**
Traditional tea in charming "British" house with pasties (meat pies), scones plus delicious teas/coffees at gourmet breakfast. Luncheon Tea $7. Also Italian offerings. Formal tea with shepherds or meat pies and unlimited desserts $14. Breakfast/Lunch $1.75-$7. Dinner $6-$17.

Dingbat's
200 Park Manor Drive, Robinson Twp. Mon-Sat 11:30-2am. Sun Brunch 10-2, Dinner til 1am. AE,DC,MC,V. **787-7010.**
Casual fun, specialty menu—sandwiches, pasta, char-broiled steaks, fish, raw oyster bar. Greenhouse patio dining. Happy Hour 4-6:30. Lunch/Dinner $4-$18.

Hyeholde
190 Hyeholde Dr, Coraopolis. Lunch Mon-Fri 11:30-2, Dinner Mon-Sat 5-10. AE,D,DC,MC,V. Reser sugg. **264-3116.**
Warm Elizabethan mansion with flagstone floors, big fireplaces, tapestries. Romantic dinner by candlelight. Four-Star Mobil Award, continental cuisine, rack-of-lamb, Virginia spots, delicious desserts $12-$27. (See Rich Man's 4)

IKEA
Robinson Town Center. Mon-Sat 11-8:30. Sun til 4:30. D,MC,V. **747-0747.**
Hot/cold Swedish delicacies—meatballs, salmon, herring, great desserts in popular furniture store's sleek cafe. Outdoor deck. Sun Brunch 11-2. $3-$6.

16

West

The Irongate
Howard Johnson Pgh Airport, Rt 22/30, Oakdale. Mon-Fri 6-10, Sat & Sun 7-10. AE,DC,MC,V. **923-2244.**
Breakfast thru dinner and all-you-can-eat buffet 10-2 daily in big, casual livingroom. Lunch $4-$5, Dinner $6-$10. Sun Brunch Buffet 10-2, $7.95.

Mad Anthony's Bier Stube
13th/Merchant, Ambridge. Tues-Sat 11-2am. AE,MC,V. **266-3450.**
Rustic room with outdoor courtyard, live bands Fri-Sat. German dishes, good sandwiches, salads $3-$12. Good place to visit after touring nearby Old Economy.

Maggie Mae's Creekhouse
288 W Steuben Street, Crafton. Mon-Thur 11:30-11, Fri til 12, Sat 3-12. Sun 12-9. AE,MC,V. **922-1662.**
A charming Victorian-style renovated 1890 bridgehouse. Fun food, dinners in casual atmosphere. Try 'taste of honey' fried chicken, Cajun. Entrees $7-$12.

Papa J's
200 E Main, Carnegie. Mon-Thur 11-10, Fri-Sat til 11. Sun 11-9. AE,CB,DC,MC,V. Reser sugg. **429-7272.**
Tempting seafood grills, pasta, veal in European cafe atmosphere. Lunch $4-$6, Dinner $10-$20.

Pastels, Royce Hotel
1160 Thorn Run Rd Ext, Coraopolis. 7 days Break/Lunch Mon-Fri 7-2, Dinner 5-11. AE,DC,MC,V. **262-2400.**
Minutes from Airport; Continental cuisine in soothing peach/cream decor. Sun Brunch 10-2. Lunch $6-$7, Dinner $12-$23.

La Primadonna
801 Broadway Ave, McKees Rocks. Mon-Sat 4-11, Lounge til 12. AE,CB,BC,MC,V. **331-1001.**
Neighborhood eatery making gastronomic waves for hearty Italian dishes—mouth-watering pasta, seafood, chicken, veal at wonderful prices. No reser, worth the wait. $8-$17. (See Review)

River Room
Sewickley Country Inn, 801 Ohio River Blvd. Sun-Thur 6:30am-10pm, Fri-Sat 7-11. AE,D,DC,MC,V. **741-4300.**
Warm, comfortable setting for veal, seafood, pasta. $4-$17.

Seasons Cafe
1100 Fifth Ave, Coraopolis. Tues-Sat 5-10. AE,DC,MC,V. **264-7004.**
Gourmet treat in neighborhood setting. Extraordinary food/wine with superb delicacies ie. homemade duck sausage, barley salad. $10-$17.

Sgro's
4400 Campbell's Run Rd, Robinson Twp. Dinner Tues-Sat 5-10. AE,DC, MC,V. **787-1234.**
Big pleasant room, modern decor with well-rounded menu—good fish, lobster, steak, homemade soups, pastries. Dinner $15-$25 inc relish tray, dessert.

Tambellini Bridgeville
413 Railroad St, Bridgeville. Mon 11-9, Tues-Thur til 10, Fri til 11, Sat 4-11, Sun 4-9. AE,DC,MC,V. **221-5202.**
Fine dining in handsome rooms; speciallizing in veal, seafood. Lunch $4.25-$8, Dinner $8-$24.

Wooden Angel
West Bridgewater, Beaver. Tues-Fri 11:30-11. Sat 5-12. AE,DC,MC,V. **774-7880.**
Award-winning wine cellar, American wines & cuisine in intimate rooms, classical music; veal, seafood. Lunch $4.50-$10, Dinner $14-$30. (See Rich Man's Guide 3)

Wright's Seafood Inn
1837 Washington St, Heidelberg. Mon-Thur 11-10, Fri-Sat til 11. AE,D,DC, MC,V. **279-7900.**
Big sprawling restaurant with some of city's best seafood—lobster, crab, Norwegian salmon $17, great bouillabaisse. Lunch $4-$7, Dinner $8-$22.

Bob Evans
Sun-Thur 5am-10, Fri-Sat til 11:30. MC,V. Century III Mall, Coraopolis, Monroeville, N Hills, Warrendale, Washington Mall, N Huntingdon.
Casual, country style, famous for sausage with eggs, gravy, grits; good ribs, BBQ chicken, peanut butter pie, dinners under $5. $1-$6. Discounts child, Srs.

Chi-Chi's Mexican Restaurants
Mon-Thur 11-11, Fri-Sat til 12. Sun til 10. AE,DC,MC,V. South Hills: Washington Rd 833-8886. Greentree: McKinney Lane 937-0818. Monroeville: Wm Penn Hwy 856-8860. North Hills: 7201 McKnight Rd 364-2414. Pleasant Hills: 500 Clairton Blvd 653-6000.
Popular, bustling Tex-Mex—from tostados to special chimichangas—all under $8. Children's $2 menu opens into sombrero! Mexican beer, desserts.

Chuck E. Cheese
7 days 11-9, Fri-Sat til 11. MC,V. Monrv: Wm Penn Highway 856-5044. Bridgeville: Wash Pike 257-2570. W Mifflin: Lebanon Church Rd 655-8840.
Birthday favorite—kids have time of their lives—puppet show, video games, big mouse Chuck E Cheese himself. Burgers, pizza $6-9; salad bar $3.29. Beer/wine for grown-ups.

Eat 'n Park
7 days, many 24 hrs. 54 sites. Some take credit cards. 923-1000.
Favorite family place for big Soup 'n Salad bars, Sunday Buffets, great breakfasts under $2, economical meals, famous strawberry pies. Many sites have bakeries. $3-$7.

Ground Round
Mon-Sat 11-1. Sun 12-12. AE,MC,V. Coraopolis: Narrows Run Rd 269-0644. Monroeville: Wm Penn Hwy 856-0385. Mt Leb: Washington Rd 833-7580. Scott: Greentree Rd 561-2187. Wexford: Perry Hwy 935-4290.
Kid's delight, fun decor, old time flicks some locations. Varied menu—beef, chicken, fish, spaghetti, Mexican. Lunch/Dinner $4-$12. Kids 1¢/lb Thur.

HOSS'S Steak & Sea House
Sun-Thur 10:30-9:30, Fri-Sat til 10:30. MC,V. Allison Park: Rt 8 486-9291. Belle Vernon: Finley Rd 929-9249. Murrysville: Rt 22 733-2090. Penn Hills: Frankstown/Rodi 241-7522.
Big family places, good home cooking— chicken, fish, steak, seafood with veg/potato, salad bar $7-$11; Salad Bar only $6. Great Sunday stop.

King's Family Restaurants
7 days 7-11, 24 hrs Fri-Sat (except Upper St Clair.) MC,V. Bridgeville, Coraopolis, Cranberry, Fox Chapel Monrv, N Versailles, Penn Hills, Plum Steubenville Pike, Upper St Clair.
Family favorite, fast service, senior specials. Complete dinners $4-$6, great breakfasts $2-$4, huge sundaes.

Olive Garden
Mon-Thur 11-10, Fri-Sat til 11. AE,DC,MC,V. Greentree: 971 Greentree Rd 922-7200. Monrv: 260 Mall Blvd 372-5017; Pleasant Hills: 527 Clairton Blvd 653-5897.
Popular Italian, nice decor; pastas, chicken, veal, fish, unlimited soup/salad. Lunch $4-$7, Dinner $6-$12.

Pappan's
7 days, Most 9-9. Sun til 7. Allegheny Center 321-8151. Century III 655-7220. Northway Mall 364-2345. Robinson Town Ctr 788-0155. McMurray 942-0401. Aliquippa 375-9827.
'You're gonna like this' locally-owned chain with home cooking, good service. Specialty—Chicken Dinner $4.19 to varied menus $6.69. Senior specials.

Red Lobster
Sun-Thur 11-10, Fri-Sat til 11. AE,DC,MC,V. Monrvoeville: Wm Penn Hwy 372-5591. Mt Lebanon: Washington Rd 831-7373. N Hills: McKnight Rd 367-2998. Robinson Twp: Rt 30 788-8700. Pleasant Hills: Clairton Blvd 653-3552.
Seafood lover's haven—fish, lobster, crab legs any way you like. Informal, friendly. Lunch $4-$7, Dinner $8-$21.

16

TEAS

Who takes tea? In a town proud of its work image, an old tradition, tea time, is returning with its civilized charm and late-afternoon goodies that have made it a continental institution. It's a wonderful way to relax and become aware of the new Pittsburgh pleasures around us. Tea for you too!

Cafe Azure
317 S Craig Street, Oakland.
AE,DC,MC,V. **681-3533.**
Hours: Mon-Sat 3-5.
A most unusual tea, a French 'cafe break' on the terrace of this sophisticated restaurant in the museum/ university center. 'High tea' with soup, smoked salmon, duck gallantine, tart with creme Anglaise, luscious cheese & fruit plate, fresh strawberries/raspberries and a froth of French desserts including house-made ice cream & sorbets, espresso $3-$6. Deliciously different.

Cathy's Windsor Tea Room
515 Locust Place, Sewickley. MC,V.
741-6677.
Hours: Mon 11-4, Tues-Sun 11-4.
A luncheon tea in the British tradition in elegant Victorian house with homemade scones, British biscuits, tea sandwiches and desserts $7. There's a lovely High Tea—complete with silver service, fine china—with scones, tea sandwiches, shepherd's or meat pie and unlimited dessert—$14. Weekends you might run into Owner Cathy Milton, well-known TV personality and British buff. Be sure to browse through the English/ American antiques at Cathy's Corner on the second floor.

Kaufmann's Dining Room
5th/Smithfield. Mon-Sat 2:30-4.
Kaufmann's charge. **232-2682.**
Shoppers—there's a beautiful tea in this department store's 11th floor dining room with shining silver service, petite sandwiches, petit-fours, scones, pastries, cookies, gourmet teas & coffees. All for the great price of $4.50!

Promenade Cafe
Pittburgh Hilton, Gateway Center.
AE,DC,MC,V. **391-4600.**
Hours: 2-5.
No set tea but delightful afternoon snacking in the diningroom looking out on Gateway Center or the green & white umbrellaed patio. Light sandwiches, six-grain bread, yummy desserts, cheesecake. $3-$7.

A Holiday Tradition —Now Year Around
Westin William Penn Hotel
Downtown. AE,DC,MC,V.
553-5235.
Hours: 7 days 2:30-4:30.
Tea is a Pittsburgh holiday tradition in the chandeliered Palm Court Lobby of this grand hotel with elegant atmosphere, gleaming silver service and music performed on Andre Previn's concert grand piano. Choice of three items—tea sandwiches, scones, gateau/Greek pastry with your coffee/tea—an affordable luxury at $7.95 a person.

Shadyside Balcony
The Theatre Mall, Walnut St, Shadyside.
AE,DC,MC,V. **687-0110.**
Hours: Mon-Sat 3-5.
Modern tea & conversation on the Balcony overlooking Walnut Street for a well-earned shopping break. The whole lunch menu to choose from—appetizers, salads, soup/salad/quiche combinations, sandwiches and delicious desserts. How about ice cream with your own pitcher of chocolate sauce—all from $2-$6. Lovely way to while away an afternoon!

Warburton's
Oxford Centre lower level, Fifth Avenue Place Food Gallery, PPG Food Court, and USX Tower Downtown.
Hours: Weekdays til 6. Sat Oxford/PPG til 4.
You can make up your own tea at these British eateries. Choice of scones, big cranberry/blueberry muffins, savouries —hot meat/cheese puffed pastries— great teas/coffees for a relaxing, inexpensive break, $2-$5.

INDEX

INDEX

FANTASTIC GIFTS FOR PITTSBURGH LOVERS

PGH GUIDE/WALKING MAP

Discover Pittsburgh's hidden secrets...places to go, best restaurant values, romantic hideaways, waterfront/outdoor eateries, sightseeing in new 200p Guide...PLUS unique four-color "Pgh Walking Map" & mini-guide...400 bldgs, parking right ON the map. Singly or the pair, gold-ribboned, gift-wrapped with big "For Pgh Lovers" gift tag. Save on the pair!

PITTSBURGH PLACEMATS/PRINTS

Favorite, well-loved scenes of old and new Pittsburgh from "Pittsburgh Pleasures" Events Calendars with the spectacular photographs by Herb Ferguson - glossy, laminated finish, 12 x 16 1/2. View from Ft Pitt Bridge, Point, Incline, Fireworks. Wonderful gift...great for framing!

PITTSBURGH PLEASURES EVENTS CALENDAR

Plan your social schedule with this beautiful calendar listing 850 wonderful things to do in Pittsburgh area day by day, month by month. A collector's item with 13 spectacular color photos of the city. Perfect for friends, employees, customers, students, Pittsburghers away from home.

BEAUTIFUL PITTSBURGH SCENES

NOTECARDS

Favorite Pittsburgh scenes – Full color photo scenes of the Point/Golden Triangle, View from the Incline, Phipps Flower Show, Univ of Pgh. 10 cards (2 each of 5 scenes.) Folds to 4 1/4 x 5 1/2.

HOLIDAY GREETING CARDS

A unique Pittsburgh holiday greeting with full color photo of the Heinz Hall Christmas tree in its resplendent glory, a Pgh tradition. Inside message "Holiday Greetings." Box of 12. 4 1/4 x 5 1/2.

POSTCARDS

12 full color photos, favorite Pgh scenes inc. Incline, Pitt, Golden Triangle, View from Ft Pitt Tunnels, Regatta, Station Sq, PPG Plaza. Wonderful mementos of city change.

NEW PITTSBURGH PUBLICATIONS   Box 81875   Pittsburgh PA 15217   (412) 681-8528   681-0601

Enclosed is a check/money order for:

_____ "Perfect Pair"-Rich/Poor Man's Guide/ Walking Map sets $12.95 ea   _____
_____ copies "Rich/Poor Man's Guide to Pittsburgh" at $9.95 ea   _____
_____ copies "Pgh Walking Map & Guide" at $2.95 ea   _____
_____ "Pittsburgh Pleasures Events Calendar" at $9.95 ea   _____
_____ Pittsburgh Placemats/Prints at $3.50 ea, 4 for $12   _____
_____ boxes of Beautiful Pgh Notecards at $5.99 ea   _____
_____ boxes of Holiday Cards at $6.50 ea   _____
_____ dozen of assorted postcards at $4.00 doz.   _____

_____ Shipping
_____ Sub Total:
_____ 6% Sales Tax (PA residents)

= = = = = = = = = TOTAL
TOTAL AMOUNT ENCLOSED _____

PLEASE SHIP TO:_____ Date:_____

Address:_____
City/Zip_____Phone:_____
        (If gift specify "Gift card to read":)

_____ Please send me information on business bulk rates, imprinting

I Love Pittsburgh! Downtown

Famous Addresses

Business decisions made in Pittsburgh are heard around the world. 4th largest corp headquarters, the city is home base to 12 "Fortune 500" firms. Famous downtown hdq bldgs are: **USX Tower,** 600 Grant St. 64 steel stories, tallest between NY & Chicago. **Westinghouse Bldg,** Gateway. Home of world-famous logo. **Alcoa Bldg,** 425 Sixth Ave. 30-story aluminum showcase. **PPG Industries,** 4th/Mkt. 6 shimmering Gothic towers. Other notable downtown bldgs are **One Mellon Bank Center,** Grant, **CNG Tower,** Liberty Ave., **Gulf Tower,** Grant/7th with its weather beacon pyramid top & **Koppers Bldg,** 436 7th Ave—with fine art deco lobby.

Quaint Old Pittsburgh

One of town's few remaining residential bldgs (1894) is picturesque Harvard-Yale-Princeton Club, Wm Penn Way/7th, its flagstone courtyard, red brick facade untouched by city bustle. Nearby is narrow, arcaded Strawberry Way.

*Civic Arena

Uptown. Dome home of Penguins hockey, concerts. Stainless steel roof, world's largest retractable, rolls back on balmy nights — moving experience.

View From the Bluff

High above city off Forbes is Duquesne U, famed for music, law, Mies van der Rohe's Mellon Hall. Panoramic view from Bluff — on clear day you can see far down river.

Mellon Square

A shady in-city parklet across from Wm Penn Hotel. Closest thing to a Pittsburgh promenade as office workers stroll, meet and eat around square fountain.

Market Square

Off 5th/Forbes below Wood. This famous square, site of Pgh's old marketplace, is a grassy park with benches, friendly pigeons in midst of bustling markets, PPG complex.

Grant/Ross. One of world's finest examples of masonry architecture, this 1888 landmark is the masterpiece of famed architect H H Richardson. The Romanesque stone 'castle' with its massive towers, chain-linked iron posts and 10 Commandments in stone is connected to County Jail by 'Bridge of Sighs.' Small hideaway parklet in interior courtyard (off 5th or Forbes) can be viewed from 2nd floor corridor. Up Grant to your right is the amazing Gothic tracery of **Union Trust at Two Mellon Bank Center** with its 11-story rotunda, one of the city's best interiors.

Window Shopping

Pgh—like Paris—is a walking city, with shopping in compact 12-block area. On Smithfield bet 5th/6th are Kaufmann's, Saks & Brooks Bros. Near Gateway are Horne's Dept Store & 5th Ave Place Shops. A bridge away is Station Sq.

Gateway Center

Downtown's first Renaissance I development, newly refurbished Gateway Ctr with its fountained plaza, now has six bldgs joined by Equitable Plaza and a walkway across Blvd of Allies.

***Allegheny Courthouse

Point State Park Block House-Museum

Follow Point Park signs under wide archway for lovely stroll in park and relaxing close-up of **Point Fountain.*** This is where it all began. You're standing at strategic Gateway to the West—where swift Allegheny (right) and muddy Monongahela (left) form the Ohio. Here two centuries ago France & England battled for control of American frontier. All that remains of Ft Pitt, built by victorious British in 1764 on ruins of French Ft Duquesne, is the **Ft Pitt Blockhouse** on its original site. Nearby **Museum** tells story of pioneer/Indian life, how Pgh grew up around Fort as merchants/traders provisioned flatboats and wagons going west. **Blockhouse/Museum** Tues-Sat, Sun 12-5. **281-9284.**

Allegheny River

Monongahela River

I Love Pittsburgh! $2⁰⁰
Sightseeing Guide

☆☆☆ **Visitor's Special** ☆☆☆

Five Easy Ways to Fall in Love with the City

Renaissance II Bldgs

Explore downtown's spectacular new bldgs starting at PPG's glass palace, 4th & Market . . . on to 5th Ave Place, Stanwix/Liberty. Then past Heinz Hall Plaza to new CNG Tower . . . down Liberty to Liberty Ctr/Vista. Then up to One Mellon Bank Ctr, Grant/Fifth and Oxford Centre at 4th/Grant.

Station Square

Station Square Shops
S Side at Smithfield St Bridge
Walk, ride the "T" subway or take a Wood St bus to Pgh's famous mall in beautifully restored P & LE RR Station. Enjoy shops, museums, eateries, nite life, riverfront sights. See magnificent Grand Concourse restaurant, one of nation's finest. Watch for new River Park next to Gateway Clipper. Shops til 9, food til 12. A must. **281-3145.**

Scaife Gallery

Carnegie Museum, Forbes/Craig, Oakland. Don't let visitors leave town without slipping out to classically modern glass & granite Scaife Gallery, dazzling Hall of Minerals/Gems, world famous Dinosaurs. Dine at Gallery Cafe. You can't miss Cath of Learning, Pitt's 42-fl Gothic home.

Gateway Clipper

The best way to experience Pittsburgh—the Gateway to the West—is from famous three rivers. Sail past spuming Point Fountain. Imagine Indian, settler past in looming hills. Discover city of bridges (573—most in US), working tugs, barges, steel mills, new riverfront parks, marinas. Daily cruises from Station Sq dock $7.50, child $4.50. Kiddie cruise $5.50-$3.50. Shuttle to/from Stadium games $1.25. **355-7980.**

Duq. Incline

Ride 400 ft up the Duquesne Incline, S Side for panoramic view of the Golden Triangle —breathtaking day/night from Mt Wash observation pods. Daily 5:30am-12:45am (Sun from 7am). **381-1665.**

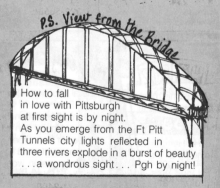

P.S. View from the Bridge

How to fall in love with Pittsburgh at first sight is by night. As you emerge from the Ft Pitt Tunnels city lights reflected in three rivers explode in a burst of beauty . . . a wondrous sight . . . Pgh by night!

*Worth Seeing **Really Worth Seeing ***Don't Miss

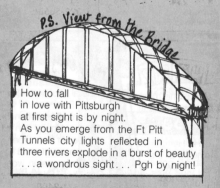 Pull Out